Sir David Lindsay

The Poetical Works of Sir David Lyndsay of the Mount, Lyon King of Arms

Vol. 2

Sir David Lindsay

The Poetical Works of Sir David Lyndsay of the Mount, Lyon King of Arms
Vol. 2

ISBN/EAN: 9783337316143

Printed in Europe, USA, Canada, Australia, Japan

Cover: Foto ©Thomas Meinert / pixelio.de

More available books at **www.hansebooks.com**

EARLY SCOTTISH POETS.

LYNDSAY.

THE
POETICAL WORKS

OF

SIR DAVID LYNDSAY

OF THE MOUNT,

LYON KING OF ARMS.

A NEW EDITION CAREFULLY REVISED.

IN TWO VOLUMES.—VOL. II.

EDINBURGH: WILLIAM PATERSON.

MDCCCLXXI.

TABLE OF CONTENTS.

Ane Dialog betuix Experience and ane Courteour.
    The Thrid Buke, ... 1
    The Fourt Buke, ... 57
    Ane Exhortation, &c., ... 102

Ane Pleasant Satyre of the Thrie Estaitis in commendatioun of Vertew and vituperatioun of Vyce, 107
    Part the First, ... 113
    The Puir Man and the Pardoner, an Interlude, . 197

Ane Pleasant Satyre of the Thrie Estaitis, &c.
    Part the Second, ... 215
    Appendix,—The Auld Man and his Wife, a Preliminary Interlude, ... 315

NOTES, ... 329

GLOSSARY, ... 355

ANE DIALOG BETUIX EXPERIENCE AND ANE COURTEOUR.

[CONTINUED.]

ANE DIALOG

BETUIX EXPERIENCE AND ANE COURTEOUR.

THE THRID BUKE.

AND IN THE FIRST, MAKAND NARRATIONE OF THE MISERABILL DISTRUCTIOUN OF THE FYVE CIETIES CALLIT SODOME, GOMORRE, SEBOIM, SEGORE, AND ADAMA, ETC.

COURTEOUR.

FATHER, I pray yow, to me tell
Quhat notabyll thyngis that befell
Duryng the ryng of Assyriens,
Quhilk had so lang prehemynens;
I mene of uther Nationis
Under thare dominationis.

EXPERIENCE.

That may be done in termys schorte,
Said he, as storyis doith reporte:
Induryng this First Monarchie
Become that wofull miserie

Of Sodome, Gomorre, and thare regione,
As Scripture makis mentione ;
Quhose peple wer so sensuall
In fylthie synnis unnaturall,
The quhilk in to my vulgar veirs
My toung abhorris to reheirs :
Lyke brutall beistis, by thare myndis,
Unnaturally abusit thare kyndis
By fylthie stynkand lychorie,
And most abhominabyll sodomie.
As holy Scripture doith discryve,
In that countrie wer Cieteis fyve,
Quhilk wer Sodome, and Gomorra,
Seboim, Segore, and Adama :
Amang thame all funde wes thare none
Undefylit, bot Lott allone.
 Holy Abraham dwelt neir hand by,
Quhilk prayit for Lott effectuously :
For God maid hym advertysment,
That he wald mak sic punyschement.
To Lott two Angellis God did sende,
Hym frome that furye tyll defende.
Quhen the peple of that regioun
Saw the Angellis cum to toun,
Transformit in to fair young men,
Thay purposit thame for to ken,
And abuse thame unnaturallye
With thare foule stynkand sodomye.
Of that gude Lott wes wounder woo,
And offerit thame his douchteris twoo,
Thame at thare plesour for tyll use :

Bot thay his douchteris did refuse.
And than the Angellis, be thare mycht,
Those men depryvit of thare sycht;
And so, perfors, leit thame allone.
To Lottis lugyng quhen thay wer gone,
Thay hym commandit haistelie
For tyll depart of that Cietie.
That foule unnaturall lychorie
A vengeance to the Hevin did crye;
The quhilk did mufe God tyll sic yre,
That frome the Hevin brintstone and fyre,
With awfull thoundryng, ranit doun,
And did consume that hole regioun.
Of all that land chapit no mo
Except Lott and his douchteris two:
His wyfe wes turnit in a stone,
So wyfeless wes he left allone,
For scho wes inobedient,
And kepit no commandement.
Quhen the Angell gif thame command
Sone tyll depart out of that land,
He monyste thame, under gret pane,
Never to luke bakwart agane.
Quhen Lottis wyfe hard the thoundring
Of flammand fyre and lychtnyng,
The ugly cryis lamentabyll
Of peple most espoventabyll,
For none of thame had fors to flee,
Scho yarnit that sorrowfull sycht to see;
And, as scho turnit hir, anone
Scho wes transformit in a stone;

Quhare scho remanis tyll this daye,
Of hir I have no more to saye.
   To schaw at leynth I am nocht abyll
That pietuous proces lamentabyll,
Quhow cieteis, castellis, tounis, and towris,
Villagis, bastailyeis, and bowris,
Thay wer all into poulder drevin ;
Forrestis be the ruttis uprevin ;
Thare Kyng, thare Quene, and peple all,
Yong and auld, brynt in poulder small :
No creature wes left in lyfe,
Foulis, beistis, man, nor wyfe ;
The erth, the corne, herb, frute and tre,
The babbis upone the noryse kne,
Rycht suddantlye, in one instant,
Unwerly come thare jugement ;
As it come in the tyme of Noye,
Quhen God did all the warld distroye ;
For that self syn of sodomye,
And most abhominabyll bewgrye :
That vyce at lenth for tyll declare
I thynk it is nocht necessare.
   Quhen all wes brynt, flesche, blud, and bonis,
Hyllis, valais, stokis, and stonis,
The cuntre sank, for to conclude,
Quhare now standith ane uglye flude,
The quhilk is callit the Dede See,
Nixt to the cuntre of Judee,
Quhose stynkand strandis, blak as tar,
The flewre of it men felith on far.
In tyll Orosius thow may reid

Of that countre the lenth and breid ;
Of lenth, fyftye mylis and two,
And fourtene myle in breid also.
   Lott of his Wyfe wes so agast
That he tyll a wyld montane past :
Of cumpanye he had no mo
Except his lustye douchteris two ;
And, be thare provocatioun,
As Moyses makith narratioun,
Allone in to that montane wylde,
His douchteris boith he gat with chylde.
For thay belevit, in thare thocht,
That all the warld wes gone to nocht,
As it become of that Natioun ;
Thynkand that generatioun
Wald faill, withoute thay craftellye
Gar thare Father with thame to lye :
And so thay fand ane craftye wyle,
Quhow thay thare Father mycht begyle,
And causit hym to drynk wycht wyne,
Quhilk men to lychorye doith inclyne.
Quhen he wes full, and fallin on sleip,
His douchteris quyetlye did creip
In tyll his bed, full secreitlye,
Provokand hym with thame to lye :
And knew nocht quhow he wes begylde,
Tyll boith his douchteris wer with chylde :
And bure two sonnis, in certane,
Thay beand in that wyld montane,
Of quhome two Nationis did proceid,
As in the Scripture thow may reid ;

In the quhilk Scripture thow may se
At lenth this wofull miserie.

This miserie become, but weir,
From Noyis flude thre hundreth yeir,
Togidder with four score and alevin,
As comptit Carione, full evin
And efter Noyis deith, I ges,
Ane and fourtye yeir thare wes;
Quhen Abraham was of aige, I wene,
Foure score of yeris and nyntene:
Quhen this foule syn of sodomye
Was puneisit so regorouslye.
Gret God preserve us, in our tyme,
That we commit nocht sic ane cryme.

 Teddious it wer for me to tell,
This Monarchie duryng, quhat befell,
And wounderis that in erth wer wrocht,
Quhilk to thy purpose langith nocht:
As quhow the peple of Israell,
Did lang tyme in to Egypt dwell;
And of thare gret puneisioun,
Throuch Pharois persecutioun;
And quhow Moyses did thame convoye
Throuch the Reid Sey, with mekle joye,
Quhare kyng Pharo, rycht misarably,
Wes drownit with all his huge army;
And quhow that peple wanderand wes
Fourtye yeris in wyldernes:
Moyses, that tyme, as I heir saye,
Ressavit the Law on Mont Sinay;
That tyme, Josue throuch Jordan

Led those peple to Canaan;
Quhare Saule, David, and Salamone,
With Hebrew kyngis mony one,
Did rychelye ryng in that countre,
Induryng this First Monarchie.
The Sege of Thebes, miserabyll.
Quhare blude wes sched incomparabyll
Of nobyll men, in to those dayis,
With utheris terribyll affrayis:
As quhow the Grekis wrocht vengeance
Apone the nobyll Troyiance,
Because that Pareis did convoye,
Perfors, fair Helena to Troye,
Quhilk wes king Menelaus wyfe,
Quhare mony one thousand lost thare lyfe.
 That tyme, the valyeant Hercules
Out throuch the warld did hym addres,
Quhare he did mony ane douchtye deid,
As in his storye thow may reid;
And quhow, throuch Dyonere, his wyfe,
That campione did lose his lyfe:
In flammand fyre full furiouslye
The deith he sufferit creuellye.
 That tyme Remus and Romulus
Did found that Cietie most famous
Of Rome, standing in Italie,
As in thare storye thow may se.
Wald thow reid Titus Levius,
Thow suld fynd warkis wounderus;
Quhose douchtye deidis ar weill kende,
And salbe to the warldis ende;

Thocht thay began with creueltie,
And endit with miseritie :
As bene the maner, to conclude,
Of all scheddaris of saikles blude.
  In Grece the ornat Poetry,
Medecene, Musike, Astronomy.
Duryng this First Monarchie began ;
Be Homerus, that famous man,
Togydder with Hesiodus,
As divers Auctouris schawis us :
It wer to lang to put in ryme
The bukis quhilk thay wret in thare tyme.
  Thir wer the actis principall,
That Monarchye duryng, quhilk befell.
As for gude Abraham and his seid,
In to the Bibyll thow may reid
Quhow, in this tyme, as I heir tell
Began the Kyngdome Spirituall,
As I have schawin to thee affore ;
Quharefor I speik of thame no more.

ANE SCHORT DISCRIPTIOUN OF THE SECUND, THRID, AND FERD MONARCHIE.

COURTEOUR.

Father, said I, quhilk wes the man
That the nyxt Monarchye began ?

EXPERIENCE.

Cyrus, said he, the Kyng of Pers,
As Cronicles hes done rehers,
Prudent, and full of pollicye,

Began the secunde Monarchye;
For he wes the most godly kyng
That ever in Pers or Mede did ryng;
For he, of his benygnitie,
Delyverit frome captyvitie
The hole peple of Israell,
In to the tyme of Daniell,
The quhilkis had bene presoneris,
In Babilone, sevin score of yeris:
Tharefor God, of his grace benyng,
Gaif hym ane divyne knawleging.
Duryng his tyme as I heir tell,
He usit counsall of Daniell.
Carione at lenth doith specifie
Of his marvellous natyvitie,
And of his vertuous upbrynging,
And quhow he vincuste Cresus king,
With mony uther valyeant deid;
As in to Carione thow may reid,
Quhose successioun did indure
Tyll the tent kyng, thareof be sure.

 Bot, efter his gret conquessyng,
Rycht miserabyll wes his endyng.
As Herodotus doith discryfe.
In Scythia he lost his lyfe,
Quhare the undantit Scythianis,
Vincuste those nobyll Persianis:
And, efter that Cyrus was dede,
Quene Tomyre hakkit off his hede,
Quhilk wes the Quene of Scythianis,
In the dispyte of Persianis:

Scho kest his heid, for to conclude,
In tyll ane vessell full of blude,
And said thir wourdis, creuellye :
Drynk, now, thy fyll, gyf thow be drye ;
For thow did aye blude schedding thryste,
Now drynk at laser, gyf thow lyste.

 Efter that, Cyrus successioun
Of all the warld had possessioun,
Tyll Alexander, with sweird and fyre,
Obtenit perfors, the Thrid Impyre,
Quhilk wes the king of Macedone :
With valyeant Grekis mony one,
In battell fell and furious,
Vincuste the mychtie Darius,¶
Quhilk wes the tent and the laste kyng
Quhilk did efter king Cyrus ryng.
As for this potent Empriour,
Alexander the Conquerour,
Geve thow at lenth wald reid his ryng,
And of his creuell conquessyng,
In Inglis toung, in his gret Buke,
At lenth his Lyfe thare thow may luke ;
Quhow Alexander, that potent Kyng,
Wes twelf yeris in his conquessyng ;
And quhow, for all his gret conquest,
He levit bot ane yeir in rest,
Quhen be his servand secretlye
He poysonit wes, full pietuouslye.

 Lucane doith Alexander compair
Tyll thounder, or fyreflaucht in the air,
One creuell planeit, a mortall weird

Doun thryngand peple with his sweird.
Ganges, that moste famous flude,
He myxit with the Indianis blude;
And Euphrates, with the blude of Pers:
Quhose creueltie for to rehers,
And saikles blude quhilk he did sched,
War rycht abhominabyll to be red.
Efter his schort prosperitie,
He deit with gret miseritie.
It wer too lang for to dissyd it.
Quhow all his realmes wer devydit.

   Aye quhill that Cesar Julyus,
Quhen he had vincust Pompeyus,
Wes chosin Empriour and Kyng,
Abufe the Romanis for tyll ryng,
That potent Prince wes the first man
Quhilk the Ferd Monarchie began;
And had the hole dominioun
Of everilk land and regioun:
Quhose successouris did ryng, but weir,
Ouer the warld, mony one hundreth yeir,
Bot gentyll Julyus, allace!
Rang Empriour bot lytill space,
Quhilk I thynk pietye tyll deplore:
In fyve moneth and lytill more,
By fals exhorbitant treasoun,
That prudent Prince wes trampit doun
And murdrest, in his counsall hous,
By creuell Brutus and Cassius.

   Efter that Julyus wes slane,
Did ryng the gret Octaviane,

Of Empriouris one of the best :
Duryng his tyme wes peace and rest
Ouer all the warld, in ilk regioun,
As storyis makith mentioun.
And als I mak it to thee plane,
Duryng the tyme of Octaviane,
The Sonne of God, our Lord Jesew,
Tuke mankynd of the Virgine trew,
And wes that tyme, in Bethelem borne,
To saif mankynde, quhilk wes forlorne ;
As Scripture makith narratioun
Of his blyst Incarnatioun.

Now haif I tald thee as I can,
Quhow the Foure Monarchyis began.
Bot, in thy mynd, thow may consydder
Quhow warldly power bene bot slydder ;
For all thir gret Impyris ar gone :
Thow seis thair is no Prince allone
Quhilk hes the hole dominioun,
This tyme, of every Regioun.

COURTEOUR.

Father, quhat reasone had those Kyngis
Rewarris to be of utheris Ryngis,
But ony rycht or juste querrell,
Quhairthrouch that thay mycht mak battell,
And commoun pepyll to doun thryng ?
To this, said I, mak answeryng.

EXPERIENCE.

My Sonne, said he, that sall be done
As I best can, and that rycht sone.

Thir Monarcheis, I understand,
Preordinat wer by the command
Of God, the Plasmatour of all,
For to doun thryng and to mak thrall
Undantit peple vitious,
And als for to be gratious
To thame quhilk vertuous wer and gude :
As Daniell heth done conclude,
At lenth, in tyll his Propheseis,
Quhow thare suld be Foure Monarcheis.
His secund chepture thow maye see :
Quhow, efter the First Monarchie,
Quhen Nabuchodonosor kyng
Ane ymage sawe, in his slepyng,
With austeir luke, boith heych and breid
And of fyne pure gold wes his heid,
His breist and armes of sylver brycht,
His wambe of copper, hard and wycht,
His loynis and lymmis of irne rycht strong,
His feit of clay, irne mixt among.
Frome a montane thare come allone,
But hand of man, a mekle stone,
Quhilk on that figouris feit did fall,
And dang all doun in poulder small.
Of quhose interpretatioun
Doctouris doith mak narratioun :
The hede of gold did signifye,
First, of Assyrianis Monarchye ;
The sylver breist thay did apply
To Persianis, quhilk rang Secundly ;
The wambe of copper or of brasse,

Thridly, to Greikis comparit was ;
His loynis and lymmis of irne and steill,
Clerkis hes thame comparit weill
To Romanis, throuch thare diligence
To have the Feird preemynence
Abufe all uther Natioun.
Be this interpretation,
The myxit feit with irne and clay
Did signifye this letter day,
Quhen that the warlde sulde be devydit,
As efterwart salbe disydit,
To Christ is signifyit the stone,
Quhose Monarchie sall never be gone ;
For under his dominioun
All Princis sall be trampit doun.
Quhen that gret Kyng Omnipotent
Cumis to his Generall Jugement,
His Monarchie, than, salbe knawin,
As efter sall be to thee schawin.
 And als the Scripture sall thee tell
Quhow in the aucht of Daniell,
He saw, in to his visioun,
Be ane plane expositioun,
Quhow that the Grekis sulde wyrk vengeance
Upone the Medis and Persience ;
Comparand Grekis tyll ane goate
With ane horne, feirs, furious, and hote,
Quhilk slew the ram with hornis two,
Comparit tyll Pers, and Mede also.
And so, be Daniellis prophesyis,
All thir gret mychtie Monarchyis,

The quhilkis all uther realmes supprysit,
Be the gret God thay wer devysit :
As He of Tytus the Romane,
Sonne and air to Vespasiane,
Maid hym ane furious instrument,
To put the Jowis to gret torment ;
Quhilk I purpose, or I hyne fair,
Schortlie that processe to declair.

OF THE MOSTE MISERABILL AND MOST TERRABILL DISTRUCTIOUN OF JERUSALEM.

COURTEOUR.

Father, said I, declare to me
Induryng this Ferd Monarchie
The maist infortune that befell.

EXPERIENCE.

My Sonne, said he, that sall I tell.
The moist and manyfest misarie
Became apon the gret cietie
Jerusalem, quhen it wes supprest,
As storyis makis manifest.
Bot, as the Scripture doith devyse,
Jerusalem wes distroyit twyse ;
First, for the gret idolatrye
Quhilk thay commyttit in Jowrye :
The honour aucht to God allone
Thay gaif figuris of stoke and stone.
Affore Christis Incarnatioun

Come this first desolatioun,
Fyve hundreth yeris, four score, and ten,
In Cronicles as thow may ken:
Quhow Nabuchodonosor kyng
That famous citie did doun thryng;
Thare Kyng, with peple mony one,
Brocht thame, all bound, to Babilone,
Quhare thay remanit presoneris
The space of thre score and ten yeris:
And that first desolatioun
Wes callit the Transmigratioun.
Wes no man left, in all thare landis,
Bot purellis lauborand with thare handis,
Tyll mychtie Cyrus, king of Pers,
As Daniell heth done rehers,
Wes movit, be God, for tyll restore
The Jowis quhare that thay wer afore.
 Geve I neglect, I wer to blame,
The last Sege of Jerusalem,
Quhose rewyne wes most miserabyll,
And for to tell rycht terrabyll;
Wes never, in erth, citie nor toun,
Gatt sic extreme distructioun:
The townis of Tyre, Thebes, nor Troye,
Thay sufferit never half sic noye:
The Emprioure Vespasiane
He did devyse that Sege certane.
 Thare wes the Prophesie compleit
Quhilk Christ spake on Mont Olyveit.
Quhen he Jerusalem beheld,
The teiris frome his eine disteld:

Seand, be Divyne prescience,
The gret distructioun and vengence
Quhilk wes to cum on that cietie,
His hart wes persit with pietie,
Sayand, Jerusalem, and thow knew
The gret rewyne, sore wald thow rew;
For no thyng I can to thé schaw,
The veritie thow wyll nocht knaw,
Nor hes in consydderatioun
Thy holy visitatioun;
Thy peple wyll no way consydder.
Quham gadderit I wald haif togidder,
As errand scheip bene with thare hirdis;
Or as the hen gadderis hir byrdis
Under hir wyngis, tenderlye,
Quhilk thay refusit dispitfullye:
Quharefor sall cum that dulefull day,
That no remedy mak thow may;
Thy dungeounis sall be dung in schounder,
So that the warld sall on thé wounder;
Thy Tempyll, now most tryumphand,
Sall be tred doun amang the sand.
And, as he said, so it befell,
As heir efter I sall thé tell.

COURTEOUR.

Schaw me, said I, with circumstance,
The speciall cause of that myschance.

EXPERIENCE.

Quod he, As Scripture doith conclude,

For scheddyng of the saikles blude
Of Prophetis, quhilkis God to thame send,
And, als, because that thay myskend
Jesu, the Sonne of God Soverane,
Quhen he amang thame did remane,
For all the myraklis that he schew,
Maliciouslye thay hym mysknew;
Thocht, be his gret power divyne,
The walter cleir he turnit in wyne,
And, be that self power and mycht,
To the blynde born he gaif the sycht,
And gaif the crukit men thair feit,
And maid the lippir haill compleit;
He hailit all, and raisit the dede;
Yit held thay hym at mortall fede.
Because he schew the veritie,
Thay did conclude that he sulde dé.

 The Byschoppis, princis of the preistis,
Thay grew so boldin, in thare breistis;
The Scrybis, the Doctouris of the law,
Of God nor man quhilkis stude none aw
On Christ Jesu to wyrk vengeance;
Rycht so, the fals Pharesiance,
Ane sect of fenyeit religioun,
Devysit his confusioun,
And send thare servandis, at the last,
And with strang cordis thay band hym fast,
Syne scurgit hym, boith bak and syde,
That none for blude mycht se his hyde:
Thare wes nocht left ane penny broid
Unwoundit, frome his feit tyll heid.

In maner of derisioun,
Thay plett for hym ane creuell croun
Of prunyeand thornis, scharpe and lang,
Quhilk on his hevinlye heid thay thrang;
Syne gart hym, for the gretter lack,
Beir his awin gallous on his back,
Tyll the vyle place of Calvarie,
Quhare mony ane thousand man mycht se.
That Innocent thay tuke, perforce,
And platt hym bakwart to the Croce;
Throuch feit and handis greit nalis thay thryst.
Tyll blude aboundantlye out bryst:
Without grunschyng, clamor, or crye,
That pane he sufferit patientlye.
And, for agmentyng of his grefis,
Thay hangit hym betuix two thefis;
Quhare men mycht se the bludy strandis
Quhilkis sprang furth of his feit and handis:
Frome thornis thristit on his heid,
Ran doun the bulryng stremis reid:
In the presens of mony one man,
That blude royall on roches ran.
Schortly to say, that hevinlye Kyng
In extreme dolour thare did hyng,
Tyll he said, *Consummatum est.*
With a loud crye, he gaif the gaist.
Quhen he was dede, thay tuke one dart,
And peirst that Prence outthrouch the hart,
Fra quham thare ran walter and blude.
    The eirth than trymblit, to conclude;
Phebus did hyde his beymes brycht,

That throuch the warld thare wes no lycht;
The gret vaill of the tempyll rave;
The dede men rais out of thare grave,
And in the Citie did appeir,
As in the Scripture thow may heir,
    Than Joseph, of Abarimathie,
Did bury him rycht honestlie:
Bot yit he rose, full gloriouslye,
On the third day, tryumphaudlye.
With his Disciplis, in certane,
Fourtye dayis he did remane;
Efter that, to the Hevin ascendit.
Thir Jowis no thyng thare lyfe amendit,
Nor gaif no credens tyll his sawis,
As at more lenth the storye schawis,
Bot cruellye thay did oppres
All men that Christis name did profes,
And persecutit mony one:
Thay presonit boith Peter and Johne;
And Stewin thay stonit to the dede;
Frome James the less thay straik the hede.
This wes the cause, in conclusioun,
Of thare creuell confusioun.
    The prudent Jow, Josephus, sayis
That he wes present in those dayis;
And, in his buke, makith mentioun,
Quhow, efter Christis Ascensioun
The space of twa and fourty yeris,
Began those creuell mortall weris,
The secund yeir of Vespasiane,
Quhare mony takin wer and slane.

Josephus planely doith conclude,
Wes never sene sic one multytude,
Affore that tyme, in to the toun,
Quhilk come for thare confusioun.
Thare gret infortune so befell,
That all the Princis of Israell
Convenit agane the tyme of Pace,
Bot tyll returne thay had no grace.
The bald Romanis, with thare chiftane,
Tytus, the sonne of Vespasiane,
Thare army ouer Judea spread:
Than all men to the cietie fled,
Belevand thare to get releif;
Bot all that turnit to thare myschief.
 The Romanis lappit thame about,
That be no waye thay mycht wyn out.
Sax moneth did that Sege indure,
Quhare loste wer mony one creature,
Quhilkis thare in misary did remane,
Tyll thay wer takin, all, or slane.
Duryng the tyme of this assailye,
Thare meit, and drynk, and all did failye;
For thare wes sic ane multytude,
That thousandis deit for falt of fude.
Necessitie gart thame eit, perforsse,
Dog, catt, and rattone, asse, and horsse.
Ryche men behuffiit tyll eate thare gold,
Syne deit of hunger mony fold.
Sic hunger wes without remeid
The quick behuffit tyll eate the deid:
The fylth of closettis mony eit;

To lenth thare lyfe thay thocht it sweit.
 The famous ladyis of the toun,
For falt of fude, thay fell in swoun :
Quhen thay mycht gett none uther meit,
Thay slew thare propir bairnis to eit ;
Bot all for nocht, dispytfullye,
Thare awin sowldiouris, full gredelye,
Reft thame that flesche most miserabyll ;
And thay, with murnyng lamentabyll,
For extreme hunger, zald the spreit.
 Thare wes the Prophesie compleit,
As Christ affore made narratioun,
The day of his grym Passioun.
Quhen that the ladyis for hym murnit,
Full pietuouslye he to thame turnit,
And said, Douchteris, murne nocht for me ;
Murne on your awin posteritie :
Within schort tyme sall cum the day
That men of this Cietie sall say,
Quhen thay ar trappit in the snair,
Blyst be the wambe that never bair ;
The barren paupis, than thay sall blys :
That dulefull day ye sall nocht mys.
 This Prophesie it come to pas,
That day, with mony lowde Allas !
Sic sorrowfull lamentatioun
Wes never hard in that natioun.
Seand those lustye ladyis sweit
Deand for hunger in the streit,
Thare husbandis, nor thare chyldring,
Mycht geve to thame na comfortyng,

Nor yit releif thame of thir harmis,
Bot atheris deand in utheris armis.
Efter this wofull indigence,
Amang thame rose sic pestilence,
Quharein thair deit mony hounder,
Quhilk tyll declare it wer gret wounder.
   And, for fynall conclusioun,
Those weirlyke wallis thay dang doun.
Prince Tytus, with his chevalrye,
With sound of trompe, triumphandlye
He enterrit in that gret Cietie.
Bot tyll declare I thynk pietie
The panefull clamour horribyll.
Of woundit folk most miserabyll.
Thare wes nocht ellis bot tak and slay;
For thare mycht no man wyn away.
The strandis of blude ran throuch the streitis
Of ded folk trampit under fetis;
Auld wedowis in the preis wer smorit;
Young virginis, schamefullye deflorit;
The gret Tempyll of Salamone,
With mony a curious carvit stone,
With perfyte pynnakles on hycht,
Quhilkis wer rycht bewtyfull and wycht,
Quhare in ryche jowellis did abound,
Thay ruscheit rudlye to the ground,
And sett, in tyll thare furious yre,
Sancta Sanctorum in to fyre;
And, with extreme confusioun,
All thare gret dungeounis thay dang doun.
   Thare bursin wer the boldin breistis

Of byschoppis, princis of the preistis :
Thare takin wes the great vengeance
On fals scrybis and pharisience.
All thare payntit ipocrasie,
That tyme, mycht mak thame no supplie.
That day thay dulefullye repentit
That to the deith of Christe consentit :
Thocht it wes our salvatioun,
It wes to thare dampnatioun.
The vengeance of the blude saikles,
From Abell tyll Zacharies,
That day apone Jerusalem fell.
Bot teddious it wer to tell
The gret extreme confusioun,
And of blude sic effusioun :
Wes never slane so mony ane man,
. At one tyme, sen the warld began.
The Jowis, that day, gat thare desyre,
Quhilk thay did aske, in to thare yre,
As bene in Scripture specifyit,
The day quhen Christe wes crucifyit.
Quhen Ponce Pylat, the president,
Said to thame, I am innocent
Of the just blude of Christ Jesus,
Thay cryit, His blude lycht upon us,
And on our generatioun :
Thay gat thare supplicatioun :
That day, with mony cairfull cry,
Thare blude was sched aboundantly.

 Josephus wryttith, in his buke,
His Cronicle quho lyste to luke

Duryng that creuell sege, certane,
Wer alewin hundreth thowsand slane;
Of presonaris, weill tauld and sene,
Foure score of thousandis, and sevintene.
Out of the land thay did expell
All the peple of Israell,
And for thare gret ingratytude,
Thay leif yit under servytude.
Thare is no Jow, in no countre,
Quhilk hes one fute of propertie,
Nor never had, withouttin weir,
Sen this day fyftene hundreth yeir,
Nor never sall, I to thé schaw,
Tyll that thay turne to Christis law.
 Sum sayis that Jowis mony fald
Wer thretty for ane penny sald;
As Judas sauld the Kyng of Glore
For thretty pennyis, and no more.
 Efter that mony wer myschevit,
Quhen novellis past quhow lang thay levit
Apone thare gold, withouttin doute
Thay slyt thare bellyis, to sers it oute.
The rest in Egypt thay did sende,
Presonaris to thare lyvis ende.
Tytus tuke in his cumpanye,
Gret nummer of the most worthye,
With him to Rome, he led thame bound,
Syne creuelly did thame confound :
His victory for tyll decore,
And for agmentyng of his glore,
Gart put thame in to publict placis,

Quhare all folk mycht behald thare facis;
Syne with wyld lyonis creuellye
He gart devore thame dulefullye.
　This hie, tryumphand, mychtie Toun
At Pasche wes put to confusioun,
Because that in the tyme of Pace
Thay crucifyit the Kyng of Grace.
Sum hes this mater done indyte
More ornatly than I can wryte;
Quharefor I speik of it no more:
Onely to God be laude and glore.

OF THE MISERABILL END OF CERTANE TYRANE PRINCIS; AND SPECIALLYE THE BEGYNNARIS OF THE FOURE MONARCHEIS.

EXPERIENCE.

Now have I done declare, at thy desyris,
　As thow demandit, in to termys schort,
And quhow began the principall Impyris,
　As Cronicle and Scripture dois report:
　Quhairfor, my Sone, I hartly thee exhort,
Perfytlie prent in thy remembrance
Of this inconstante warld the variance.

The Princis of thir Foure gret Monarcheis,
　In thare most hiest pompe Imperiallis,
Traistyng to be moist sure sett in thare seis,
　The fraudful warld gaif to thame mortall fallis,
　For thare rewarde, bot dyrk memoriallis:

Thocht ouir the warld thay had preheminence,
Of it thay gat none uther recompence.

For, siclyke as the snaw doith melt in May,
    Throuch the reflex of Phebus bemys brycht,
Thir gret Impyris rycht so ar went away:
    Gone bene thare glore, thair power, and thare mycht,
Because thay wer revaris withouttin rycht,
And blude scheddaris full creuell, to conclude:
Rycht creuellye, tharefor, wes sched thare blude.

Behald quhow God, aye sen the warld began,
    Hes maid of Tyrrane Kyngis instrumentis
To scurge peple, and to keill mony one man,
    Quhilkis to his law wer inobedientis:
    Quhen thay had done perfurneis his ententis,
In dantyng wrangus peple schamefullye,
He sufferit thame be scurgit creuellye;

Evin as the scule maister doith mak ane wand,
    To dant and dyng scollaris of rude ingyne,
The quhilkis wyll nocht study at his command:
    He scurgis thame, and only to that fyne,
    That thay suld to his trew counsall inclyne;
Quhen thay obey, and meisit bene his yre,
He takis the wand and castis in to the fyre.

God of kyng Pharo maid one instrument,
    Quhilk wes the gret kyng of Egyptience.
His awin peculiar peple to torment:

That beand done, he wrocht on hym vengence,
And leit hym fall throuch inobedience;
And, fynallie, he, with his gret armye,
In the Reid Sey thame drownit dulefullye.

Rycht so, of Nabuchodonosor kyng,
God maid of hym ane furious instrument,
Jerusalem and the Jowis to doun thryng,
Quhen thay to God wer inobedient;
Syne reft hym frome his ryches and his rent,
And hym transformit in ane beist brutell,
Sevin yeris and more, as wryttis Daniell.

Alexander, throuch prydefull tyrranye,
In yeris twelf did mak his gret conquest,
Aye scheddand saikles blude full creuellye;
Tyll he wes Kyng of kyngis, he tuke no rest:
In all the warld quhen he wes full possest,
In Babilone thronit tryumphantlye,
Throuch poysoun strang, deceisit dulefullye.

Duke Hanniball, the strang Cartagiane,
The danter of the Romanis pompe and glorye,
Be his power were mony one thousand slane,
As may be red at lenth in tyll his storye.
At Cannas, quhare he wan the victorye,
On Romanis handis that dede lay on the ground,
Three heipit buschellis wer of ryngis found.

In to that mortall battell, I heir sane,
Of the Romanis moste worthy weriouris,

By presonaris, wer fourty thousand slane;
  Of quhom thare wes thretty wyse Senatouris,
  And twentye Lordis, the quhilkis had bene Pretouris,
That deit in to defence of thare countre,
And for tyll hald thare lande at lybertie.

Quhat rewarde gatt this creuell campioun,
  Quhen he had slane so gret one multytude,
And quhen the glasse of his glorye wes roun?
  Ane schamefull deith, and, schortlye to conclude,
  This bene reward of all scheddaris of blude;
For he gat sic extreme confusioun,
He slew hymself in drynking strang poysoun.

Behald the twa moste famous campionis,
  That is to say, Julyus and Pompey,
Quhilkis did conquesse all erthly Regionis,
  Alsweill maine land as Ylis in the sey,
  And to the toun of Rome gart thame obey:
For Pompeyus subdewit the Orient;
And Julyus Cesar, all the Occident.

Bot fynaly, thir two did stryve for stait,
  Quhare throw three hundreth thowsand men were slane;
Bot Pompeyus, efter that gret debait,
  He murdreist wes, the story tellis plane.
  Than Julyus wes prince and soverane,
Abufe the hole warld Empriour and Kyng;
Bot, in to rest, schorte tyme indurit his ryng:

For, within fyve moneth and lytill more,
   Amyd his Lórdis in the counsall hous.
He murdreist wes, quhat nedeth proces more?
   As I have said, be Brute and Cassius.
   Geve thow wald knaw thare dethis dolorous,
Thow most lenth go reid the Romane storye,
Quhilk hes this mater put in memorye.

Gone is the Goldin warld of Asserianis,
   Of quhome kyng Nynus wes first and principall;
Gone is the Sylver warld of Persianis;
   The Coppar warld of Grekis now is thrall;
   The warld of Irne, quhilk wes the last of all,
Comparit to the Romanis in thare glore,
Ar gone, rycht so, I heir of thame no more.

Now is the warld of irne myxit with clay,
   As Daniell at lenth hes done indyte:
The gret Impyris ar meltit clene away;
   Now is the warld of dolour and dispyte.
   I se nocht ellis bot troubyll infinyte:
Quharefor, my Sonne, I mak it to thé kend,
This Warld, I wait, is drawand to ane end.

Tokynnis of darth, hunger, and pestilence,
   With creuell weris, boith be sey and land,
Realme aganis realme with mortall violence,
   Quhilk signifyis the last day evin at hand:
   Quharefor, my Sonne, be in thy faith constand,
Rasyng thy heart to God, and cry for grace,
And mend thy lyfe, quhill thow hes tyme and space

HEIR FOLLOWIS THE FYRST SPIRITUALL AND PAPALL MONARCHIE.

COURTEOUR.

FATHER, Is thare no Prynce ringand,
Quhilk hes the Warld now at command;
As had the Kyngis of Asserianis,
The Persis, Grekis, or the Romanis?
Quho hes now, most dominioun
Of everilk land and regioun?

EXPERIENCE.

Thare is no Prince, my Sonne, said he,
That hes the principall Monarchie
Abufe the warld universall,
With hole power Imperiall,
As Alexander, or Darius,
Or as had Cesar Julyus:
For Orient and Occident
To thame wer all obedient.
Nochtwithstandyng, I find one kyng
Quhilk in tyll Europe doith ryng,
That is, the potent Pope of Rome,
Impyrand ouir all Christindome,
To quhome no Prince may be compare,
As Canon Lawis can declare.
All Princis of the Occident
Ar tyll his Grace obedient;
For he hes hole power compleit

Boith of the body and the spreit,
Quhilk never had no Prince affore,
Except the mychtie Kyng of Glore :
To Christe he is gret Lewtennand,
In holy Peteris saitt syttand :
So he is of all kyngis Kyng
Quhilkis in to Europe now doith ryng.
 And, as the Romane Empriouris,
Havyng the Warld under thare curis,
Had princis, knychtis, and campiounis,
Rewlaris in tyll all Regiounis,
Uphaldyng thare auctoritie,
Usyng justice and policie ;
Rycht so, this potent Pope of Rome,
The soverane kyng of Christindome,
He hes, in tyll ilk countré,
His Princis of gret gravytie ;
In sum countreis, his Cardinallis,
In thare moste precious apparallis ;
Archbyschoppis, byschoppis, thow may se,
Defendyng his auctoritie,
With uther potent patriarkis ;
Collegis full of cunnyng clerkis ;
Abbottis and priouris, as ye ken,
Misrewlaris of religious men ;
Officiallis, with thare procuratouris,
Quhose langsum law spoilyeis the puris ;
Archidenis and denis of dignitie ;
Gret doctouris of divynitie ;
Thare chantouris, and thare sacristanis,
Thare tresouraris, and thare subdenis ;

Legionis of preistis seculeris,
Personis, vicairis, monkis, and freris,
Óf divers Ordouris mony one,
Quhilk langsum wer for tyll expone,
In syndrie habitis, as ye ken,
Different from uther Christin men;
Fair ladyis of religioun
Proffessit, in every regioun;
Fals heremitis, fassionit lyke the freris;
Proude parische clerkis, and pardoneris,
Thare gryntaris, and thare chamberlanis,
With thare temporall courtissianis,
Thus, all the warld, be land and sey,
His Sanctitude thay do obey:
Nocht onely his Spirituall kyngdome,
Bot the gret Empriour of Rome,
And Kyngis of everilk regioun,
That day quhen thay resave thare crown,
Thay mak aith of fidelytie
Tyll defende his auctorytie:
Moreovir, with humyll reverence,
Thay mak tyll hym obedience,
Be thare selfis, or ambassadouris,
Or utheris ornate oratouris.
   Quho doith ganestand his Majestie,
His lawis, or his lybertie,
Or haldis ony opinioun
Contrar his gret dominioun,
Outher be way of deid or wordis,
Ar put to deith, be fyre or swordis:
Sanct Peter stylit wes *Sanctus;*

Bot he is callit *Sanctissimus:*
His style at lenth gyf thow wald knaw,
Thow moste go luke the Canon Law,
Boith in the Sext and Clementene :
His staitly style thare may be sene:
Thare sall thow fynd, reid gyf thow can,
Quhow he is nother God nor man.

COURTEOUR.

Quhat is he than, be your jugement ?
Quod I, me thynk hym different,
Far from our Soverane, Lord Jesus,
And tyll his kynd contrarious :
For Christ wes God and naturall man.
Gyf he be nother, quhat is he than ?

EXPERIENCE.

The Canon Law, my Sonne, said he,
That questioun wyll declare to thé.
It doith transcend my rude ingyne
His Sanctitude for tyll defyne,
Or to schaw the auctoritie
Pertenyng to his Majestie.
So gret one Prince quhare sall thow fynd,
That spiritually may lowse and bynd ;
Nor be quhame synnis ar forgyffin,
Be thay with his disciplis schrevin ?
Quhame ever he byndis by his mycht,
Thay boundin ar in Goddis sycht ;
Quhame ever he lousis in erth heir doun,
Ar lousit be God in his regioun.

Als he is Prince of Purgatorie,
Delyvering saulis from paine to glorie :
Of that dirke dungeoun, but doute,
Quham evir he plesis he takis thame oute.
Oure secreit synnis, every yeir,
We mon schaw to sum preist or freir,
And tak thare absolutioun,
Or ellis we gett no remissioun ;
So, be this way, thay cleirly ken
The secretis of all seculare men ;
Thare secretis we knaw nocht at all :
Thus ar we to thame bound and thrall.
Quhat evir thare ministeris commandis
Most be obeyit, without demandis.
Quharefor, my Sonne, I say to thé,
This is ane marvellous Monarchie,
Quhilk hes power Imperiall
Boith of the body and the saull.

COURTEOUR.

Father, quod I, declare to me
Quhow did begyn this Monarchie.

EXPERIENCE.

Quod he, Christ Jesus, God and Man,
That Impyre gratiouslye began,
Nocht be the fyre, nor be the swourde ;
Bot be the vertew of his wourde ;
And left, in tyll his Testament,
Mony ane devote document,
With his successouris to be usit,

Thocht mony of thame be now abusit.
For Peter and Paull, with all the rest
Of thare brethrin, maid manifest
The law of God, with trew intent,
Precheing the Auld and New Testament.
Thay led thair lyfe in povertie,
Devotioun, and humilytie,
As did thare maister, Christ Jesus;
And war nocht half so glorious
As thare successouris now in Rome,
Impyrand ouer all Christindome.
Efter the deth of Peter and Paull,
And Christis trew disciplis all,
Thare successouris, within few yeris,
As at more lenth thare storye beris,
Full craftelye clam to the heycht,
Frome Spirituall lyfe to Temporall mycht.

COURTEOUR.

Father, or we passe forthermore,
Quhen did begyn thare Temporall glore?

EXPERIENCE.

Sonne, said he, thow sall understand,
Or ever ane Pape gat ony land,
Twa and thretty gude Papis in Rome
Ressavit the Crown of martyrdome,
Bot nocht the thrinfald diademe;
To weir thré crownis thay thocht gret schame:
Tyll Sylvester the Confessoure
Frome Constantene the Emprioure
Ressavit the Realme of Italie,

Rycht so, of Rome the gret cietie.
That wes the rute of thare ryches :
Then sprang the well of welthynes.
Quhen that the Pape wes maid ane kyng,
All Princis bowit at his biddyng :
This act wes done, withouttin weir,
Frome Christis deith thre hundreth yeir.
   Than Lady Sensualitie
Tuke lugeing in that gret Cetie,
Quhare scho sensyne hes done remane,
As thare awin lady Soverane.
Than Kyngis, in tyll all Nationis,
Maid Preistis gret fundationis :
Thay thocht gret mereit and honour
To contrafait the Empriour ;
As did David, of Scotland kyng,
The quhilk did founde, duryng his ryng,
Fyftene Abbayis, with temporall landis,
Withouttin teindis and offerandis ;
Be quhose holy simplicitie
He left the Crown in povertie.
   Now haif I schawin thee as I can,
Quhow thare Temporall impyre began,
Ascendyng up, aye gre by gre,
Abufe the Empriouris Majestie.
So, quhen thay gat amang thare handis
Of Italie all the Empriouris landis,
Efter that, in ilke countrie
Sprang up thare temporalitie,
With so gret ryches and sic rent,
That thay gan to be negligent
In makyng ministratioun

To Christis trew Congregatioun,
And tuke no more paine in thair precheing,
And far les travell in thare techeing;
Changeing thare Spiritualitie
In Temporall sensualitie.

COURTEOUR.

Father, thynk ye that thay ar sure
That thare Impyre sall lang indure?

EXPERIENCE.

Apperandlye it may be kende,
Quod he, thare glore sall have ane ende:
I mene, thare Temporall Monarchie
Sall turne in tyll humylitie.
Throuch Goddis worde, without debait,
Thay sall turne to thare first estait:
As Daniellis prophesie apperis,
Thareto sall nocht be mony yeris.
Quhowbeit Christis faith sall never faill,
Bot more and more it sall prevaill;
Thocht Christis trew Congregatioun
Suffer gret trybulatioun.

COURTEOUR.

Father, said I be quhat reasoun
Thynk ye thare Impyre may cum doun?

EXPERIENCE.

Consydderyng thare preheminence,
Quod he, for inobedience

Abusyng the commandiment
Quhilk Christ left in his Testament;
Usyng thare awin traditioun
More than his institutioun:
For Christ, in his last conventioun,
The day of his Ascensioun,
Tyll his Disciplis gaif command,
That thay suld passe in every land,
To teche and preche, with trew intent,
His law and his commandiment:
None uther office he to thame gaif:
He did nocht bid thame seik nor craif
Cors presentis, nor offerandis,
Nor gett Lordschipis of temporall landis.

 Bot now it may be hard and sene,
Baith with thyne eiris and thyne eine,
Quhow Prelatis now, in every land,
Takis lytill cure of Christis command,
Nouther in to thare deidis nor sawis;
Neglectyng thare awin Canon Lawis,
Usying thame selfis contrarious,
For the maist part, to Christ Jesus.

 Christ thocht no schame to be ane precheour,
And tyll all peple of trewth ane techeour.
Ane Pope, Byschope, or Cardinall,
To teche nor preche wyll nocht be thrall:
Thay send furth Freris, to preche for thame,
Quhilk garris the peple now abhor thame.

 Christ wald nocht be ane Temporall kyng,
Rychely into no realme to ryng,
Bot fled Temporall auctoritie.

As in the Scripture thow may se.
All men may knaw quhow Popis ryngis,
In dignitie abufe all kyngis,
Als weill in Temporalitie
As in to Spiritualitie.
Thow may se, be experience,
The Popis princely preheminence.

 In Cronicles geve thow lyst to luke,
Quhow Carion wryttis, in his buke,
Ane notabyll narratioun :
The yeir of oure Salvatioun
Ellewin hundreth and sax and fyftie,
Pope Alexander, presumptuouslie,
Quhilk wes the thrid Pope of that name,
To Frederike Empriour did diffame
In Veneis, that tryumphand town :
That nobyll Empriour gart ly down
Apone his wambe, with schame and lake,
Syne treid his feit apone his bake,
In toknyng of obedience.
Thare he schew his preheminence,
And causit his Clergy for to syng
Thir wourdis efter following :

 Super Aspidem et Basiliscum ambulabis.
 Et conculcabis Leonem et Draconem.—*(That is,)*
 Thow sal gang upon the eddar and the coketrice,
 And thow sal tred down the lyoun and the dragoun.

Than said this humyll Empriour,
I do to Peter this honour !
The Pope answerit, with wordis wroith,
Thow sall me honour, and Peter boith !

Christ, for to schaw his humyll spreit,
Did wasche his pure Disciplis feit:
The Popis holynis, I wys,
Wyll suffer Kyngis his feit to kys.
Birdis had thare nestis, and toddis thare den;
Bot Christ Jesus, saiffer of men,
In erth had nocht ane penny breid
Quhare on he mycht repose his heid.

Quhowbeit, the Popis excellence
Hes castellis of magnifycence;
Abbottis, Byschoppis, and Cardinallis
Hes plesand palyces royallis:
Lyke Paradyse ar those prelattis places,
Wantyng no plesoure of fair faces.
Jhone, Androw, James, Peter, nor Paull
Had few housis amang thame all:
From tyme thay knew the veritie
Thay did contempne all propertie,
And wer rycht hartfully content
Of meit, drynk, and abuilyement.

To saif Mankynde, that wes forlorne,
Christ bure ane creuell crown of thorne;
The Pope, thre crownis, for the nonis,
Of gold, poulderit with pretious stonis.

Of gold and sylver, I am sure,
Christ Jesus tuke bot lytill cure,
And left nocht, quhen he yald the spreit,
To by hym self ane wynding scheit.
Bot his successoure, gude Pope Johne,
Quhen he deceisit in Avinione,
He left behynd hym one treassoure

Of gold and sylver, by mesoure,
Be one juste computatioun,
Weill fyve and twentye myllioun,
As dois indyte Palmerius:
Reid hym, and thow sall fynd it thus.
   Christis Disciplis wer weill knawin
Throuch vertew, quhilk wes be thame schawin,
In speciall fervent charitie,
Gret pacience, and humylitie:
The Popis floke, in all regiounis,
Ar knawin best be thare clyppit crounis.
   Christ he did honour matrimonie
In to the Cane of Galalie,
Quhare he, be his power Divyne,
Did turne the walter in to wyne;
And, als, cheisit sum maryit men
To be his servandis, as ye ken:
And Peter, duryng all his lyfe,
He thocht no syn to haif ane wyfe.
Ye sall nocht fynd, in no passage,
Quhare Christ forbiddith mariage;
Bot leifsum tyll ilk man to marye,
Quhilk wantis the gyft of chaistytie.
   The Pope hes maid the contrar lawis
In his kyngdome, as all men knawis:
None of his Priestis dar marye wyfis,
Under no les paine nor thare lyfis.
Thocht thay haif concubynis fyftene,
In to that cace, thay ar ouersene.
Quhat chaistytie thay keip in Rome
Is weill kend ouer all Christindome.

Christ did schaw his obedience
On to the Empriouris excellence,
And causit Peter for to pay
Trybute to Cesar for thame tway.
Paull biddis us be obedient
To Kyngis, as the most excellent.
  The contrar did Pope Celistene,
Quhen that his sanctytude serene
Did crown Henry the Empriour:
I thynk he did hym small honour;
For with his feit he did hym crown,
Syne with his feit the crown dang doun,
Sayand, I haif auctoritie
Men tyll exalt to dignitie,
And to mak Empriouris and Kyngis,
And syne depryve thame of thair ryngis.
Peter, be my opinioun,
Did never use sic dominioun.
Apperandlye, be my jugement,
That Pope red never the New Testament:
Gyf he had lernit at that lore,
He had refusit sic vaine glore,
As Barnabas, Peter and Paull,
And rycht so, Christis disciplis all.
  The Capitane Cornelius,
Quhen Sanct Peter come tyll his hous,
Tyll worschyp hym, fell at his feit;
Bot Sanct Peter, with humyll spreit,
Did rais hym up, with diligence,
And did refuse sic reverence.
  Rycht so, Sanct Johne the Evangelist

The Angellis feit he wald haif kist;
Bot he refusit sic honoure,
Sayand, I am bot servitoure,
Rycht so, thy fallow and thy brother:
Gyff glore to God, and to none uther.
 Alykewyis Barnabas and Paull
Sic honour did refuse at all:
In Listra, quhare thay wroucht gret workis,
The preist of Jupiter, with his clerkis,
And all the peple, with thare avyse,
Wald haif maid to thame sacrifyse;
Of quhilk thay wer so discontent,
That thay thare clothyng raif and rent;
And Paull amang thame rudely ran,
Sayand, I am ane mortall man:
Gyf glore to God, of kyngis Kyng,
That maid hevin, erth, and every thyng.
Sen Peter and Paull vaine glore refusit,
With Popis quhy sulde sic glore be usit?
 Peter, Andro, Johne, James, and Paull,
And Christis trew disciplis all,
Be Goddis worde thare faith defendit;
To byrne and skald thay never pretendit.
The Pope defendis his traditioun
Be flammand fyre, without remissioun:
Quhowbeit men breik the law Divyne,
Thay ar nocht put to so gret pyne,
For huredome, nor idolatrye,
For incest, nor adulterye;
Or quhen young virginnis ar deflorit,
For sic thyng men ar nocht abhorit.

Bot quho that eitis flesche in to Lent
Ar terriblye put to torment;
And gyf ane preist happynis to marye,
Thay do hym baneis, cursse, and warye,
Thocht it be nocht aganis the law
Of God, as men may cleirlie knaw:
Betuix thir two quhat difference bene,
Be faithfull folk it may be sene.
Sic antitheses mony mo
I mycht declare, quhilkis I lat go,
And may nocht tary to compyle
Of ilk Ordour the staitlye style.

   The seilye Nun wyll thynk gret schame,
Without scho callit be Madame;
The pure Preist thynkis he gettis no rycht,
Be he nocht stylit lyke ane knycht,
And callit Schir, affore his name,
As Schir Thomas, and Schir Wilyame.
All monkrye, ye may heir and se,
Ar callit Denis, for dignitie:
Quhowbeit his mother mylk the kow,
He mone be callit Dene Androw,
Dene Peter, Dene Paull, and Dene Robart.
With Christ, thay tak ane painfull part,
With dowbyll clethyng frome the cald,
Eitand and drynkand quhen thay wald;
With curious countryng in the queir:
God wait, gyf thay by Hevin full deir,
My lorde Abbot, rycht venerabyll,
Ay marschellit upmoste at the tabyll;
My lord Byschope, moste reverent,

Sett abufe Erlis in Parliament;
And Cardinalis, duryng thare ryngis,
Fallowis to Princis and to Kyngis;
The Pope exaltit, in honour,
Abufe the potent Empriour.
   The proude Persone, I thynk trewlye,
He leidis his lyfe rycht lustelye;
For quhy? he hes none uther pyne
Bot tak his teind, and spend it syne:
Bot he is oblyste, be resoun,
To preche untyll his perrochioun:
Thoucht they want precheing sevintene yeir,
He wyll nocht want ane boll of beir.
Sum Personis hes at thare command
The wantoun wencheis of the land;
Als thay have gret prerogatyffis,
That may depart ay with thare wyffis,
Without divorce or summondyng,
Syne tak ane uther but weddyng:
Sum man wald thynk ane lustye lyfe,
Ay quhen he lyst to chenge his wyfe,
And tak ane uther of more bewtie:
Bot Secularis wantis that lybertie,
The quhilk ar bound in mariage;
Bot thay, lyke rammis in to thair rage,
Unpissilit rynnis amang the yowis,
So lang as Nature in thame growis.
   And als the Vicar, as I trow,
He wyll nocht faill to tak ane kow,
And umaist claith, thoucht babis thame ban,
Frome ane pure selye husband man;

Quhen that he lyis for tyll de,
Haiffeing small bairnis two or thre,
And hes thre ky, withouttin mo,
The vicare moste have one of tho,
With the gray cloke, that happis the bed,
Howbeit that he be purelye cled :
And gyf the wyfe dé on the morne,
Thocht all the babis suld be forlorne,
The uther kow he cleikis awaye,
With hir pure coit of roploch graye.
And gyf, within tway dayis or thre,
The eldest chyld hapnis to de,
Of the thrid kow he wylbe sure.
Quhen he hes all than under his cure,
And father and mother boith ar dede,
Beg mon the babis, without remede:
Thay hauld the corps at the kirk style,
And thare it moste remane ane quhyle,
Tyll thay gett sufficient souertie
For thare Kirk rycht and dewitie.
Than cummis the landis lord perfors,
And cleiks tyll hym ane herield hors.
Pure laubourars wald that law wer doun,
Quhilk never was fundit be resoun :
I hard thame say, onder confessioun,
That Law is brother tyll Oppressioun.

 My Sonne, I have schawin, as I can,
Quhow this Fyft Monarchie began ;
Quhose gret Impyre for to report
At lenth, the tyme bene all too schort.

HEIR FOLLOWIS ANE DESCRIPTIOUN OF THE COURT OF ROME.

COURTEOUR.

FATHER, said I, quhat rewll keip thay in Rome,
   Quhilk hes the Spirituall dominatioun
And Monarchie abufe all Christindome?
   Schaw me, I mak yow supplicatioun.

EXPERIENCE.

My Sonne, wald I mak trew narratioun,
Said he, to Peter and Paull thocht thay succeid,
I thynk thay preve nocht that in to thare deid:

For Peter, Androw, and Johne war fyschearis fyne,
   Of men and wemen, to the Christin faith;
Bot thay haif spred thare net, with huik and lyne,
   On rentis ryche, on gold, and uther graith:
   Sic fyscheing to neglect thay wylbe laith;
For quhy? thay haif fyscheit in, ouerthort the strandis,
Ane gret part trewlye of all temporall landis:

With that, the tent part of all gude movabyll,
   For the uphaldyng of thare digniteis:
So bene thare fyscheing wounder profitabyll
   On the dry land als weill as on the seis.
   Thare herywaiter thay spread in all countreis.

And, with thare hois nett, daylie drawis to Rome
The most fyne gold that is in Christindome.

I dar weill say, within this fyftie yeir,
    Rome hes ressett, furth of this Regioun,
For Bullis and Benefyce, quhilk thay by full deir,
    Quhilk mycht ful weil haif payit a kingis ransoun.
    Bot, war I worthye for to weir ane crown,
Preistis suld no more our substance so consume,
Sendyng yeirlye, so gret ryches to Rome.

In to thare tramalt nett thay fangit ane fysche,
    More nor ane quhaill worthye of memorye,
Of quhome thay have had mony dayntay dysche,
    Be quhome thay ar exaltit to gret glorye;
    That marvelous monstour callit Purgatorye.
Howbeit tyll us it is nocht amyable,
It hes to thame bene veray profytable.

Lat thay that fructfull fysche eschaip thare nett,
    Be quhome thay haif so gret commoditeis,
Ane more fatt fysche I traist thay sall nocht gett,
    Thocht thay wald sers ouerthort the occiane seis.
    Adew the daylie dolorous Derigeis!
Selye pure preists may syng with hart full sorye,
Want thay that painefull palyce, Purgatorye.

Fairweill, monꬶyre, with chanoun, nun, and freir!
    Allace! thay wylbe lychtleit in all landis:
Cowlis wyll no more be kend in kirk nor queir,
    Lat thay that fructfull fysche eschaip thare handis.
    I counsall theme to bynd hym fast in bandis:

For Peter, Androw, nor Johne culde never gett
So profytable ane fysche in to thare nett.

Thare merchandyce, in tyll all Nationis,
    As prentit lede, thare walx, and perchement,
Thare pardonis, and thare dispensationis,
    Thay do exceid sum temporall princis rent :
    In sic trafyke thay ar nocht neglygent.
Of benefyce thay mak gude merchandyce,
Throuch symonie, quhilk thay hald lytill vyce.

Christ did command Peter to feid his scheip;
    And so he did feid thame full tenderlye :
Of that command thay take bot lytill keip;
    Bot Christis scheip thay spulye petuouslye;
    And with the woll thay cleith thame curiouslye :
Lyk gormand wolfis, thay tak of thame thare fude,
Thai eit thair flesche, and drynkis boith mylk and
    blude.

For that office thay serve bot lytill hyir :
    I thynk sic Pastouris ar nocht for to pryse,
Quhilk can nocht gyde thare scheip about the myir,
    Thay ar so besye in thare merchandyse.
    Thocht Peter wes porter of Paradyse,
That plesand passage craftelye thay close :
Throuch thame rycht few gettis entres, I suppose.

Christ Jesus said, as Matthew did report,
    Wo be to Scribes and to Pharisience,
The quhilkis did close of Paradyse the port.

Of thame we haif the same experience :
To enter thare thay mak small diligence,
Thay tak sic cure in temporall besynes ;
Rycht so, frome us thay stop the plane entres.

Those spirituall keis quhilkis Christ to Peter gaif,
    Thare colour cleir with reik and rowst ar fadit ;
Unoccupyit thay hald thame in thare neif :
    Of that office thay serve to be degradit,
With Goddis worde withoute that thay remeid it,
Oppinyng the port quhilk lang tyme hes bene closit,
That we may enter, with thame, and be rejoisit.

Contrar tyll Christis institutioun,
    To thame that deis in habit of ane freir,
Rome hes thame grantit full remissioun,
    To pass tyll hevin straucht way, withouttin weir,
    Quhilk bene in Scotland usit mony ane yeir.
Be thare sic vertew in ane Freris hude,
I thynk in vane Christ Jesus sched his blude.

Wald God the Pope, quhilk hes preheminence,
    With advyse of his Counsall Generall,
That thay wald do thare detfull deligence,
    That Christis law mycht keipit be ouir all,
    And trewlye preicheit baith to gret and small,
And geve to thame Spirituall auctoritie
Quhilk culde perfytlie schaw the veritie !

Quho can not preche, a Preist sulde not be namit,
    As may be previt be the Law Divyne ;

And, be the Canon law, thay ar defamit
    That takis Priesthood bot onely to that fyne :
    Tyll all vertew thare hartis thay suld inclyne,
In speciall, to preche with trew intentis.
And minister the neidfull Sacramentis.

As for thare Monkis, thair Chanounis, and thare
    Freris,
    And lustye Ladyis of Religioun,
I knaw nocht quhat to thare office efferis ;
    Bot men may se thare gret abusioun.
    Thay ar nocht lyke, in to conclusioun,
Nother in to thare wordis nor thare warkis,
To the Apostolis, Prophetis, nor Patriarkis.

Geve presentlye thare Prelatis can nocht preche,
    Than latt ilke Byschope haif ane Suffragane,
Or successour, quhilk can the peple teche,
    On thare expensis yeirlye to remane,
    To cause the peple frome thare vyce refrane :
And, quhen ane Prelate hapnith to deceace,
Than put ane perfyte precheour in his pleace.

Do thay nocht so, on thame sall ly the charge,
    Geveand unhable men auctoritie ;
As quho wald mak ane steirman tyll ane barge
    Of ane blynd borne, quhilk can no dainger se.
    Geve that schyp drown, forsuth, I say for me,
Quho gaif that steirman sic commissioun
Suld of the schip mak restitution.

The humane Lawis that ar contrarious
   And nocht conformyng to the Law divyne,
Thay suld expell, and hald thame odious,
   Quhen thay persave thame cum to no gude fyne,
   Inventit bot be sensuall menis ingyne,
As that law quhilk forbiddis mariage,
Causyng young Clerkis byrne in lustys rage,

Difficill is chaistitie tyll observe,
   But speciall grace, laubore, and abstinence,
In tyll our flesche aye ryngith, tyll we sterve,
   That first Originall syn, concupiscence,
   Quhilk we, throuch Adamis inobedience,
Hes done incur, and sall indure for ever,
Quhill that our saull and body Deith dissever.

Tharefor God maid of mariage the band,
   In Paradyse, as Scripture doith recorde :
In Galelie, rycht so, I understand,
   Wes mariage honourit be Christ our Lorde
   Auld Law and New thareto thay do concorde.
I thynk for me, better that thay had sleipit,
Nor tyll have maid ane law and never keip it.

Tuke nocht Christ Jesu his Humanitie
   Of ane Virgene in mariage contractit,
And of hir flesche cled his Divynitie?
   Quhy haif thay done that blysfull band dejectit,
   In thare kyngdome? wald God it wer correctit;
That young prelattis mycht marye lustye wyffis,
And nocht in sensuall luste to leid thare lyffis.

Did nocht Christ cheis of honest maryit men,
　Alsweill as thay that keipit chaistitie,
For to be his disciplis as ye ken?
　As in the Scripture cleirlye thay may se,
　Thay keipit, styll, thare wyffis, with honestie;
As Peter, and his spousit bretherin, all,
Observit chaistitie matrymoniall.

Bot now apperis the prophesie of Paull,
　Quhow sum suld ryis, in to the latter aige,
That frome the trew faithe sulde depart and fall,
　And sulde forbid the band of mariage;
　Als thow sall fynd, into that sam passage,
Thay sulde command from meitis tyll abstene,
Quhilk God creat his pepyll to sustene.

Bot, sen the Pope, our Spirituall prince and kyng,
　He dois ouersie sic vyces manifest,
And in his kyngdome sufferith for to ryng
　The men be quhome the veritie bene supprest,
　I excuse nocht hym self more than the rest.
Allace! how sulde we membris be weill usit,
Quhen so our spirituall heidis bene abusit?

The famous ancient doctor Aviceane,
　Savis, quhen evyll rewme descendis frome the heid
In to the membris, generith mekle pane,
　Without thare be maid, haistelye, remeid.
　Quhen that cald humour dounwart dois proceid,
In senownis it causis Arthetica,
Rycht so, in to the handis, crampe Chiragra.

Of maladeis it generis mony mo
  Bot gyf men gett sum soverane preserve,
As in the theis Siatica Passio,
    And in the breist, sumtyme the strang Caterve,
    Quhilk causis men rycht haistellye to sterve,
And Podagra, difficill for to cure,
In mennis feit, quhilk lang tyme dois indure.

So, to this moste tryumphant Court of Rome
    This simylitude fuill weill I may compare,
Quhilk hes bene heirschyp of all Christindome,
    And to the warld ane evyll examplare,
    That umquhyle was lod sterre and lumynare,
And the moste sapient sors of sanctytude,
Bot now, allace ! bair of beatytude.

Thare Kyngdome may be callit Babilone,
    Quhilk umquhyle was ane brycht Hierusalem,
As planelye menis the Apostill Johne.
    Thare moste famous Citie hes tynt the fame ;
    Inhabitaris thareof, thare nobyll name ;
For quhy ? thay haif of Sanctis habitacle
To Symon Magus maid ane tabernacle.

And horribyll vaill of everilk kynd of vyce,
    Ane laithlye loch of stynkand lychorye,
Ane curssit cove, corrupt with covatyce,
    Bordourit aboute with pryde and symonye,
    Sum sayis, ane systerne full of sodomye,
Quhose vyce in speciall gyf I wald declair,
It wer aneuch for tyll perturbe the air.

Of treuth the hoill Christian Religioun
   Throuch thame are scandalizat and offendit.
It can nocht faill bot thare abusioun
   Affore the Throne of God it is ascendit :
   I dreid, but doute, without that thay amend it,
The plaiges of Johnis Revelatioun
Sall fall upon thare generatioun.

O Lord ! quhilk hes the hartis of everilk kyng
   In to thy hand, I mak thee supplication,
Convert that Court, that, of thair grace benyng,
   Thay wald mak generall reformatioun
   Amang thame selfis, in everilk Natioun
That thay may be ane holy exemplair
Tyll us, thy pure lawid commoun populair,

Hungrit, allace ! for falt of Spirituall fude,
   Because from us bene hid the veritie.
O Prince ! quhilk sched for us thy precious blude,
   Kendle in us the fyre of Charitie,
   And saif us frome Eterne miseritie,
Now lauboryng in to thy Kirk Militant,
That we may, all, cum to thy Kirk Tryumphant.

FINIS.

HEIR ENDIS THE THRID PART.

THE FOURT BUKE.

MAKAND MENTIOUN OF THE DEITH: AND OF THE ANTICHRIST: AND GENERALL JUGEMENT: AND OF CERTANE PLESOURIS OF GLORYFEIT BODYIS: AND QUHOW EVERY CREATURE DE-SYRIS TO SEE THE LAST DAY: WITH ANE EXHORTATIOUN, BE EXPERIENCE TO THE COURTEOUR.

COURTEOUR.

PRUDENT Father Experience,
Sen ye, of your benevolence,
Hes causit me for to consydder
Quhow warldlye pompe and glore bene slydder,
By divers storyis miserabyll;
Quhilkis to reheirs bene lamentabyll;
Yitt, or we passe furth of this vaill,
I pray yow geve me your counsaill
Quhat I sall do, in tyme cumyng.
To wyn the glore evirlesting.

EXPERIENCE.

My Sonne, said he, sett thy intent
To keip the Lordis commandiment,

And preis thee nocht to clym ouer hie
To no warldlie auctoritie.
Quho in the warld doith moste rejose,
Ar farrest aye frome thare purpose.
Wald thow leve warldlye vaniteis,
And thynk on foure extremiteis
Quhilkis are to cum, and that schortlye,
Thou wald never syn wylfullye.
Prent thir four in thy memorye :
The Deith, the Hell, and Hevinnis Glorye,
And extreme Jugement Generall,
Quhare thow man rander compt of all ;
Thow sall nocht faill to be content
Of quyet lyffe and sobir rent ;
Considdryng no man can be sure
In erth one hour for tyll indure ;
So all warldly prosperitie
Is myxit with gret miseritie.

Wer thow Empriour of Asia,
Kyng of Europe and Affrica,
Gret dominator of the Sey,
And thocht the Hevinnis did thee obey,
All fyschis sowmyng in the strand,
All beist and fowle at thy command,
Concludyng, thow wer Kyng of all
Under the hevin Imperiall ;
In that most heych authoritie
Thow suld fynd leist tranquilitie.
Exempyll of kyng Salamone,
More prosperous lyfe had nevir none ;
Sic ryches, with so gret plesoure,

Had never Kyng nor Emprioure,
With moste profunde intelligence,
And superexcelland sapience.
His plesand habitatiounis
Precellit all utheris Natiounis;
Gardyngis and parkis for hartis and hyndis,
Stankis with fysche of divers kyndis;
Moste profunde maisteris of musike,
That in the warld wes none thame like;
Sic tresour of gold and pretious stonis
In erth had nevir no kyng att onis:
He had sevin hundreth lustye quenis,
And thre hundreth fair concubenis;
In erth thare wes no thyng plesand
Contrarious tyll his command :
Yitt all this gret prosperitie
He thoucht in vaine and vanitie,
And mycht nevir fynd repose compleit,
Without afflictioun of the spreit.

COURTEOUR.

Father, quod I, it marvellis me,
He, haveand sic prosperitie,
With so gret ryches by mesoure,
Nor he had infynite plesoure.

EXPERIENCE.

My Sonne, the suth gyf thow wald knaw,
The veritie I sall thee schaw.
Thare is no warldly thyng, at all,
May satyfie ane mannis saull;

For it is so insaciabyll,
That Heuin and Erth may nocht be abyll
One saull allone to mak content,
Tyll it se God Omnipotent :
Wes never none, nor never salbe,
Saciate, that sycht tyll that he se.
Quharefor, my Sonne, sett nocht thy cure
In Erth, quhare no thyng may be sure,
Except the Deith allanerlye,
Quhilk followis man continuallye.
Tharefor, my Sonne, remember thee
Within schorte tyme that thow mon de,
Nocht knawing quhen, quhow, in quhat place,
Bot as plesit the Kyng of Grace.

OF THE DEITH.

Of Miserie moste miserable
Is Deith, and most abhominable,
That dreidful dragone, with his dartis
Aye reddy for to peirs the hartis
Of everilk creature on lyve,
Contrar quhose strenth may no man stryve.
 Of dolent Deith this sore sentence
Wes gyffin throw inobedience
Of our parentis, allace tharefor !
As I have done declare affore,
Quhow thay and thare posteritie
Wer, all, condampnit for to dee.
Quhowbeit the flesche to deith be thrall,

God hes the saull maid immortall,
And so, of his benignytie
Hes myxit his Justice with mercie.
Tharefor, call to remembrance
Of this fals warld the variance,
Quhow we, lyke pylgramis, evin and morrow,
Ay travellyng throw this vaill of sorrow;
Sum tyme in vaine prosperitie,
Sum tyme in gret miseritie,
Sum tyme in blys, sum tyme in baill,
Sum tyme rycht seik, and sum tyme haill,
Sum tyme full ryche, and sum tyme pure.
Quharefor, my Sonne, tak lytill cure
Nother of gret prosperitie,
Nor yitt of gret miseritie,
Bot plesand lyfe and hard myschance,
Ponder thame boith in one ballance;
Considdryng none auctoritie,
Ryches, wysedome, nor dignitie,
Empyre of realmes, bewtie, nor strenth,
May nocht one day our lyvis lenth.
Sen we ar sure that we moste dé,
Fairweill all vaine felycitie!

Gretlye it doith perturbe my mynde,
Of dolent Deith the divers kynd.
Thoucht Deith tyll every man resortis,
Yitt strykith he in syndrie sortis:
Sum be hait feveris violence;
Sum be contagious pestilence;
Sum be justice execution,
Bene put to deith without remissioun;

Sum hangit; sum doith lose thare heidis;
Sum brynt; sum soddin in to leiddis;
And sum, for thare unleifsum actis,
Ar rent and revin apone the ractis;
Sum ar dissolvit by poysoun;
Sum on the nycht ar murdreist doun;
Sum fallis in to frynasie;
Sum deis in hydropesie,
And utheris strange infirmiteis,
Quharein mony ane thousand deis,
Quhilk humane Nature dois abhor,
As in the gutt, gravell, and gor;
Sum, in the flux, and fevir quartane,
Bot ay, the houre of deith uncertane.
Sum ar dissolvit suddantlye,
Be cattarve, or be poplesye;
Sum doith distroye thame self also,
As Hannibal and wyse Cato;
Be thounder Deith sum doith consume,
As he did the thrid kyng of Rome,
Callit Tullius Hostilius,
As wryttis gret Valerius;
For he and his househald attonis
Wer brynt be thounder, flesche and bonis.
Sum deith be extreme excesse
Of joy, as Valerie doith expresse;
Sum be extreme malancholye
Wyll de, but uther maladye.
In Chronicles thow may weill ken,
Quhow mony hundreth thousand men
Ar slane, sen first the warld began,

In battell; and quhow mony one man
Apone the see doith lose thare lyvis,
Quhen schyppis upone roches ryvis.
Thocht sum dé naturally, throuch aige,
For mo deis raiffand in one raige.
Happy is he the quhilk hes space
Att his last hour to cry for grace.
Quhowbeit deith be abhominabyll,
I thynk it suld be comfortabyll
Tyll all thame of the faithfull nummer;
For thay depart frome cair and cummer,
Frome trubyll, travell, sturt, and stryfe,
Tyll joy and evirlestand lyfe.

 Pollidorus Virgilius
To that effect he wryttis thus:
In Trace, quhen ony chylde be borne,
Thare kyn and freindis cumis thame beforne,
With dolent lamentatioun,
For the gret trybulatioun,
Calamitye, cummer, and cure,
That thay in erth ar to indure;
Bot, at thare deith and burying,
Thay mak gret joy and bankettyng,
That thay have past from miserie
To rest and grett felycitie.

 Sen Deith bene fynall conclusioun,
Quhat valis warldly provisioun,
Quham wysedome may not contramand,
Nor strenth that stoure may nocht ganestand
Ten thousand myleone of treasoure
May nocht prolong thy lyfe one houre;

Efter quhose dolent departyng,
Thy spreit sall passe, but taryng,
Straucht way tyll joye inestimabyll,
Or to strang pane intollerabyll :
Thy vyle corruptit carioun
Sall turne in putrefactioun,
And so remane, in pulder small,
On to the Jugement Generall.

ANE SCHORT DISCRIPTIOUN OF THE ANTICHRIST.

COURTEOUR.

Quod I, Father, I heir men say
That thair sall ryse, affore that day
Quhilk ye call Generall Jugement,
One wickit man, from Sathan sent,
And contrar to the law of Christ,
Callit the creuell Antichrist.
And sum sayis, that myschevous man
Discende sall of the trybe of Dan.
And sulde be borne in Babilone,
The quhilk dissave sall mony one,
Infydelis sall, of every art,
With that fals Propheit tak one part :
And quhow that Enoch and Elias
Sall preche contrar that fals Messias ;
Bot fynally, his fals doctryne
And he sall be put to rewyne,
Bot nother be the fyre nor swourd,
Bot be the vertew of Christis wourd :

And, gyf this be of verytie,
The suith, I pray yow, schaw to me.

EXPERIENCE.

My Sonne, said he, as wryttis Johne,
Thare sall nocht be one man allone,
Havyng that name in speciall;
Bot Antichristis in generall
Hes bene, and now ar, mony one:
And, rycht so, in the tyme of Johne
Wer Antichristis, as hym self sayis;
And presentlye, now in thir dayis,
Ar rycht mony, withouttin dout,
Wer thare fals lawis weill soucht out.

Quha wes one greter Antichrist,
And more contraryous to Christ,
Nor the fals Propheit Machomeit,
Quhilk his curste lawis maid so sweit?
In Turkye yit thay ar observit,
Quhare throuch the hell he hes deservit.
All Turkis, Sarazenis, and Jowis,
That in the Sonne of God nocht trowis
Ar Antichristis, I thee declare.
Because to Christ thay ar contrare.

Daniell sayis, in his Propheseis,
That, efter the gret Monarcheis,
Sall ryse ane marvellous potent Kyng,
Quhilk with ane schameles face sall ryng,
Mychtie and wyse in dirk speikyngis,
And prospir in all plesand thyngis:
Throuch his falsheid and craftynes,

He sall flow in to welthynes;
The godlye pepyll he sall noye
By creuell deith, and thame distroye;
The Kyng of Kyngis he sall ganestand.
Syne be distroyit withouttin hand.

 Paull sayis, Affore the Lordis cumyng,
That thare salbe one departyng,
And that man of iniquitye
Tyll all men he sall opened be,
Quhilk sall sitt in the Holy sait,
Contrary God to mak debait:
Bot that Sonne of perditioun
Salbe put to confusioun
He power of the Haly Spreit,
Quhen he his tyme hes done compleit.

 Beleve nocht that, in tyme cumyng,
One gretar Antichriste to ryng
Nor thare hes bene, and presentlye
Ar now, as Clerkis can espye.
Tharefor, my wyll is, that thow knaw,
Quhat ever thay be that makis one law,
Thocht thay be callit Christin men,
By naturall reassoun thow may ken,
Be thay never of so gret valour,
Pape, Cardinall, Kyng, or Empriour,
Extolland thare traditionis
Abufe Christis institutionis,
Makand lawis contrar to Christe.
He is ane verray Antichriste;
And quho doith fortifye or defend
Sic law, I mak it to thé kend,

Be it Pape, Empriour, Kyng, or Quene,
Gret sorrow sall be on thame sene,
Att Christis extreme Jugement,
Without that thay in tyme repent.

HEIR FOLLOWIS A SCHORT REMEMBRANCE OF THE MOST TERRABYLL DAY OF THE EXTREME JUGEMENT.

COURTEOUR.

FATHER, said I, with your lycence,
Sen ye haith sic Experience,
Yitt one thyng at yow wald I speir:
Quhen sall that dreidfull day appeir
Quhilk ye call Jugement Generall?
Quhat thyngis affore that day sall fall?
Quhare sall appeir that dreidfull Juge?
Or quhow may faltouris gett refuge?

EXPERIENCE.

Quod he, As to thy first questioun,
I can mak no solutioun:
Quharefor, perturbe nocht thyne intent
To knaw day, hour, nor moment:
To God allone the day bene knawin,
Quhilk never was to none Angell schawin.
Howbeit, be divers conjectouris,
And principall expositouris

Of Daniell and his Prophecie,
And be the sentence of Elie,
Quhilkis hes declarit, as thay can,
How lang it is sen the Warld began,
And for to schaw hes done thare cure,
How lang thay traist it sall indure,
And als, how mony ages bene,
As in thare warkis may be sene.
   Bot, tyll declare thir questionis,
Thare bene divers opinionis.
Sum wryttaris hes the Warld devidit
In sex ageis : as bene desidit
In to *Fasciculus Temporum*,
And *Cronica Cronicorum ;*
Bot, be the sentence of Elie,
The Warld devydit is in thre ;
As cunnyng Maister Carioun
Hes maid plane expositioun,
How Elie sayis, withouttin weir,
The Warld sall stand sax thousand yeir
Of quhome I follow the sentence,
And lattis the uther Bukis go hence,
From the Creatioun of Adam
Two thousand yeir tyll Abraham ;
Frome Abraham, be this narratioun,
To Christis Incarnatioun,
Rycht so, hes bene two thousand yeris ;
And, be thir Propheceis, apperis
Frome Christ, as thay mak tyll us kend,
Two thousand tyll the Warldis end,
Of quhilkis ar by gone, sickirlye,

Fyve thousand, fyve hundreth, thre and fyftie;
And so remanis to cum, but weir,
Four hundreth, with sevin and fourtye yeir:
And than the Lorde Omnipotent
Suld cum tyll his gret Jugement.
 Christ sayis, the tyme salbe maid schort,
As Matthew planelye doith report,
That, for the warldis iniquitie,
The letter tyme sall schortnit be,
For plesour of the chosin nummer,
That thay may passe from care and cummer.
So, be this compt, it may be kend,
The Warld is drawand neir ane end:
For legionis ar cum, but doute,
Of Antichristis, wer thay soucht out;
And mony toknis dois appeir,
As efter, schortlye, thow sall heir,
Quhow that Sanct Jherome doith indyte,
That he hes red, in Hebrew wryte,
Of fyftene signis in speciall,
Affore that Jugement Generall.
Off sum of thame I tak no cure,
Quhilk I find nocht in the Scripture:
One part of thame thocht I declare,
First wyll I to the Scripture fare.
 Christ sayis, Affore that day be done,
Thare sallbe signis in Sonne and Mone;
The Sonne sall hyde his beymes brycht
So that the Mone sall gyf no lycht;
Sterris, be mennis jugement,
Sall fall furth of the firmament.

Of this signis, or we forther gone,
Sum morall sence we wyll expone,
As cunnyng Clerkis hes declarit,
And hes the Sonne and Mone comparit,
The Sonne, to the stait Spirituall,
The Mone, to princis Temporall,
Rycht so the sterris thay do compare
To the lawd common populare.
The Mone and sterris hes no lycht
But the reflex of Phebus brycht :
So, quhen the Sonne of lycht is dyrk,
The Mone and sterris man be myrk.
Rycht so, quhen pastouris spirituallis,
Popis, Byschoppis, and Cardinallis.
In thare begynning schew gret lycht.
The Temporall stait wes rewlit rycht.
 Bot, now, allace ! it is nocht so :
Those schynand lampis bene ago,
Thare radious beymes ar turnit in reik :
For now in erth no thyng thay seik,
Except ryches and dignitie,
Followyng thare sensualitie.
Mony prelatis ar now ryngand,
The quhilkis no more dois understand
Quhat doith pertene to thare offyce,
Nor thow can kendyll fyre with yce.
Wo to Papis, I say for me,
Quhilk sufferis sic enormitie,
That ignorant warldly creaturis
Suld in the kirk haif ony curis !
No marvell thocht the peple slyde,

Quhen thay have blynd men to thare gyde!
For ane Prelat that can nocht preche,
Nor Goddis law to the peple teche,
Esaye compareth hym in hys wark,
Tyll ane dum dog that can nocht bark;
And Christ hym callis, in his grief,
Moste lyke ane murdrer, or ane theif.
The cunnyng doctour Augustyne
Wolfis and devyllis doith thame defyne.
The Canon Lawe doith hym defame
That of ane Prelat beris the name,
And wyll nocht preche the Divyne lawis,
As the Decreis planelye schawis.
Bot those that hes auctoritie
To provyde spirituall dignytie
Mycht, geve thay plesit to tak pane,
Gar thame lycht all thair lampis agane:
Bot ever, allace! that is nocht done,
So dirknit bene boith Sonne and Mone.

War Kyngis lyvis weill declarit,
The quhilkis ar to the Mone comparit,
Men mycht consydder thare estate
Frome charitie degenerate.
I thynk thay sulde thynk mekle schame
Of Christ for to take thare surname,
Syne leif nocht lyke to Christianis,
Bot more lyke Turkis and to Paganis.
Turke contrar Turke makis lytill weir;
Bot Christiane princis takis no feir,
Quhilkis suld aggre as brother to brother,
But now ilk ane dyngis doun ane uther.

I knaw no ressonabyll cause quharefore
Except pryde, covatyce, and vaine glore
The Empriour movis his ordinance
Contrar the potent Kyng of France;
And France, rycht so, with gret regour,
Contrar his freinde the Empriour;
And rycht swa, France agane Ingland;
Ingland alsso, aganis Scotland;
And als the Scottis, with all thare mycht,
Doith feycht, for tyll defend thare rycht:
Betuix thir realmes, of Albione,
Quhare battellis hes bene mony one,
Can be maid none affinitie,
Nor yit, no consanguinitie;
Nor, be no waye, thay can consydder
That thay may have lang peace togydder,
I dreid that weir makis none endyng,
Tyll thay be boith onder ane kyng.
Thocht Christ, the Soverane Kyng of Grace,
Left, in his Testament, lufe and peace,
Our Kyngis frome weir wyll nocht refrane,
Tyll thare be mony ane thousand slane,
Gret heirschipis maid be see and land,
As all the Warld may understand.

COURTEOUR.

Father, I thynk that temporall kyngis
May feycht, for tyll defend thare ryngis;
For I haif sene the Spirituall Stait
Mak weir, thare rychtis tyll debait.

I saw Pape Julius manfullye
Passe to the feild tryumphantlye,
With ane rycht aufull ordinance,
Contrar Lowis, the kyng of France;
And, for to do hym more dispyte,
He did his Regioun interdyte.

EXPERIENCE.

My Sonne, said he, as I suppose,
That langith weill tyll our purpose;
How Sonne and Mone ar boith denude
Of lycht, as Clerkis dois conclude,
Comparyng thame, as ye hard tell,
To Spirituall Stait and Temporell,
And commoun peple, half disparit,
Quhilk to the Sterris bene comparit.
Lawid peple followis ay thare heidis;
And speciallye, in to thare deidis,
The moste part of Religioun
Bene turnit in abusioun.
Quhat dois availl religious weidis,
Quhen thay ar contrar in thare deidis?
Quhat holynes is thare within
Ane wolf cled in ane wedderis skin?
So, be thir toknis, dois appeir,
The day of Jugement drawis neir.
Now latt us leif this morall sens,
Proceidyng tyll our purpose hens,
And of this mater speik no more,
Begynning quhare we left affore.

The Scripture sayis, efter thir signis

Salbe sene mony marvellous thyngis :
Than sall ryse trybulationis
In erth, and gret mutationis,
Als weill heir under, as above,
Quhen vertewis of the hevin sall move.
Sic creuell weir salbe, or than,
Wes never sene sen the Warld began,
The quhilk sall cause gret indigence,
As darth, hunger, and pestilence.
The horribyll soundis of the sey
The peple sal perturbe and fley.
Jerome sayis, it sall ryse on heycht
Abone montanis, to mennis sycht ;
Bot it sall nocht spred ouer the land,
Bot, lyke ane wall, evin straycht upstand,
Syne sattell doun agane so law
That no man sall the walter knaw.
Gret quhalis sall rummeis, rowte and rair,
Quhose sound redound sall in the air ;
All fysche and monstouris marvellous
Sall cry, with soundis odious,
That men sall wydder on the erd,
And wepyng, wary sall thare weird,
With lowde allace and welaway !
That ever thay baid to se that day ;
And, speciallye, those that dwelland be
Apone the costis of the see.
Rycht so, as Sanct Jerome concludis,
Sall be sene ferleis in the fludis :
The sey, with movyng marvellous,
Sall byrn with flammis furious.

Rycht so, sall byrn fontane and flude;
All herb and tre sall sweit lyk blude;
Fowlis sall fall furth of the air;
Wylde beistis to the plane repair,
And, in thare maner, mak gret mone.
Gowland with mony gryslye grone.
The bodeis of dede creaturis
Appeir sall on thare sepulturis :
Than sall boith men, wemen, and bairnis
Cum creipand furth of howe cavernis,
Quhare thay, for dreid, wer hyd affore,
With seych, and sob, and hartis sore;
Wandryng about as thay war wode,
Affamysit for falt of fude.
None may mak utheris confortyng,
Bot dule for dule, and lamentyng.
Quhat may thay do bot weip and wounder,
Quhen thay se roches schaik in schounder,
Throw trimlyng of the erth and quakyng?
Of sorrow, than, salbe no slakyng.
Quho that bene levand, in those dayis
May tell of terrabyll affrayis :
Thare ryches, rentis, nor tressour,
That tyme sall do thame small plesour.
Bot, quhen sic wonderis dois appeir,
Men may be sure the day drawis neir,
That juste men pas sall to the glore,
Injuste, to pane for ever more.

COURTEOUR.

Father, said I, we daylie reid
One Artikle, in to our Creid,

Sayand, that Christ Omnipotent,
In to that generall Jugement,
Sall juge boith dede and quick also.
Quharefore, declare me, or ye go,
Geve thare sall ony man, or wyfe,
That day be foundin upon lyve.

EXPERIENCE.

Quod he, As to that questione,
I sall mak sone solutione.
The Scripture planelye doith expone,
Quhen all tokynnis bene cum and gone,
Yitt mony one hundreth thousand
That samyn day salbe levand :
Quhowbeit, thare sall no creature
Nother of day nor hour be sure ;
For Christ sall cum so suddantlye,
That no man sall the tyme espye ;
As it wes in the tyme of Noye,
Quhen God did all the warld distroye.
Sum on the feild salbe lauborand ;
Sum in the templis mariand ;
Sum afore jugis makand pley ;
And sum men sailand on the sey.
Those that bene on the feild going
Sall nocht returne to thare luging.
Quho bene apone his hous above.
Sall haif no laser to remove.
Two salbe in the myll grindyng,
Quhilkis sall be takyng, but warnyng ;
The ane, tyll everlestyng glore,

The uther, loste for ever more.
Two salbe lying in one bed ;
The one, to plesour salbe led,
The uther, salbe left allone,
Gretand with mony gryslie grone.
And so, my Sonne, thow may weill trow,
The warld salbe as it is now,
The peple usyng thare besynes,
As Holy Scripture doith expres.
Sen no man knawis the hour, nor day,
The Scripture biddis us walk and pray,
And for our Syn be penitent,
As Christ wald cum incontinent.

THE MANER QUHOW CHRIST SALL CUM TO HIS JUGEMENT.

EXPERIENCE.

QUHEN all takinnis bene brocht tyll end,
Than sall the Sone of God discend :
As fyreflaucht haistely glansyng.
Discend sall the most Hevinly Kyng,
As Phebus, in the Orient,
Lychtnis in haist the Occident,
So plesandlye he sall appeir
Amang the hevinlye cluddis cleir,
With gret power and majestie,
Above the countrie of Judee,
As Clerkis doith concludyng, haill,
Direct above the lustye vaill

Of Josaphat and Mont Olyveit:
All prophesie thare salbe compleit.
The Angellis of the Ordoris Nyne
Inviron sall that throne Divyne
With hevinlye consolatioun,
Makand hym ministratioun.
In his presens thare salbe borne
The signis of cros, and croun of thorne,
Pillar, nalis, scurgis, and speir,
With everilk thyng that did hym deir,
The tyme of his grym Passioun;
And, for our consolatioun,
Appeir sall, in his handis and feit,
And in his syde, the prent compleit
Of his fyve woundis precious,
Schynand lyke rubeis radious,
Tyll reprobatt confusioun;
And, for fynall conclusioun,
He, sittand in his tribunall,
With gret power Imperiall.
There sall ane Angell blawe a blast
Quhilk sall mak all the Warld agast,
With hyddeous voce, and vehement
Ryse, Dede folk, cum to Jugement!
With that, all reassonabyll creature
That ever was formit be Nature
Sall suddantlye start up attonis,
Conjunit with saull, flesche, blude, and bonis.
That terribyll trumpet, I heir tell,
Beis hard in Hevin, in Erth, and Hell:
Those that wer drownit in the sey

That boustious blast thay sall obey;
Quhare ever the body buryit wase,
All salbe fundyng in that plase.
Augellis sall passe in the four airtis
Of Erth, and bryng thame frome all partis,
And, with one instant diligence,
Present thame to his Excellence.
  Sanct Jerome thoucht continuallye
On this Jugement, so ardentlye,
He said, quhidder I eit, or drynk,
Or walk, or sleip, forsuth me thynk
That terrabyll trumpat, lyke ane bell,
So quiklye in my eir doith knell,
As instantlye it wer present,
Ryse, Dede folk, cum to Jugement!
Geve Sanct Jerome tuke sic ane fray,
Allace! quhat sall we synnaris say?
  All those quhilk funding bene on lyve
Salbe immortall maid belyve;
And, in the twynkling of one Ee,
With fyre thay sall translatit be,
And never for to dee agane,
As Divyne Scripture schawis plane,
Als reddy, boith for pane and glore,
As thay quhilk deit lang tyme affore.
  The Scripture sayis, thay sall appeir
In aige of thre and thretty yeir,
Quhidder thay deit young or auld,
Quhose gret nummer may nocht be tauld.
That day sall nocht be myst one man
Quhilk borne wes sen the warld began.

The Angellis sall thame separait,
As hird the scheip doith frome the gait;
And those quhilk bene of Beliallis band
Trymling apone the erth sall stand,
On the left hand of that Gret Juge,
But esperance to get refuge.
  Bot those quhilk bene predestinate
Sall frome the erth be elevate:
And that moste happy cumpanye
Sall ordourit be triumphantlye,
At the rycht hand of Christe, our Kyng,
Heych in the air, with loude lovyng.
  Full gloriouslye thare sall compeir,
More brycht than Phebus in his speir,
The Virgene Marie, quene of quenis,
With mony ane thousand brycht Virgenis.
The Fatheris of the Auld Testament,
Quhilk wer to God obedient.
Father Adam sall thame convoye,
With Abell, Seth, Enoch, and Noye;
Abraham, with his faithfull warkis,
With all the prudent Patriarkis;
Johne the Baptiste thare sall compeir,
The principall and last messyngeir,
Quhilk come bot half ane yeir affore
The cumyng of that Kyng of Glore;
Moyses, Esayas, honorabyll,
With all trew Prophetis venerabyll;
David, with all the faithfull Kyngis
Quhilk verteouslye did rewle thare ryngis
The nobyll cheiftane Josue,

With gentyll Judas Machabé,
With mony one nobyll campioun,
Quhilk, in thare tyme, with gret renoun,
Manfullye tyll thare lyvis ende,
The law of God thay did defende.
 With Eve, that day, salbe present
The Ladyis of the Auld Testament:
Delbora, Adamis douchter deir,
With the four lusty ladyis cleir
Quhilk keipit wer in the Ark with Noye.
Sara and Cithara, with joye,
The quhilkis to Abraham wyffis bene;
With gude Rebecka, thare salbe sene
The prudent wyffis of Israell.
Gude Lya, and the fair Rachell;
With Judeth, Hester, and Susanna,
And the rycht sapient Quene Saba.
 Thare sall compeir Peter and Paull,
With Christis trew disciplis all,
Lawrence and Stevin, with thare blyst band
Of Martyris, mo than ten thousand;
Gregore, Ambrose, and Augustyne,
With confessouris, ane tryumphand tryne;
With Sanct Francis, and Dominick,
Sanct Bernard, and Sanct Benedick;
With small nummer of Monkis, and Freiris,
Of Carmeletis, and Cordeleiris,
That, for the lufe of Christ onlye,
Renuncit the warld unfenyeitlye.
 With Elizabeth and Anna,
All gude wyffis sall compeir that day;

The blyst and holy Magdelane,
That day, affore hir Soverane,
Rycht plesandlye scho sall present
All synnaris that wer penitent,
Quhilk of thare gylt heir askit grace:
In Hevin, with hir, sall have ane place.
 But wo beis to that bailfull band
Quhilk sall stand lawe at his left hand!
Wo, than, to Kyngis and Empryouris
Quhilkis wer unrychteous conquerouris;
For thare glore and perticular gude,
Gart sched so mekle saikles blude!
But sceptour, crown, and robe royall,
That day thay sall mak compt of all,
And, for thare creuell tyrannye,
Sall punyste be perpetuallye.

 Ye Lordis and Barronis, more and les,
That your pure tennantis dois oppres,
Be gret gyrsome, and dowbyll maill,
More than your landis bene availl,
With sore exhorbitant cariage,
With Merchetis of thare Mariage,
Tormentit boith in peace and weir,
With burdyngis more than thay may beir;
Be thay haif payit to yow thare maill,
And, to the Preist, thare teindis haill,
And, quhen the land agane is sawin,
Quhat restis behynd I wald wer knawin!
I traist thay and thare pure househauld
May tell of hunger and of cauld.

Without ye haif of thame pieté,
I dreid ye sall gett no mercie,
That day, quhen Christ Omnipotent
Cumis tyll his Generall Jugement.
  Wo beis to publict oppressouris,
To tyrannis, and to transgressouris,
To murderaris, and commoun theifis,
Quhilk never did mend thare gret mischeifis!
Fornicatouris, and ockararis.
Commoun publict adulteraris,
All pertinat wylfull heretykis,
All fals dissaitfull scismatykis,
All salbe present in that place,
With mony lamentabyll Allace!
  The cursit Cayn, that never wes gude,
With all scheddaris of saikles blude;
Nemrod, fundar of Babilone,
With fals ydolateris mony one;
Nynus, the kyng of Asseriay,
With gret dule shall compeir that day,
Quhilk first inventit ymagery,
Quharethrouch come gret ydolatry:
For makyng of the image, Bell,
That day his hyre salbe in hell.
  The gret oppressour, kyng Pharo,
The tyrrane Empriour Nero,
Sall with thame cursit Kyng Herode bryng,
With mony uther cairfull kyng.
The cruell kyng Antiochus.
With the moste furious Olofernus,
Gret oppressouris of Israell,

That day thare hyre salbe in Hell.
With Judas sall compeir ane clan
Of fals tratouris to God and man.
Thare sall compeir, of everilk land,
With Ponce Pylat, one bailfull band
Of Temporall and of Spirituall statis;
Fals jugis, with thare advocatis.
Thare sall our Senyeouris of the Sessioun
Of all thare faltis mak cleir confessioun.
Thare salbe sene the fraudfull failyeis
Of Schireffis, Provestis, and of Bailyeis;
Officiallis, with thare Constry clerkis,
Sall mak compt of thare wrangous werkis;
Thay, and thare perverst Procuratouris,
Oppressouris boith of ryche and puris,
Throw delatouris full of dissait,
Quhilk mony one gart beg thare meit.
Gret dule, that day, to Jugis bene,
That cumis nocht with thare conscience clene:
That day sall pas be Peremptouris,
Without cawteill or dillatoris;
No Duplicandum, nor Triplicandum,
But schortlye pas to Sentenciandum,
Without continuatiounis,
Or ony appellatiounis:
That sentence sall nocht be retraitit,
Nor with no man of Law debaitit.

Ye Lauboraris be sey and landis,
Perfyte craftismen, and ryche merchandis,
Leif your dissait and crafty wylis,
Quhilk syllie simpyll folk begylis

Mak recompence heir, as ye may,
Remembryng on this dreidfull day.

  With Machomeit sall compeir, but doute,
Of Antichristis one hydduous route:
Byschope Annas, and Cayphas,
With hym in cumpany sall pas:
With Scrybis and fals Pharisianis,
Quhilk wrocht on Christ gret violencis;
With mony one Turk and Sarracene,
With gret sorrow thare salbe sene:
Papis, for thare traditionis
Contrar Christis institutionis,
With mony one cowle and clyppit crown,
Quhilk Christis lawis strampit down,
And wald nocht suffer for to preche
The veritie, nor the peple teche,
Bot Lawit men pat to gret torment,
Quhilk usit Christis Testament.
All Kyngis and Quenis thare salbe kend,
The quhilk sic lawis did defend.
In that Court sall cum mony one
Of the blak byik of Babilone.
The innocent blude, that day, sall crye
Ane loude vengeance, full pietuouslye,
On those creuell bludy bowchouris,
Martyris of propheteis and prechouris,
Sum with the fyre, sum with the sworde,
Quhilk planelye precheit Goddis worde;
That day thay sall rewardit be,
Conforme to thare iniquitie.

The Sodomitis and Gomoreance,
On quhome God wrocht so gret vengeance,
With Chore, Dathan, and Abyrone,
With thare assistance, mony one,
The holy Scripture wyll thee tell,
Quhow thay sank all doun to the hell.
With Symon Magus sall resort
Of proude Preistis ane schamefull sort.
 That samyn day thare salbe sene
Mony one creuell cairfull Quene :
Quene Semirame, kyng Nynus wyfe,
Ane tygir full of sturt and stryfe,
Togydder with Quene Jezabell,
Quhilk wes boith covetous and creuell ;
The fals dissaitfull Dalyla ;
The creuell Quene Clytemnestra,
The quhilk did murdreis, on the nycht
Agamemnon, boith wyse and wycht,
The quhilk wes hir awin soverane lorde,
As Grekis storyis dois recorde.
With creuell Quenis mony one,
Quhilk langsum wer for tyll expone.

 Ye wantoun Ladyis, and Burges wyvis,
That now for sydest taillis stryvis,
Flappand the fylth amang your feit,
Rasyng the duste in to the streit,
That day, for all your pompe and pryde,
Your tailis sall nocht your hyppis hyde :
Thir vaniteis ye sall repent,
Without that ye be penitent.

With Phitonissa, I heir tell,
Quhilk rasit the Spreit of Samuell,
That day, with hir, thare sall resorte
Of rank wytcheis one sorrowfull sorte,
Brocht frome all partis, mony one myle,
Frome Savoy, Atholl, and Argyle,
And frome the Ryndes of Galloway,
With mony wofull wallaway!

Ye Brether of Religioun,
In tyme leif your abusioun,
With quhilk ye haif the warld abusit,
Or ye, that day, salbe refusit.
I speik to yow all, generallye,
Nocht till one Ordoure speciallye.
That day, all creature sall ken
Geve ye war sanctis, or warldly men,
Or gyf ye tuk the skapellarye,
That ye mycht leif more plesandlye,
And gett ane gude gross portioun,
Or for godlye devotioun;
That day, your faynit sanctytudis
Sail nocht be knawin be your hudis:
Your superstitious ceremoneis,
Participand tyll ydolatreis,
Corde, cuttit schone, nor clippit hede,
That day sall stande yow in no stede:
For cowlis blak, gray, nor begaird,
Ye sall, that day, get no rewaird.
Your polit payntit flatterye,
Your dissimulat ypocrasye,

That day thay sall be cleirlye knawin,
Quhen ye sall scheir as ye have sawin.
Tharefore, in tyme be penitent,
Or ellis that day ye wylbe schent.
  I pray yow hartlie, as I may,
Remember on that dreidfull day,
Ye Abbot, Pryour, and Pryores:
Consydder quhat ye did profes,
And quhow that your promotioun
Wes no thyng for devotioun;
Bot tyll obtene the Abbacye.
Ye maid your vow of Chaistitye,
Of Povertie, and Obedience:
Tharefor, remord your conscience,
Quhow thir thre vowis bene observit,
And quhat rewarde ye have deservit.
Quharefore, repent, quhill ye have space;
Sen God is lyberall of his grace.

COURTEOUR.

  Father, quod I, declare to me
Quhare sall our Prelatis ordourit be,
Quhilk now bene in the warld levand:
With quhome sall cum that Spirituall band?

EXPERIENCE.

  Quod he, As Sanct Barnard discryvis,
Without that thay amend thare lyvis,
And leve thair wantoun vicious warkis,
Nocht with Prophetis nor Patriarkis,
Nocht with Martyris nor Confessouris,

The quhilkis to Christ wer trew prechouris :
Thare predecessouris, Peter and Paull,
That day wyll theme mysken, at all;
So sall they nocht, I say for me,
With the Apostillis ordourit be.
I traist thay sall dwell on the bordour
Of Hell, quhare thare salbe non ordour.
Endlang the flude of Phlegetone,
Or on the brayis of Acherone ;
Cryand on Charon, I conclude,
To ferrie thame ouer that furious flude,
Tyll eternall confusioun,
Without thay leif thare abusioun.
I traist those Prelatis, more and les,
Sall mak cleir compt of thare ryches,
That dreidfull day, with hartis sore,
And quhat service thay did tharefore.
The princely pomp nor apparell
Of Pope, Byschope, nor Cardinall,
Thare Royall rentis, nor dignitie,
That day sall nocht regardit be.
Thare sall no tailis, as I heir say,
Of Byschoppis be borne up that day.
Cum thay nocht with thare conscience clene,
On thame gret sorrow salbe sene,
Without that thay thare lyfe amend
In tyme : And so I mak ane end.

HEIR FOLLOWIS THE MANER QUHOW CHRIST SALL GIVE HIS SENTENCE.

EXPERIENCE.

Quhen all thir Congregatiounis
Beis brocht furth frome al natiounis,
Quhilk wilbe without lang process,
Thocht I haif maid sum lang degress;
For, in the twinkling of one E,
All mankind sall presentit be
Affore that Kyngis Excellence,
Than schortlye sall he geve sentence;
First sayand to that blysfull band,
Quhilk beis ordourit at his rycht hand,
Cum, with my Fatheris benysoun,
And ressave your possessioun,
Quhilk bene for yow preordinat,
Affore the Warld wes first creat.
Quhen I wes hungry, ye me fed;
Quhen I was naikit, ye me cled:
Oftymes ye gave me herberye,
And gaif me drynk, quhen I was drye,
And vesyit me with myndis meik,
Quhen I was presonar and seik:
In all sic trybulatioun,
Ye gaif me consolatioun.
  Than sall thay say, O potent Kyng,
Quhen saw we thé desyre sic thyng?

We never saw thyne excellence
Subdewit to sic indigence.
Yes, sall he say, I yow assure,
Quhen ever ye did ressave the pure,
And, for my saik, maid thame supplie,
That gyft, but doute, ye gaif to me:
Tharefor sall now begyn your glore,
Quhilk sall indure for ever more.
  Than sall he luke on his left hand,
And say unto that bailfull band,
Pas, with my maledictioun,
Tyll eternall afflictioun,
In cumpany with feindis fell,
In everlestyng fyre of Hell:
Quhen I stude, naikit, at your yett,
Houngry, thristy, cauld, and wett,
Rycht febyll, seik, and lyke to dé,
I never gatt of yow supplie;
And, quhen I lay in presoun strang,
For yow I mycht haif lying full lang,
Without your consolatioun,
Or ony supportatioun.
  Trymbling for dreid, than sall thay say,
With mony hydduous harmissay,
Allace! gude Lorde, quhen saw we thee
Subject to sic necessitie?
Quhen saw we thee cum to our dure,
Houngry, thristy, naikit, pure?
Quhen saw we thee in presoun ly,
Or thee refusit herbery?
  Than sall that most precelland Kyng

Tyll those wretchis mak answeryng,
That tyme quhen ye refusit the puris
Quhilkis neidfull cryit at your duris,
And of your superfluitie
For my saik maid thame no supplie,
Refusand thame, ye me refusit,
With wrecheitness so ye wer abusit,
Tharefor ye sall have, to your hyre,
The everlestyng byrning fyre,
But grace, but peace, or confortyng.
Than sall thay cry, full sore weipyng,
That we were maid, allace ! gude Lorde !
Allace ! is thare non misericorde ?
But thus, withouttin hope of grace,
Tyne presens of thy plesand face ?
Allace for us ! it had bene gude,
We had bene smorit in our cude.

 Than, with one rair, the erth sall ryve,
And swallow thame, boith man and wyve ;
Than sall those creaturis forlorne
Warie the hour that thay wer borne,
With mony yamer, yowt, and yell,
Frome tyme thay feill the flammis fell
Apone thare tender bodeis byte ;
Quhose torment salbe infinyte :
The erth sall close, and frome thare sycht
Sall takin be all kynde of lycht.
Thare salbe gowlyng and gretyng,
Bot hope of ony confortyng :
In that inestimabyll pane
Eternallye thay sall remane,

Byrnand in furious flammys rede,
Ever deand, but never be dede;
That the small minute of one hour
To thame salbe so gret dolour,
Thay sall thynk thay haif done remane
Ane thousand yeir in to that pane.
Allace ! I trimbyll tyll heir tell
The terribyll tormentyng of Hell.
That panefull pytt quho can deplore,
Quhilk mon indure for evermore ?
  Than sall those glorifyit creaturis,
With myrth and infinyte plesouris,
Convoyit with joy angelical,
Passe to the Hevin imperiall.
With Christ Jesu, our Soverane Kyng,
In glore eternallye to ryng,
Of man quhilk passis the ingyne
The thousand part for tyll defyne
Allanerlie of the leist plesoure
Preordinat for ane creature.
  Than sall ane fyre, as Clerkis sane,
Mak all the hyllis and valeyis plane.
Frome Erth, up to the Hevin impyre,
All beis renewit by that fyre,
Purgeyng all thyng materiall
Under the Hevin imperiall:
Boith erth and water, fyre and air,
Salbe more perfyte maid, and fair,
The quhilkis affore had myxit bene,
Sall than be purifyit and maid clene.
The Erth lyke christall salbe cleir;

And everilk Planeit in his speir
Sall rest, withouttin more moveyng.
Boith Sterny Hevin and Christellyng,
The first and hiest Hevin movabyll,
Sall stand, but turnyng, firme and stabyll.
The Sonne in to the Orient
Sall stand, and in the Occident
Rest sall the Mone, and be more cleir
Nor now bene Phebus in his speir.
And, als, that lantern of the Hevin
Sall gyf more lycht, by greis sevin,
Nor it gave sen the Warld began.
The Hevin renewit salbe than ;
Rycht so the Erth, with sic devyse,
Compair tyll hevinlye Paradyse.

So Hevin and Erth salbe all one,
As menith the Apostill Johne.
The gret Sey sall no more appeir,
Bot lyke the christall pure and cleir,
Passing imaginatioun
Of man to mak narratioun,
Of glore, quhilk God haith done prepair
Tyll every one that cummis thare,
The quhilk with eiris, not with eine
Of man, may nocht be hard nor sene.
With hart it is unthynkabyll,
And with toungis inpronunciabyll ;
Quhose plesouris salbe so perfyte,
Haveyng in God so gret delyte,
The space now of one thousand yeir,

That tyme sall nocht one hour appeir;
Quhilk can nocht comprehendit be,
Tyll we that plesand sycht shall se.
   Quhen Paull wes revyst, in the spreit,
Tyll the thrid Hevin, of glore repleit,
He sayith, the secretis quhilk he saw
Thay wer nocht leifsum for to schaw
To no man on the erth leveand:
Quharefor, preis nocht tyll understand,
Quhowbeit thareto thow haif desyre,
The secretis of the Hevin impyre.
The more men lukis on Phebus brycht,
The more febyll salbe thare sycht:
Rycht so, latt no man sett thare cure
To sers the heych Divyne nature:
The more men studye, I suppose,
Salbe the more frome thare purpose.
To knaw quhareto sulde men intend,
Quhilk Angellis can nocht comprehend?
Bot, efter this gret Jugement,
All thyng tyll us salbe patent.
   Latt us, with Paull our mynde addres,
He, beand full of hevinlynes,
Full humilye he techeit us,
Nocht for to be too curious
Quhowbeit men of gret ingyne
To seik the heych secretis divyne,
Quhose jugementis ar unsercheabyll,
And strange wayis investigabyll,
That is to say, past out fynding,
Of quhome no man may fynd endyng.

It sufficeth us for tyll implore
Greit God, to bryng us to that glore!

OF CERTANE PLESOURIS OF THE GLORIFEIT BODEIS.

EXPERIENCE.

SEN thare is none, in erth, may comprehend
  The Hevinlye glore and plesouris infinyte,
Quhairfor, my Sone, I pray thee not pretend
  Ouer far to seik that maner of delyte
  Quhilk passit naturall reasoun to indyte,
That God, affore that He the Warld creat,
Preparit to thame quhilk ar predestinat.

All mortall men salbe maid immortall,
  That is to say, never to dé agane,
Impassabyll, and so celestiall
  That fyre nor swerd may do to thame no pane;
  Nor hete, nor cald, nor frost, nor wynd, nor rane,
Thocht sic thyng wer, may do to thame no deir.
Those creaturis, rycht so, salbe als cleir

As flammand Phebus in his mansioun:
  Considder than, gyf thare salbe gret lycht,
Quhen every one in to that regioun
  Sall schyne lyke to the Sonne, and be als brycht;
  Lat us, with Paull, desyre to se that sycht:
To be dissolvit Paull had a gret desyre,
With Christ to be in tyll the Hevin impyre.

And, more attour, as Clerkis can discryve,
　Thare marvellous myrthis beis incomparabyll:
Amang the rest, in all thare wyttis fyve
　Thay sall have sensuall plesouris delectabyll.
　The hevinlye sound, quhilk salbe innarrabyll,
In thare eris continuallye sall ryng.
And, als, the sycht of Christ Jesus, our Kyng.

In his tryumphant throne Imperiall,
　With his Mother, the Virgene Quene of quenis,
Thare salbe sene: the Court Celestiall,
　Apostolis, Martyris, Confessouris, and Virgenis,
　Brychtar than Phebus in his speir that schynis,
The Patriarkis, and Prophetis venerabyll,
Thare salbe sene, with glore inestimabyll.

And with thare Spirituall Eis, salbe sene
　That sycht quhilk bene most superexcelland,
God, as he is and evermore hes bene.
　Continuallye that sycht contempland,
　Augustyne sayis, he had lever tak on hand
To be in Hell, he seying the essence
Of God, nor be in Hevin but his presence.

Quho seis God in his divynitie,
　He seis, in hym all uther plesand thyngis,
The quhilk with toung can nocht pronuncit be.
　Quhat plesour bene to se that Kyng of Kyngis!
　The gretest pane the dampnit folk doun thryngis,
And, to the Devyllis, the most punytioun,
It is of God to want fruitioun.

And mairattour, thay sall feill sic ane smell
　　Surmountyng far the fleure of erthly flouris,
And, in thare mouth, ane taist, as I heir tell,
　　Of sweit and supernaturall sapouris;
　　Als thay sall se the hevinlye brycht colowris
Schynyng amang those creaturis divyne.
Quhilk tyll discryve transcendith mannis ingyne.

And als, thay sall haif sic agilitie,
　　In one instant to passe, for thare plesour,
Ten thousand mylis in twynkling of one E:
　　So thare joyis salbe without mesour.
　　Thay sall rejois to se the gret dolour
Of dampnit folk in hell, and thare torment;
Because of God it is the juste jugement.

Subtellytie thay sall have marvellouslye:
　　Supponyng that thare wer ane wall of bras.
One glorifeit body may rycht haistellye
　　Out throw that wall without impediment, pas,
　　Siclyke as doith the sonne beime throw the glas;
As Christ tyll his Disciplis did appeir,
All entres clois, and none of thame did steir.

Quhowbeit, in Hevin, thocht everilk creature
　　Have nocht alyke felicitie, nor glore,
Yitt everilk one sall haif so gret plesure,
　　And so content, thay sall desyre no more:
　　To have more joye thay sall no way implore;
Bot thay salbe all satysfeit and content,
Lyke to this rude exempyll subsequent.

Tak ane crowat, one pynt stope, and one quart,
   One gallon pitchair, one punsioun, aud one tun,
Of wyne, or balme; gyf everilk one thare part,
   And fyll thame full, tyll that thay be ouir run:
   The lytill crowat, in comparisoun,
Salbe so full, that it may hald no more
Of sic misouris, thocht thare be twenty score.

In to the tun, or in the punsioun,
   So all those vesschellis, in one qualitie,
May hald no more, without thay be ouir run:
   Yitt haif thay nocht alyke in quantitie:
   So, be this rude exempyll, thow may se,
Thocht everilk one be nocht alyke in glore,
Ar satysfeit so that thay desyre no more.

Thocht presentlye, be Goddis proviance,
   Beistis, fowlis, and fyschis in the seis,
Ar necessar, now, for mannis sustenance,
   With cornis, herbis, flowris, and fructfull treis,
   Than sall thare be non sic commoditeis:
The Erth sall beir no plant, nor beist brutall,
Bot, as the Hevinnis, brycht lyke burall.

Suppone sum be on erth, walkand heir doun,
   Or heycht abone, quhare ever thay pleis to go,
Of God thay have, ay, cleir fruitioun,
   Boith, Est, or West, up, doun, or to or fro.
   Clerkis declaris plesouris mony mo,
Quhilk dois transcend al mortal mennis ingyne
The thousand part of those plesouris divyne.

In to the Hevin thay sall perfytlie knaw
  Thare tender freindis, thare father, and thare
    mother,
Thare predecessouris quhilkis thay never saw,
  Thare spousis, bairnis, syster, and thare brother;
  And everilk one sall have sic lufe tyll uther,
Of utheris glore and joy thay sall rejoyse,
As of thare awin, as Clerkis doith suppose.

Than salbe sene that brycht Jerusalame
  Quhilk Johne saw, in his Revelatione.
We mortall men, allace! ar far to blame,
  That wyll nocht haif consideratione,
  And one continuall contemplatione,
With hote desyre to cum on to that glore,
Quhilk plesour sall indure for ever more.

O Lorde, our God and Kyng Omnipotent,
  Quhilk knew, or thow the hevin and erth creat,
Quho wald to thee be inobedient,
  And so disarve for to be reprobat,
  Thou knew the noumer of predestinat,
Quhome thow did call, and hes thame justifeit,
And sall, in Hevin, with thee be glorifeit.

Grant us to be, Lorde! of that chosin sort
  Quhome, of thy mercy superexcellent,
Did purifie, as Scripture doith report,
  With the blude of that holy Innocent,
  Jesu, quhilk maid hym self obedient
On to the deth, and stervit on the Rude:
Latt us, O Lord! be purgit with that blude.

All creature that ever God creat,
　　As wryttis Paull, thay wys to se that day
Quhen the childryng of God, predestinat,
　　Sall do appeir in thare new fresche array;
　　Quhen corruptioun beis clengit clene away,
And changeit beis thare mortall qualitie
In the gret glore of immortalitie.

And, moreattour, all dede thyngis corporall,
　　Onder the concave of the Hevin impyre,
That now to laubour subject ar, and thrall,
　　Sone, mone, and sterris, erth, walter, air, and fyre,
　　In one maneir thay have ane hote desyre,
Wissing that day, that thay may be at rest,
As Erasmus exponis manifest.

We sé the gret Globe of the Firmament
　　Continuallie in moveyng marvellous;
The sevin Planetis, contrary thare intent,
　　Ar reft about, with course contrarious;
　　The wynd, and see, with stormys furious,
The trublit air, with frostis, snaw, and rane,
Unto that day thay travell ever in pane.

And all the Angellis of the Ordouris Nyne,
　　Haveand compassioun of our misereis,
Thay wys efter that day, and to that fyne,
　　To sé us freed frome our infirmiteis,
　　And clengit frome thir gret calamiteis
And trublous lyfe, quhilk never sall have end
On to that day, I mak it to thee kend.

ANE EXHORTATIOUN
GYFFIN BE FATHER EXPERIENCE, UNTO HIS SONNE THE COURTEOUR.

EXPERIENCE.

My Sonne, now mark weil in thy memory,
Of this fals Warld the trublous transitory,
  Quhose dreidfull dayis drawis neir aue end.
Tharfor, call God to be thy adjutory;
And every day, my Sonne, *Memento Mori;*
  And watt not quhen, nor quhare that thow sal wend.
  Heir to remaine I pray thee nocht pretend;
And, sen thow knawis the tyme is verray schort,
In Christis blude sett all thy hole comfort.

Be nocht too myche solyst in temporall thyngis;
Sen thow persavis Pape, Empriour, nor Kyngis
  In to the erth haith no place permanent,
Thow seis that Deith thame dulefully doun thryngis,
And reivis thame from thare rent, ryches, and ringis,
  Tharefor, on Christ confirme thyne hole intent;
  And of thy callyng be rycht weill content.
Than God, that fedis the fowlis of the air,
All neidfull thyng for thee he sall prepair.

Consydder, in thy contemplatioun,
Ay, sen the warldis first creatioun,
   Mankynd hes tholit this misery mortall,
Ay tormentit with trybulatioun,
With dolour, dreid, and desolatioun.
   Gentiles, and chosin peple of Israell,
   To this unhap, all subject ar, and thrall;
Quhilk misery, but doute, sall ever indure,
Tyll the last day : my Sonne, thareof be sure.

That day, as I have maid narratioun,
Salbe the day of consolatioun
   Tyll all the childryng of the chosin noumer :
Thare endit beis thare desolatioun.
And als, I mak thee supplycatioun,
   In erthlye materis tak thee no more cummer.
   Dreid nocht to dee; for Deith is bot ane slummer :
Leve ane just lyfe, and with ane joyous hart,
And of thy guddis tak plesandlye thy part.

Of our talkeing now latt us mak ane end.
Behald quhow Phebus dounwart dois discend,
   Towart his palyce in the Occident.
Dame Synthea, I se, scho dois pretend
In tyll hir wattry regioun tyll ascend,
   With vissage paill, up frome the Orient.
   The dew now donkis the rosis redolent :
The mareguildis, that all day wer rejosit
Of Phebus heit, now craftelly ar closit.

The blysfull byrdis bownis to the treis,
And ceissis of thare hevinlye armoneis :
  The cornecraik in the crofte, I heir hir cry ;
The bak, the howlat, febyll of thare eis,
For thair pastyme, now in the evenyng fleis ;
  The nychtyngaill, with myrthfull melody,
  Hir naturall notis persith throw the sky,
Tyll Synthea, makand hir observance,
Quhilk on the nycht dois tak hir dalyance.

I se Pole Artike in the North appeir,
And Venus rysing, with hir bemis cleir :
  Quharefor, my SONNE, I hald it tyme to go.

COURTEOUR.

Wald God, said I, ye did remane all yeir,
That I mycht of your hevinlye lessonis leir :
  Of your departyng I am wounder wo.

EXPERIENCE.

  Tak pacience, said he ; it mone be so :
Perchance, I sall returne with deligence.—
Thus I departit frome EXPERIENCE :

And sped me home, with heart sychyng full sore,
And enterit in my quyet Oritore.
  I tuke paper, and thare began to wryt
This Miserie, as ye have hard afore.
All gentyll Redaris hertlye I implore
  For tyll excuse my rurall rude indyte,
  Thoucht Phareseis wyll have at me dispyte,

Quhilkis wald not that thare craftynes wer kend:
Latt God be Juge! And so I mak ane end.

FINIS.

QUOD LYNDESAY.

1552.

ANE PLEASANT SATYRE OF THE THRIE ESTAITIS.

ANE SATYRE
OF THE THRIE ESTAITIS.

NAMES OF PERSONS IN THE PLAY.

PART THE FIRST.—

Rex Humanitas.
Diligence, *the Messenger.*
Wantonnes.
Placebo.
Solace, *called* Sandie.
The Vyces *in the habit of Friars :*—
    Flatterie (*alias* Devotioun).
    Falset (*alias* Sapience).
    Dissait (*alias* Discretioun).
Divyne Correctioun (*or* King Correctioun).
Correctioun's Varlet.
Gude Counsall.
Spiritualitie :—
    The Bishop.
    The Abbot.
    Schir Parson, a Persone.
Temporalitie.
Sensualitie.
Hamelines.
Danger.

Fund Jonet.
Dame Chastitie.
Dame Veritie.
Prioress or Abbess.

The First Interlude.—

Dame Chastitie.
The Sowtar.
The Sowtar's Wyfe.
The Taylour.
The Taylour's Wyfe.
Jennie the Taylour's Daughter.
Diligence.

The Second Interlude.—

Pauper, the Pure Man.
Diligence.
The Pardoner, *called* Schir Robert Rome-raker.
The Sowtar.
The Sowtar's Wyfe.
Wilkin, the Pardoner's Boy.

Part the Second—

Rex Humanitas.
Diligence, *the Messenger*.
The Three Estaitis :—
    Spiritualitie (or the Clergy).
    Temporalitie (or Landholders).
    The Burgesses (or Merchants).

Johne the Common-weill.
Divyne Correctioun.
Pauper.
The Abbot.
The Parson.
Placebo.
Wantones.
Solace.
Covetice.
Sensualitie.
Gude Counsell.
First and Second Sarjeant.
The Scrybe, or Notar.
Commoun Thift.
Oppressioun.
Doctour of Divinity.
First Licentiate.
Batchelor.
Flatterie, the Freir.
The Taylor.
The Sowtar.
Dissait.
Dame Veritie.
Dame Chastitie.
The Abbess or Prioress.

THE THIRD INTERLUDE.—

Rex Humanitas.
Folie.
Diligence.

ANE PLEASANT SATYRE OF THE THRIE ESTAITIS IN COMMENDATIOUN OF VERTEW AND VITUPERATIOUN OF VYCE, AS FOLLOWIS.

[PART THE FIRST.]

DILIGENCE.

THE FATHER, and founder of faith, and felicitie,
   That your fassioun formed to his similitude;
And his SONE, our Saviour, scheild in necessitie,
   That bocht yow from baillis, ransonit on the Rude,
   Repleadgeand his presonaris with his hart blude; 5
The HALIE GAIST, governour, and grounder of grace,
   Of wisdome and weilfair baith fontane and flude,
Saif yow all that I sie seisit in this place,
   And scheild yow from sinne;
And with his spreit yow inspyre,   10
Till I have schawin my desyre:
Silence, Soveraine, I requyre:
   For now I begin.   [*Pausa.*

TAK tent to me, my freinds, and hald yow coy,
   For I am sent to yow, as messingeir,   15
From ane nobill and rycht redoubtit Roy,
   The quhilk hes bene absent this monie yeir;
   Humanitie, give ye his name wald speir,
Quha bade me schaw to yow, but variance,

That he intendis amang yow to compeir,
With ane triumphand awfull ordinance :
With crown, and sword, and scepter, in his hand,
    Temperit with mercie, quhen penitence appeiris :
Howbeit, that he lang tyme hes bene sleipand,   5
    Quhairthrow misreull hes rung thir monie yeiris ;
    That innocentis hes bene brocht on thair beiris,
Be fals reporteris of this natioun ;
    Thocht young oppressouris at the elder leiris ;
Be now assurit of reformatioun.   10

Sie no misdoeris be sa bauld,
As to remaine into this hauld :
For quhy, be him that Judas sauld,
    They will be heich hangit ;
Now faithfull folk for joy may sing :   15
For quhy, it is the just bidding
Of my soveraine lord the King,
    That na man be wrangit,
Thocht he ane quhyll into his flouris,
Be governit be vile trompouris,   20
And sumtyme lufe his paramouris,
    Hauld ye him excusit ;
For quhen he meittis with Correctioun,
With Veritie, and Discretioun,
Thay will be banisched aff the toun,   25
    Quhilk hes him abusit.

And heir, be oppin Proclamatioun,
    I wairne, in name of his magnificence,
The THRIE ESTAITIS of this Natioun,

That thay compeir, with detfull diligence,
And till his Grace mak thair obedience.
And first, I wairne the Spiritualitie,
And se the Burgessis spair not for expence,
Bot speid thame heir, with Temporalitie. 5

Als I beseik yow, famous Auditouris,
  Conveinit in this congregatioun,
To be patient, the space of certaine houris,
  Till ye have hard our schort narratioun:
  And als we mak yow supplicatioun, 10
That na man tak our wordis intill disdaine;
  Althocht ye heir be declamatioun,
The Common-weill richt pitiouslie complaine.
Richt so the verteous ladie Veritie
  Will mak ane pitious lamentatioun: 15
Als for the treuth scho will impresonit be,
  And banisched lang tyme out of the Toun:
  And Chastitie will mak narratioun,
How scho can git na lugeing in this land,
  Till that the heavinlye king Correctioun 20
Meit with the King, and commoun hand for hand.

  Prudent Peopill I pray yow all,
  Tak na man greif, in speciall;
  For wee sall speik in generall,
    For pastyme, and for play: 25
  Thairfoir till all our rymis be rung,
  And our mistoinit sangis be sung,
  Let everie man keip weill ane toung,
    And everie woman tway.

REX HUMANITAS.

O Lord of lords, and King of kingis all,
    Omnipotent of power, Prince but peir,
Ever ringand, in gloir celestiall,
    Quha be great micht, and haifing na mateir,
    Maid heavin, and eird, fyre, air, and watter cleir ; 5
Send me thy grace, with peace perpetuall,
    That I may rewll my realme to thy pleaseir,
Syne bring my saull to joy angelicall.

Sen thow hes givin mee dominatioun,
    And rewll of pepill subject to my cure,   10
Be I nocht rewlit be counsall, and reasoun,
    In dignitie I may nocht lang indure.
    I grant my stait my self may nocht assure,
Nor yit conserve my lyfe in sickernes :
    Have pitie, Lord, on mee, thy creature,   15
Supportand me in all my busines.

I thé requeist, quha rent was on the Rude,
    Me to defend from the deids of defame ;
That my pepill report of me bot gude,
    And be my saifgaird baith from sin, and shame. 20
    I knaw my dayis induris bot as ane dreame ;
Thairfor, O Lord, I hairtlie thé exhort,
    To gif me grace to use my diadeame
To thy pleasure, and to my gret comfort.
        [*Heir sall the King pass to the Royall sait, and sit
        with ane grave countenance, till Wantonness cum.*

WANTONNES.

My Soveraine Lord, and Prince but peir,   30

THE THRIE ESTAITIS.

Quhat garris yow mak sic dreirie cheir?
Be blyth, sa lang as ye ar heir,
    And pas tyme, with pleasure:
For als lang leifis the mirrie man,
As the sorie for ocht he can,   5
His banis full sair, Sir, sall I ban,
    That dois yow displeasure.
Sa lang as Placebo, and I,
Remaines into your company,
Your Grace sall leif richt mirrely;   10
    Of this haif ye na dout.
Sa lang as ye haif us in cure,
Your Grace, Sir, sall want na pleasure:
War Solace heir, I yow assure,
    He wald rejoyce this rout.   15

PLACEBO.

Gude brother myne, quhare is Solace?
The mirrour of all mirrines?
I have gret mervell, be the Mess,
    He taries sa lang.
Byde he away, wee ar bot shent,   20
I ferlie how he fra us went:
I trow he hes impediment.
    That lettis him nocht gang.

WANTONNES.

I left Solace, that same greit loun,
Drinkand into the burrows toun,   25
It will cost him halfe of ane croun,

Althocht he had na mair.
And als hee said, he wald gang see
Fair Ladie Sensualitie,
The beriall of all bewtie,
 And portratour preclair.   5

PLACEBO.

Be God, I see him, at the last,
As he war chaist, rynnand richt fast,
He glowris, evin as he war agast,
 Or fleyit of ane gaist.
Na, he is wod drunkin, I trow, 10
Sie ye not that he is wod fow :
I ken weill, be his creischie mow,
 He hes bene at ane feast.

SOLACE.

Now, quha saw ever sic ane thrang;
Me thocht sum said I had gaine wrang; 15
Had I help, I wald sing ane sang,
 With ane richt mirrie noyse.
I have sic pleasure at my hart,
That garris me sing the tribill pairt,
Wald sum gude fallow fill the quart, 20
 It wald my hart rejoyce.
Howbeit, my coat be short, and nippit,
Thankis be to God I am weill hippit,
Thocht all my gold may sone be grippit
 Intill ane pennie pursse; 25
Thocht I ane servand lang haif bene,
My purchais is nocht worth ane preine;

I may sing, Peblis on the Greine,
    For ocht that I may tursse.
Quhat is my name? can ye not gesse,
Sirs, ken ye nocht Sandie Solace?
Thay callit my mother bonie Besse,   5
    That dwelt betwene the Bowis.

. . . .

And gif I lie, sirs, ye may speir:
Bot, saw ye nocht the King cum heir?
I am ane sportour, and playfeir
    To that royall young King.   10
He said, he wald within schort space,
Cum pas his tyme into this place:
I pray the Lord to send him grace,
    That he lang time may ring.

PLACEBO.

Solace, quhy taryit ye sa lang?   15

SOLACE.

The feind a faster I micht gang:
I micht not thrist out throw the thrang,
    Of wyfes fyftein fidder:
Than for to rin I tuik ane rink,
Bot I felt never sik ane stink: 20
For our Lordis luif gif me ane drink,
    Placebo, my deir brother.
        [*Heir sall Placebo gif Solace ane drink.*

REX HUMANITAS.

My servant Solace, quhat gart you tarie?

SOLACE.

I wait nocht, Sir, be sweit Saint Marie!
I have bene in ane feirie farie,
    Or ellis intill ane trance:
Sir, I have sene, I yow assure,
The fairest earthlie creature,   5
That ever was formit be nature,
    And maist for to advance.
To luik on hir is great delyte,
With lippis reid, and cheikis quhyte,
I wald renunce all this warld quyte,   10
    For till stand in hir grace:
Scho is wantoun, and scho is wyse;
And cled scho is on the new gyse,
It wald gar all your flesche up ryse,
    To luik upon hir face.   15
War I ane king it sould be kend,
I sould not spair on hir to spend;
And this same nicht for hir to send,
    For my pleasure.
Quhat rak of your prosperitie,   20
Gif ye want Sensualitie?
I wald nocht gif ane sillie flie,
    For your treasure.

REX HUMANITAS.

Forsuith, my freinds, I think ye ar nocht wyse,
    Till counsall me to break commandement,   25
Directit be the Prince of Paradyse:
    Considdering ye knaw that my intent
    Is for till be to God obedient,

Quhilk dois forbid men to be lecherous:
  Do I nocht sa, perchance, I will repent;
Thairfoir, I think your counsall odious,
    The quhilk ye gaif mee till;
  Because I haif bene, to this day,   5
Tanquam tabula rasa:
That is als mekill as to say,
    Redie for gude, and ilL

PLACEBO.

Beleive ye, that we will begyll yow?
Or from your vertew we will wyle yow?   10
Or with evill counsall overseyll yow?
    Both, into gude and evill:
To tak your Graces part wee grant,
In all your deidis participant;
Sa that ye be nocht ane young sanct,   15
    And syne ane auld devill.

WANTONNES.

Beleive ye, Sir, that lecherie be sin?
  Na, trow nocht that, this is my ressoun quhy;
First, at the Romane Kirk will ye begin,
  Quhilk is the lemand lamp of lechery: 20
  Quhair Cardinalis, and Bischopis, generally,
To luif ladies, thay think ane plesaud sport,
  And out of Rome hes baneist Chastity,
Quha with our Prelats can get na resort.

SOLACE.

Sir, quhill ye get ane prudent Queine,   25

I think your Majestie serein
Sould haif ane lustie concubein,
    To play yow withall:
For, I knaw, be your qualitie,
Ye want the gift of chastitie;   5
Fall to *in nomine Domini:*
    This is my counsall.
I speik, Sir, under protestatioun,
That nane at me haif indignatioun:
For all the Prelats of this natioun,   10
    For the maist part,
Thay think na schame to have ane huir,
And sum hes thrie under thair cuir:
This to be trew, I'le yow assuir,
    Ye sall heir efterwart.   15
Sir, knew ye all the mater throch,
    To play ye wald begin;
Speir at the Monks of Bamirrinoch,
    Gif lecherie be sin.

PLACEBO.

Sir, send ye for Sandie Solace,   20
Or ells your monyeoun Wantonnes,
And pray my ladie Priores,
    The suith till declair:
Gif it be sin to tak Kaity,
Or to leif like ane bummill baty?   25
The buik sayis, *Omnia probate,*
    And nocht for to spair.
    [*Heir sall entir Dame Sensualitie, with hir
        Madynnis Hamelines and Danger.*

SENSUALITIE.

Luifers awalk ! behald the fyrie spheir,
    Behauld the naturall dochter of Venus :
Behauld luifers, this lustie Ladie cleir,
    The fresche fonteine of knichtis amorous,
    Repleit with joyis dulce and delicious.   5
Or quha wald mak to Venus observance,
    In my mirthfull chalmer melodious,
There sall thay fynd all pastyme, and pleasance;

Behauld my heid, behauld my gay attyre,
    Behauld my halse, lusum and lilie quhyte ;   10
Behauld my visage, flammand as the fyre,
    Behauld my papis, of portratour perfyte.
    To luik on mee luiffers hes greit delyte,
Rycht sa hes all the kinges of Christindome ;
    To thame I haif done pleasouris infinyte,   15
And speciallie unto the Court of Rome.

Ane kis of me war worth, in ane morning,
A milyioun of gold to knight, or king :
And yit, I am of nature sa towart,
I lat na luiffer pas with ane sair hart.   20
Of my name, wald ye wit the veritie,
Forsuith thay call me Sensualitie.
I hauld it best now, or we farther gang,
To dame Venus let us go sing ane Sang.

HAMELINESS.

    Madame but tarrying,   25
        For to serve Venus deir,

We sall fall to, and sing,
  Sister Danger, cum neir.

DANGER.

Sister, I was nocht sweir,
  To Venus observance.
Howbeit, I mak Dangeir,
  Yit, be continuance,
  Men may have thair pleasance:
Thairfoir lat na man fray,
  We will tak it, perchance,
Howbeit that wee say nay.

HAMELINESS.

Sister, cum on your way,
  And let us nocht think lang,
In all the haist wee may,
  To sing Venus ane Sang.

DANGER.

Sister, sing this Sang I may not,
Without the help of gude Fund-Jonet.
Fund-Jonet, hoaw! cum tak a part.

FUND-JONET.

That sall I do, with all my hart,
Sister, howbeit, that I am hais,
I am content to beir a bais.
Ye twa suld luif me as your lyfe,

*[Ye know I lernit you baith to sing:
In my chalmer, ye wat weill quhare,
San syne the pynt ane man ye spare.

Fund-Jonet; fy, ye ar to blame!
To speik fowll words, think ye not schame?]*

[*Exeunt.*

REX HUMANITAS.

Up, Wantonnes, thow sleipis too laug!
Me thocht I hard ane mirrie sang:
I thee command, in haist to gang,
   Se quhat yon mirth may meine.

WANTONNES.

I trow, Sir, be the Trinitie,   5
Yon same is Sensualitie,
Gif it be scho, sune sall I sie
   That Soverane sereine.
    [*Heir sall Wantonnes go spy thame, and come
      agane to the King.*

REX HUMANITAS.

Quhat war thay yon, to me declair.

WANTONNES.

Dame Sensuall, baith gude and fair.   10

PLACEBO.

Sir, scho is mekill to avance,
For scho can baith play, and dance:
   That perfyte patron of plesance,
    Ane perle of pulchritude:
Soft as the silk is hir quhite lyre,   15
Hir hair is like the goldin wyre:
My hart burnis in ane flame of fyre,
   I sweir yow, be the Rude!
I think scho is sa wonder fair,
   That in earth scho has na compair,   20

War ye weill lernit at luifis lair
    And syne had hir anis sene:
I wait, be cokis passioun,
Ye wald mak supplicatioun,
And spend on hir ane millioun,   5
    Hir lufe for till obteine.

SOLACE.

Quhat say ye, Sir, ar ye content,
That scho cum heir incontinent?
Quhat vails your kingdome, and your rent,
    And all your great treasure;   10
Without ye he haif ane mirrie lyfe,
And cast asyde all sturt, and stryfe?
And sa lang as ye want ane wyfe,
    Fall to, and tak your pleasure.

REX HUMANITAS.

Gif that be trew, quhilk ye me tell,   15
    I will not langer tarie:
Bot will gang preif that play my sell,
    Howbeit the warld me warie.
    Als fast as ye may carie,
        Speid with all diligence: 20
    Bring Sensualitie,
        Fra hand to my presence.
Forsuth, I wait not how it stands,
Bot sen I hard of your tythands,
My bodie trimblis, feit and hands,   25
    And quhiles is hait as fyre:
I trow Cupido, with his dart,

Hes woundit me out-throw the hart;
My spreit will fra my bodie part,
    Get I nocht my desyre.
Pas on away, with diligence,
And bring hir heir, to my presence: 5
Spair nocht for travell, nor expence,
    I cair not for na cost.
Pas on your way schone Wantonnes,
And tak with you Sandie Solace,
And bring that Ladie to this place,   10
    Or els I am bot lost.
Commend me to that sweitest thing,
And present hir with this same ring,
And say, I ly in languisching,
    Except scho mak remeid.   15
With siching sair, I am bot schent,
Without scho cum incontinent,
My heavie langour to relent,
    And saif me now fra deid.

WANTONNES.

Dout ye nocht, Sir, bot wee will get hir,   20
Wee sall be feirie for till fetch hir,
Bot faith wee wald speid all the better
    Till gar our pursses rout.

SOLACE.

Sir, let na sorrow in yow sink,
Bot gif us ducats for till drink,   25
And wee sall never sleip ane wink
    Till it be back, or eadge:

ANE SATYRE OF

Ye ken weill, Sir, we haif no cunzie.

REX HUMANITAS.

Solace, sure that sall be no sunzie,
Beir ye that bag upon your lunzie,
    Now sirs, win weill your wage;
I pray yow speid yow sone agane.   5

WANTONNES.

Ye, of this sang, Sir, we are fane,
Wee sall nether spair [for] wind, nor raine,
    Till our days wark be done:
Fairweill, for wee are at the flicht,
Placebo rewll our Roy at richt: 10
We sall be heir, man, or midnicht,
    Thocht wee marche with the Mone.
    [*Heir sall thay depairt, singand mirrely.*

WANTONNES.

Pastyme, with pleasance, and greit prosperitie,
Be to yow, soveraine Sensualitie.

SENSUALITIE.

Sirs, ye ar welcum: quhair go ye? eist or west   15

WANTONNES.

In faith, I trow we be at the farrest.

SENSUALITIE.

Quhat is your name, I pray you, sir, declair?

WANTONNES.

Marie! Wantonnes, the Kings Secretair!

SENSUALITIE.

Quhat King is that, quhilk hes sa gay a boy?

WANTONNES.

Humanitie, that richt redoutit Roy,
Quhilk dois commend him to yow hartfullie,
And sendis yow heir ane ring with ane rubie,   5
In takin, that abuife all creatour,
He hes chosen yow to be his paramour:
He bade me say, that he will be bot deid,
Without that ye mak haistelie remeid.

SENSUALITIE.

How can I help him, althocht he suld forfair,   10
Ye ken richt weill, I am na medcinair.

SOLACE.

Yes, lustie Ladie, thocht he war never sa seik,
I wait ye beare his health into your breik:
Ane kis of your sweit mow, in ane morning,
Till his seiknes micht be greit comforting,   15
And als he maks yow supplicatioun,
This nicht, to mak with him collatioun.

SENSUALITIE.

I thank his Grace, of his benevolence,
    Gude sirs, I sall be reddie evin fra hand;
In me, thair sall be fund na negligence,   20

Baith nicht, and day, quhen his Grace will demand.
Pas ye befoir, and say, I am cummand,
And thinks richt lang to haif of him ane sicht
And I to Venus do mak ane faithfull band,
That in his arms I think to ly all nicht. 5

WANTONNES.

That sal be done, bot yit, or I hame pass,
Heir I protest for Hamelynes, your lass.

SENSUALITIE.

Scho sal be at command, sir, quhen ye will,
I traist, scho sall find yow flinging your fill.

WANTONNES.

Now hay for joy, and mirth, I dance. 10
Tak thair ane gay gamond of France :
Am I nocht worthie till avance,
    That am sa gude a page ?
And that sa spedelie can rin,
To tyst my maister unto sin : 15
The feind a penny he will win
    Of this his mariage.
. . . .

I think this day, to win greit thank,
Hay ! as an brydlit cat I brank :
Alace ! I haif wrestit my schank, .20
    Yit I gang, be Sanct Michaell.
Quhilk of my leggis, Sirs, as ye trow,
Was it that I did hurt evin now ?
Bot, quhairto sould I speir at yow,
    I think thay baith ar haill. 25

Gude morrow, Maister, be the Mes!

REX HUMANITAS.
Welcum, my minyeon, Wantonnes,
How hes thow speid, in thy travell?

WANTONNES.
Rycht weill, be Him that herryit hell:
    Your erand is weill done.   5

REX HUMANITAS.
Then, Wantonnes, how weill is mee,
Thow hes deservit baith meit, and fie,
    Be him that maid the Mone:
Thare is ane thing that I wald speir,
Quhat sall I do quhen scho cums heir?   10
For I knaw nocht the craft perqueir
    Of lufferis gyn:
Thairfoir, at lenth, ye mon me leir,
    How to begin.

WANTONNES.
To kis hir, and clap hir,   15
    Sir, be not affeard,
Scho will not schrink, thocht ye kis hir,
    Ane span within the baird:
Gif ye think, that scho thinks shame,
    Then hyd the bairns eine,   20
With hir taill, and tent hir weill,
    Ye wait quhat I meine.
Will ye leif me, Sir, first for to go to,
And I sall leirne yow all kewis how to do.

REX HUMANITAS.

God forbid, Wantonnes, that I gif thé leife;
Thou art ouer perillous ane page, sic practiks to preife.

WANTONNES.

Now, Sir, preife as ye pleis: I se hir cumand,
Use yourself gravelie, wee sall by yow stand.
   [*Heir sall Sensualitie cum to the King and say*:

SENSUALITIE.

O Queene Venus! unto thy celsitude,   5
 I gif gloir, honour, laud, and reverence,
Quha grantit me sic perfite pulchritude,
 That Princes of my persone have pleasance.
  I mak ane vow, with humbill observance,
Richt reverentlie thy tempill to visie   10
With sacrifice unto thy dyosie.
Till everie stait I am so greabill,
 That few or nane refuses me at all;
Paipis, patriarks, or prelats venerabill,
 Common pepill, and princis temporall,   15
  Ar subject all to me Dame Sensuall:
Sa sall it be ay quhill the warld indures,
And speciallie quhair youthage hes the cures.
   Quha knawis the contrair?
  I traist few in this companie,   20
  Wald thay declair the veritie,
  How thay use Sensualitie,
   Bot with me maks repair.
  And now my way I man avance,
  Unto ane Prince of great puissance,   25

Quhom young men hes in governance,
   Rolland into his rage:
I am richt glaid, I yow assure,
That potent Prince to get in cure;
Quhilk is of lustines the lair,   5
   And greitest of curage.
     [*Heir sall scho mak reverence, and say
       to the King.*
O potent Prince, of pulchritude preclair,
   God Cupido, preserve your celsitude!   10
And Dame Venus mot keip your Court from cair;
   As I wald scho suld keip my awin hart-blud.

REX HUMANITAS.

Welcum to me peirles in pulchritude;
Welcum to me thow sweiter nor the lamber,
Quhilk hes maid me of all dolour denude.   15
   Solace, convoy this Ladie to my chamber.
     [*Heir sall scho pass to the chalmer, and say,*

SENSUALITIE.

I gang this gait with richt gude will:
Sir Wantonnes, tarie ye still,
And Hamelines the cap yeis fill,
   And beir him cumpanie.   20

[HAMELINES.]

That sall I do, withouttin dout,
And he and I sall play cap out.

WANTONNES.

Now, Ladie, len me that batye tout;

Fill in for I am dry.
Your Dame, be this trewlie,
Hes gotten upon the gumis;
Quhat rak thocht ye, and I,
Go junne our justing lumis. 5

HAMELINES.

Content I am, with gude will,
Quhenever ye ar reddie,
Your pleasure to fulfill.

WANTONNES.

Now, weill said, be our Ladie;
I'le bear my maister cumpanie, 10
Till that I may indure:
Gif ye be quhisland wantounlie,
We sall fling on the flure.

*[Heir sall thay pas all to the chalmer;
and Gude Counsall sall say:*

GUDE COUNSALL.

Immortall God! maist of magnificence,
Quhais Majestie na clark can comprehend: 15
Must save yow all that givis sic audience,
And grant yow grace Him never till offend,
Quhilk on the Croce did willinglie ascend,
And sched his pretious blude, on everie side:
Quhais pitious passioun from danger yow defend, 20
And be your gratious governour, and gyde.

Now my gude friendis considder, I yow beseik,
The caus maist principall of my cumming,

Princes, or potestatis, ar nocht worth ane leik,
  Be thay not gydit, be my gude governing;
  Thair was nevir Empriour, Conquerour, nor King,
Without my wisdome, that micht thair wil avance,
  My name is GUDE COUNSALL, without feinzeing, 5
Lords, for lack of my lair, ar brocht to mischance.

  Finallie, for conclusioun,
  Quha haldis me at delusioun
  Sall be brocht to confusioun :
    And this I understand,   10
  For I have maid my residence,
  With hie Princes of greit puissance,
  In Ingland, Italie, and France,
    And monie uther land.
Bot, out of Scotland, wa, allace !   15
I haif bene fleimit lang tyme space,
That garris our gyders all want grace,
    And die, befoir thair day ;
Becaus thay lichtlyit Gude Counsall,
Fortune turnit on thame hir saill,   20
Quhilk brocht this Realme to meikill baill,
    Quha can the contrair say !
My Lords, I came nocht heir to lie :
Wais me ! for King Humanitie,
Overset with Sensualitie,   25
    In th' entrie of his ring.
Throw vicious counsell insolent,
Sa thay may get riches, or rent.
To his weilfair thay tak na tent,
    Nor quhat sal be th' ending.   ·   30

Yit, in this Realme, I wald mak sum repair,
Gif I beleifit my name suld nocht forfair,
For wald this King be gydit yit with ressoun,
And on misdoars mak punitioun :
Howbeit, I haif lang tyme bene exyllit,
I traist in God my name suld yit be styllit : 5
Sa till I se God send mair of his grace,
I purpois till repois me in this place.

   [*Heir enteris Flatterie, new landit out of France ;
     and stormesteid at the May.*

FLATTERIE.

Mak roume, sirs, hoaw ! that I may rin,
Lo se quhair I am new cum [in],
  Begaryit all with sindrie hewis: 10
Let be your din, till I begin,
  And I sall schaw yow of my newis.
Throuchout all Christindome I have past,
And am cum heir now at the last,
  Tostit on sea, ay sen Yuill day : 15
That wee war faine to hew our mast,
  Nocht half ane myle beyond the May.
Bot, now amang yow, I will remaine,
I purpois never to sail againe ;
  To put my lyfe, in chance of watter : 20
Was never sene sic wind, and raine,
  Nor of schipmen sic clitter clatter :
Sum bade haill, and some bad stand by,
On steirburd, hoaw ! aluiff ! fy ! fy !
  Quhill all the raipis beguith to rattil : 25
Was never Roy sa fleyd as I,

Quhen all the sails playd brittill brattill.
To see the wavis it was ane wonder,
And wind that raif the sails in sunder,
    Bot, I lay braikand like ane brok :
And shot sa fast above, and under,   5
    The Devill durst not cum neir my dok.
Now, am I scapit fra that effray,
Quhat say ye, Sirs; am I nocht gay?
    Se ye not, Flatterie, your awin fuill,
That yeid to mak this new array,   10
    Was I not heir with yow at Yuill?
Yes, be my faith, I think on weill.
Quhair ar my fallows that wald nocht faill?
    We suld have cum heir for ane cast.
Hoaw! Falset, hoaw!   15

FALSET.

            Wa sair the Devill!
Quha is that, that cryis for me sa fast?

FLATTERIE.

Quhy Falset, brother knawis thou not me?
Am I nocht thy brother Flatterie?

FALSET.

Now, welcome, be the Trinitie,
    This meitting cums for gude: 20
Now, let me bresse thé in my armis,
Quhen freinds meits hartis warmis,
    Quod Jok, that frelie fude.
How happinit yow into this place?

FLATTERIE.

Now, be my saul, evin on a cace,
I come in sleipand at the port,
Or evir I wist, amang this sort.
Quhair is Dissait, that limmer loun?

FALSET.

I left him drinkand in the Toun : 5
He will be heir incontinent.

FLATTERIE.

Now be the haly Sacrament,
That tydingis comforts all my hart :
I wait Dissait will tak my part.
He is richt craftie, as ye ken, 10
And counsallour to the Merchandmen :
Let us ly doun heir baith, and spy,
Gif wee persave him cummand by.
                  [*Heir sall Dissait entir.*

DISSAIT.

Stand by the gait, that I may steir,
I say, Koks bons! how cam I heir? 15
I can not mis, to tak sum feir,
    Into sa gret ane thrang :
Marie! heir ane cumlie congregatioun,
Quhat ar ye, sirs, all of ane natioun?
Maisters, I speik be protestatioun, 20
    In dreid ye tak me wrang.
Ken ye nocht, sirs, quhat is my name?
Gude faith! I dar nocht schaw it for schame :

Sen I was clekit of my dame,
    Yit was I never leill;
For, Katie unsell was my mother,
And Common Theif my father brother;
Of sic freindship I had ane fither,   5
    Howbeit I can not steill.
Bot yit, I will borrow, and len,
As be my cleathing ye may ken,
That I am cum of nobill men;
    And als I will debait,   10
That querrell with my feit, and hands:
And I dwell amang the merchands,
My name, gif onie man demands,
    Thay call me Dissait.
Bon jour! brother, with all my hart!   15
Heir I am cum to tak your part,
    Baith into gude and evill:
I met Gude Counsall be the way,
Quha pat me in ane felloun fray,
    I gif him to the Devill!   20

FALSET.

How chaipit ye, I pray yow tell?

DISSAIT.

I slipit into ane bordell,
And hid me in ane bawburds bed;
Bot, suddenlie hir schankis I sched,
With hoch hurland amang hir howis,   25
God wait, gif wee maid monie mowis.
How came ye heir, I pray yow tell me?

FALSET.
Marie! to seik King Humanitie.

DISSAIT.
Now, be the gude ladie, that me bair,
That samin hors is my awin mair.
Now with our purpois, let us mell.
Quhat is your counsall, I pray yow tell? 5
Sen we thrie seiks yon nobill King,
Let us devyse sum subtill thing:
And als I pray yow, as my brother,
That we ilk ane be trew to uther.
I mak ane vow, with all my hart, 10
In gude, and evill to tak your part.
I pray to God, nor I be hangit,
Bot I sall die, or ye be wrangit.

FALSET.
Quhat is my counsall that wee do?
Marie! Sirs, this is my counsall lo, 15
Till tak our tyme, quhill wee may get it,
For now thair is na man to let it:
Fra tyme, the King begin to steir him,
Marie! Gude Counsall, I dreid cum neir him,
And be wee knawin with Correctioun, 20
It will be our confusioun:
Thairfoir, my deir brother, devyse,
To find sum toy of the new gyse.

FLATTERIE.
Marie! I sall finde ane thousand wyles,
Wee man turne our claithis, and change our styles: 25

And disagyse us that na man ken us :
Hes na man Clarkis cleathing to len us ?
And let us keip grave countenance,
As wee were new cum out of France.

DISSAIT.

Now, be my saull ! that is weill devysit,   5
Ye sall se me sone disagysit.

FALSET.

And sa sall I man, be the Rude !
Now sum gude fallow len me ane hude.
    [*Heir sall Flatterie help his twa marrowis.*

DISSAIT.

Now, am I buskit, and quha can spy,
The Devill stik me, gif this be I !   10
If this be I, or not, I can not weill say ;
Or hes the Feind, or Farie folk, borne me away.

FALSET.

And gif my hair war up in ane how,
The feind ane man wald ken me, I trow.
Quhat sayis thou of my gay garmoun ?   15

DISSAIT.

I say, thou luiks evin lyke ane loun.
Now, brother Flatterie, quhat do ye,
Quhat kynde of man schaip ye to be ?

FLATTERIE.

Now be my faith ! my brother deir,
I will gang counterfit the Freir.   20

DISSAIT.

A Freir! quhaireto? ye can not preiche!

FLATTERIE.

Quhat rak, bot I can richt weill fleich!
Perchance I'le cum to that honour,
To be the Kings Confessour,
Pure Freirs ar free at any feist, 5
And marchellit ay amang the best.
Als God hes lent to tham sic graces,
That Bischops puts them in thair places,
Out-throw thair dioceis to preiche,
Bot ferlie nocht howbeit thay fleich: 10
For schaw thay all the veritie,
Thai'll want the Bischops charitie.
And thocht the corne war never sa skant,
The gudewyfis will not let Freiris want:
For quhy, thay ar thair confessours, 15
Thair heavinlie prudent counsalours:
Thairfor the wyfis plainlie taks thair parts,
And schawis the secreits of thair harts
To Freirs, with better will, I trow,
Nor thay do to thair bed-fallow. 20

DISSAIT.

And I reft anis ane Freirs coull,
Betwixt Sanct Johnestoun, and Kinnoul:
I sall gang fetch it, gif ye will tarie.

FLATTERIE.

Now play me that of companarie:

Ye saw him nocht, this hundreth yeir,
That better can counterfeit the Freir.

DISSAIT.

Heir is thy gaining, all and sum,
This is ane koull of Tullilum.

FLATTERIE.

Quha hes ane portouns for to len me ? 5
The feind ane saull, I trow, will ken me.

FALSET.

Now gang thy way quhairever thow will,
Thow may be fallow to freir Gill :
Bot, with Correctioun, gif wee be kend,
I dreid wee mak ane schamefull end. 10

FLATTERIE.

For that mater, I dreid nathing,
Freiris ar exemptit fra the King :
And Freiris will reddie entreis get,
Quhen Lords are haldin at the yet.

FALSET.

Wee man do mair yit, be Sanct James ! 15
For wee mon all thrie change our names.
Hayif me, and I sall baptize thee.

DISSAIT.

Be God ! and thair-about may it be.
How will thou call me, I pray the tell ?

FALSET.
I wait not how to call my sell.

DISSAIT.
Bot, yit anis name the bairns name!

FALSET.
Discretioun, Discretioun, in God's name!

DISSAIT.
I neid nocht now to cair for thrift
Bot quhat sal be my God bairne gift ?   5

FALSET.
I gif yow all the devillis of hell.

DISSAIT.
Na Brother, hauld that to thysell:
Now, sit doun, let me baptize thé,
I wait not quhat thy name sould be.

FALSET.
Bot, yit anis name the bairns name.   10

DISSAIT.
Sapience, in ane warlds-schame.

FLATTERIE.
Brother Dissait, cum baptize me.

DISSAIT.
Then sit doun lawlie on thy kné.

THE THRIE ESTAITIS.

FLATTERIE.

Now, brother, name the bairns name.

DISSAIT.

Devotioun, in the Devillis name!

FLATTERIE.

The Devill resave thé, lurdoun loun!
Thow hes wet all my new schavin croun.

DISSAIT.

Devotioun, Sapience, and Discretioun, 5
Wee thrie may rewll this Regioun:
Wee sall find monie craftie things,
For to begyll ane hundreth kings;
For thow can richt weill crak, and clatter,
And I sall feinze, and thow sall flatter. 10

FLATTERIE.

Bot, I wald have, or wee depairtit,
Ane drink to mak us better hartit.

DISSAIT.

Weill said, be Him that herryit hell!
I was evin thinkand that mysell.
Now, till we get the Kings presence, 15
Wee will sit doun, and keip silence.
[Heir sall they drink; till the King sall cum furth of his chamber, and call for Wantonnes.

I se ane yeoman, quhat ever he be,
I'le wod my lyfe, yon same is he.

Feir nocht Brother, bot hauld yow still,
Till wee have hard quhat is his will.
  [*Heir the King has bene with his Concubyne, and
    thairefter returns to his young company.*

REX HUMANITAS.
Now quhair is Placebo, and Solace?
Quhair is my minzeoun Wantonnes?
Wantonnes, hoaw! cum to me sone.   5

WANTONNES.
Quhy cryit ye, Sir, till I had done?

REX HUMANITAS.
Quhat was ye doand, tell me that?

WANTONNES.
Mary! leirand how my father me gat.
I wait nocht how it stands, bot doubt,
Me think the warld rinnis round about.   10

REX HUMANITAS.
And sa think I, man, be my thrift,
I se fyfteine Mones in the lift.

HAMELINES.
Gat ye nocht that, quhilk ye desyrit?
Sir, I beleif, that ye ar tyrit.

[WANTONNES.
Lat Hamelines my lass allane;   15
Scho bendyt up aye twa for ane.]

DANGER.

Bot, as for Placebo, and Solace,
I held them baith in mirrines.

SOLACE.

Now, schaw me, Sir, I yow exhort,
How ar ye of your luif content;
   Think ye not this ane mirrie sport ?   5

REX HUMANITAS.

Yea! that I do, in verament.
Quhat bairnis ar yon upon the bent?
   I did nocht se them all this day.

WANTONNES.

Thay will be heir incontinent:
   Stand still, and heir quhat thay will say.   10
      [*Now the Vycis cums, and maks
        salutatioun to the King, saying,*

DISSAIT.

Laud, honor, gloir, triumph, and victory,
Be to your maist excellent Majestie.

REX HUMANITAS.

Ye ar welcum, gude freinds, be the Rude!
Appeirandlie ye seime sum men of gude;
   Quhat ar your names? tell me without delay.   15

DISSAIT.

Discretioun, Sir, is my name, perfay.

REX HUMANITAS.
Quhat is your name, Sir, with the clippit croun?

FLATTRIE.
But dout, my name is callit Devotioun.

REX HUMANITAS.
Welcum Devotioun, be Sanct Jame.
Now, sirray, tell quhat is your name.

FALSET.
Marie! Sir, thay call me, quhat call thay me? 5
[I wait not weill, but gif I lie!]

REX HUMANITAS.
Can ye nocht tell, quhat is your name.

FALSET.
I kend it, quhen I cam fra hame.

REX HUMANITAS.
Quhat gars ye can nocht schaw it now?

FALSET,
Marie! thay call me Thin Drink, I trow. 10

REX HUMANITAS.
Thin Drink! quhat kynde of name is that?

DISSAIT.
Sapiens, thow servis to beir ane plat:
Me think thow schawis thé not weill wittit.

FALSET.

Sypeins, Sir, Sypeins, Marie! now ye hit it.

FLATTRIE.

Sir, gif ye pleis to let him say,
His name is Sapientia.

FALSET.

That same is it, be Sanct Michell.

REX HUMANITAS.

Quhy could thou not tell it thy sell?   5

FALSET.

I pray your grace appardoun me,
And I sall schaw the veritie:
I am sa full of Sapience,
That sumtyme, I will tak ane trance.
My spreit was reft fra my bodie,   10
Now heich abone the Trinitie.

REX HUMANITAS.

Sapience suld be ane man of gude.

FALSET.

Schir, ye may ken that be my hude.

REX HUMANITAS.

Now have I Sapience, and Discretioun;
How can I faill, to rewll this Regioun?   15

And Devotioun, to be my confessour,
Thir thrie came in ane happie hour.
Heir, I mak thé my Secretar;
And thow salbe my Thesaurar;
And thow salbe my Counsallour 5
In spirituall things, and Confessour.

FLATTRIE.

I sweir to you, Sir, be Sanct An,
Ye met never with ane wyser man,
For monie a craft, Sir, do I can,
    War thay weill knawin : 10
Sir, I have na feill of flattrie,
Bot fosterit with philosophie,
Ane strange man in astronomie,
    Quhilk sal be schawin.

FALSET.

And I have greit intelligence, 15
In quelling of the quintessence;
Bot to preif my experience,
    Sir, len me fourtie crownes,
To mak multiplicatioun,
And tak my obligatioun: 20
Gif wee mak fals narratioun,
    Hauld us for verie lownes.

DISSAIT.

Sir, I ken, be your physnomie,
Ye sall conqueis, or els I lie,
Danskin, Denmark, and Almane, 25
Spittelfeild, and the realme of Spane.

Ye sall have at your governance,
Ranfrow, and all the realme of France,
Yea, Rugland, and the toun of Rome,
Corstorphine, and all Christindome.
Quhairto, Sir, be the Trinitie, 5
Ye ar ane verie A per se.

FLATTRIE.

Sir, quhen I dwelt in Italie,
I leirit the craft of palmistrie,
Schaw me the lufe, Sir, of your hand,
And I sall gar yow understand, 10
Gif your Grace be infortunat,
Or gif ye be predestinat.
I see ye will haif fyfteine Queenes,
And fyfteine scoir of concubeines:
The Virgin Marie saife your Grace! 15
Saw ever man sa quhyte ane face,
Sa greit ane arme, sa fair ane hand,
Thair's nocht sic ane leg in al this land,
War ye in armis, I think na wonder,
Howbeit, ye dang doun fyfteine hunder. 20

DISSAIT.

Now, be my saull, that's trew thow sayis,
Wes never man set sa weill his clais:
Thair is na man in Christintie,
Sa meit to be ane King as ye.

FALSET.

Sir, thank the Haly Trinitie, 25
That send us to your cumpanie:

For, God, nor I gaip in ane gallows,
Gif ever ye fand thrie better fallows.

REX HUMANITAS.

Ye ar richt welcum, be the Rude !
Ye seime to be thrie men of gude.
    [*Heir sall Gude Counsell schaw himself in the feild.*
Bot, quha is yon, that stands sa still ?   5
Ga spy, and speir quhat is his will :
And, gif he yearnis my presence,
Bring him to mee, with diligence.

DISSAIT.

That sall wee do, be God's breid,
We's bring him eather quick, or deid.   10

REX HUMANITAS.

I will sit still heir, and repois :
Speid yow agane to me, my jois.

FALSET.

Ye, hardlie, Sir, keip yow in clois
    And quyet, till wee cum againe.
Brother, I trow, be Coks toes !   15
    Yon bairdit bogill cums fra ane traine.

DISSAIT.

Gif he dois sa, he salbe slaine,
    I doubt him nocht, nor yit ane uther :
Trowit I that he come for ane traine,
    Of my friendis, I sould rais ane futher.   20

FLATTRIE.

I doubt full sair, be God him sell!
That yon auld churle be Gude Counsell:
Get he anis to the King's presence,
We thrie will get na audience.

DISSAIT.

That matter, I sall tak on hand,   5
And say, it is the King's command,
That he anone devoyd this place,
And cum nocht neir the King's grace;
And that under the paine of tressoun.

FLATTRIE.

Brother, I hald your counsell ressoun.   10
Now, let us heir quhat he will say:
Auld lyart beird, gude day, gude day!

GUDE COUNSELL.

Gude day againe, Sirs, be the Rude,
The Lord mot mak yow men of gude.

DISSAIT.

Pray nocht for us to Lord, nor Ladie,   15
For we ar men of gude alreadie.
Sir, schaw to us, quhat is your name?

GUDE COUNSELL.

Gude Counsell, thay call me at hame.

FALSET.

Quhat says thow, Carle, ar thow Gude Counsell?
Swyith! pak thé sone, unhappie unsell,
Gif ever tho cum this gait againe,
I vow to God thou sall be slaine.

GUDE COUNSELL.

I pray yow, Sirs, gif me licence,   5
To cum anis to the King's presence;
To speik bot twa words to his Grace.

FLATTRIE.

Swyith! hursone Carle devoyd this place.

GUDE COUNSALL.

Brother, I ken yow weill aneuch,
Howbeit ye mak it never sa teuch: 10
Flattrie, Dissait, and Fals Report,
That will not suffer to resort
Gude Counsall to the King's presence.

DISSAIT.

Swyith! hursone Carle, gang pak thé hence:
Gif ever thou cum this gait agane,   15
I vow to God thou sall be slane!
    [*Heir sall thay hurle away Gude Counsall.*

[GUDE COUNSALL.]

Sen, at this tyme, I can get na presence,
Is na remeid bot tak in patience:
Howbeit Gude Counsell haistelie be nocht hard,
With young Princes, yit sould thay nocht be skard: 20

Bot, quhen youthheid hes blawin his wanton blast,
Then sall Gude Counsell rewll him at the last.
                [*Now the Vyces gangs to ane counsall.*

FLATTRIE.

Now quhill Gude Counsall is absent,
Brother, wee mon be diligent:
And mak betwix us sikker bands,   5
Quhen vacands fallis in onie lands;
That everie man help weill his fallow.

DISSAIT.

I hauld, deir brother, be Alhallow!
Sa, ye fische nocht within our bounds.

FLATTRIE.

That sall I nocht, be God's wounds!   10
Bot, I sall plainlie tak your partis.

FALSET.

Sa, sall wee thyne, with all our hartis.
Bot, haist us, quhill the King is young,
Lat everie man keip weill ane toung;
And, in ilk quarter have ane spy,   15
Us till adverteis haistelly,
Quhen ony casualities
Sall happin into our countries;
And lat us mak provisioun.
Or he cum to discretioun: 20
Na mair he waits now, nor ane Sant,
Quhat thing it is to haif, or want.
Or he cum till his perfyte age,

We sall be sikker of our wage :
And then, lat everie carle craif uther.

DISSAIT.

That mouth speik mair, my awin dear brother,
For God, nor I rax in ane raip !
Thow may gif counsall to the Paip. 5
   [*Now thay returne to the King.*

REX HUMANITAS.

Quhat gart you byde sa long lang fra my presence?
I think it lang since ye departit thence.
Quhat man was yon, with an greit bostous beird;
Me thocht he maid yow all thrie very feard.

DISSAIT.

It was ane laidlie lurdan loun, 10
Cumde to brek buithis into this toun :
Wee have gart bind him with ane poill,
And send him to the theifis hoill.

REX HUMANITAS.

Let him sit thare with ane mischance;
And let us go to our pastance. 15

WANTONNES.

Better go revell at the rackat,
Or ellis go to the hurlie hackat;
Or then, to schaw our curtlie corsses,
Ga se, quha best can rin thair horsses.

SOLACE.

Na, Soveraine, or wee farther gang,
Gar Sensualitie sing ane sang.
> [*Heir sall the Ladies sing ane sang, the
> King sall ly doun amang the Ladies
> and then Veritie sall enter.*

VERITIE.

Diligite justitiam qui judicatis terram.
Luif justice, ye quha hes ane judges cure,
   In earth, and dreid the awfull judgement
Of Him, that sall cum judge baith rich and pure,   5
   Rycht terribilly, with bludy woundis rent.
That dreidfull day into your harts imprent:
Belevand weill how, and quhat maner, ye
   Use justice heir til uthers, thair at lenth
That day, but doubt, sa sall ye judgit be.   10

Wo than, and duill, be to yow Princes all!
   Sufferand the pure anes, for till be opprest:
In everlasting burnand fyre, ye sall,
   With Lucifer, richt dulfullie be drest;
Thairfoir in tyme, for till eschaip that nest,   15
Feir God, do law, and justice equally
   Till everie man; se that na puir opprest
Up to the Hevin, on yow ane vengence cry.

Be just judges, without favour or fead,
   And hauld the ballance evin till everie wicht;   20
Let not the fault be left into the head,
   Then sall the members reulit be at richt:

For quhy, subjects do follow, day and nicht,
Thair governours in vertew, and in vyce.
Ye ar the lamps that sould schaw them the licht,
To leid thame on this sliddrie rone of yce.

Mobile mutatur semper cum Principe vulgus.
And gif ye wald your subjectis war weill gevin,   5
   Then verteouslie begin the dance your sell:
Going befoir; then they auone, I wein,
   Sal follow yow, eyther till hevin, or hell.
   Kings sould of gude exempils be the well;
Bot, gif that your strands be intoxicate,   10
   Insteid of wyne, thay drink the poyson fell:
Thus pepill followis ay thair principate.

Sic luceat lux vestra coram hominibus, ut videant
    opera vestra bona.
And, specially, ye Princes of the preists;
   That of peopill hes Spiritual cure,
Dayly ye sould revolve into your breistis,   15
   How that thir haly words ar still maist sure,
   In verteous lyfe, gif that ye do indure,
The pepill wil tak mair tent to your deids,
   Then to your words, and als baith rich, and puir,
Will follow yow baith in your warks, and words.   20
    [*Heir sall Flattrie spy Veritie with ane dum*
    countenance.

Gif men of me wald haif intelligence,
   Or knaw my name, thay call me Veritie:
Of Christis law I haif experience,

And hes over saillit many stormie sey.
Now, am I seikand King Humanitie;
For, of his Grace, I have gude esperance,
    Fra tyme that he acquaintit be with mee,
His honour, and heich gloir, I sall avance.   5
            [*Heir sall Veritie pas to hir sait.*

DISSAIT.

Gude day, Father, quhair have ye bene?
    Declair till us of your novells.

FLATTRIE.

Thare is now lichtit on the grene,
    Dame Veritie, be buiks and bells.
Bot cum scho to the King's presence,   10
    Thair is na buit for us to byde;
Tharfoir, I red us all go hence.

FALSET.

That will we nocht yit be Sanct Bryde,
    Bot, wee sall ather gang, or ryde,
        To Lords of Spiritualitie;   15
    And gar them trow, yon bag of pryde,
        Hes spokin manifest heresie.
            [*Heir thay cum to the Spiritualitie.*

FLATTRIE.

O reverent Fatheris of the Spiritual State,
    Wee counsall yow, be wyse, and vigilant:
Dame Veritie hes lychtit now of lait,   20
    And, in hir hand, beirand the New Testament:
Be scho ressavit, but dout, wee ar bot schent,

Let hir nocht ludge, thairfoir, into this Land,
  And this wee reid yow do incontinent,
Now, quhill the King is with his lufe sleipand.

SPIRITUALITIE.

Wee thank yow, Freindis, of your benevolence:
  It sall be done even as ye haif devysit; 5
Wee think ye serve ane gudlie recompence,
  Defendand us, that wee be nocht supprysit.
  In this mater, wee man be weill avysit,
Now, quhill the King misknawis the Veritie:
  Be scho ressavit, then wee will be deprysit; 10
Quhat is your counsell, Brother, now let se?

ABBOT.

I hauld it best, that wee incontinent,
  Gar hauld hir fast into captivitie,
Untill the thrid day of the Parlament:
  And then, accuse hir of hir heresie; 15
  Or than banische hir out of this cuntrie;
For, with the King, gif Veritie be knawin,
  Of our greit gloir we will degradit be,
And all our secreits to the commouns schawin.

PERSONE.

Ye se the King is yit effeminate, 20
  And gydit be Dame Sensualitie,
Richt sa with young counsall intoxicate;
  Swa at this tyme ye haif your libertie.
  To tak your tyme, I hald it best for me,
And go distroy all thir Lutherians; 25
  In speciall, yon ladie Veritie.

SPIRITUALITIE.

Schir Persone, ye sall be my commissair,
   To put this matter till executioun;
And ye, Sir Freir, becaus ye can declair
   The haill processe, pas with him in commissioun;
   Pas all togidder, with my braid bennisoun,   5
And gif scho speiks against our libertie,
   Then, put hir in perpetuall presoun,
That scho cum nocht to King Humanitie.
              [*Heir sall thay pas to Veritie.*

PERSONE.

Lustie Ladie, we wald faine understand
   Quhat errand ye haif in this Regioun?   10
To preich, or teich, quha gaif to yow command;
   To counsall kingis, how gat ye commissioun?
   I dreid, without ye get ane remissioun,
And syne renunce your New Opiniones,
   The Sprituall Stait sall put yow to perditioun;   15
And, in the fyre, will burne yow flesche and bones.

VERITIE.

I will recant nathing that I have schawin,
   I have said nathing bot the veritie;
Bot, with the King, fra tyme that I be knawin,
   I dreid, ye spaiks of Spiritualitie   20
   Sall rew, that ever I came in this cuntrie:
For, gif the veritie plainlie war proclamit,
   And speciallie to the King's Majestie,
For your traditions ye wilbe all defamit.

FLATTRIE.

Quhat buik is that, harlot, into thy hand ?
   Out, walloway ! this is the New Test'ment,
In Englisch toung, and printit in England :
   Herisie, herisie ! fire, fire ! incontinent.

VERITIE.

Forsuith, my friend, ye have ane wrang judgement,
For, in this Buik, thair is na herisie :   [5
   Bot our Christ's word, baith dulce and redolent,
Ane springing well of sinceir veritie.

DISSAIT.

Cum on your way, for all your yealow locks,
   Your wantoun words, but doubt ye sall repent : 10
This nicht ye sall forfair ane pair of stocks,
   And syne the morne be brocht to thoill judgement.

VERITIE.

For our Christ's saik, I am richt weill content
To suffer all thing that sall pleis his Grace,
   Howbeit, ye put ane thousand till torment,   15
Ten hundreth thowsand sall ryse into thair place,
     [*Veritie sits down on hir knies, and sayis;*

Get up, thow sleipis all too lang, O Lord !
   And mak sum ressonabill reformatioun,
On thame that dois tramp doun thy gracious word,
   And hes ane deidlie indignatioun,   20
   At them, quha maks maist trew narratioun :
Suffer me not, Lord, mair to be molest,

Gude Lord, I mak thé supplicatioun,
With thy unfriends let me nocht be supprest.

   Now, Lordis, do as ye list,
      I have na mair to say.

FLATTRIE.

Sit doun, and tak yow rest,   5
   All nicht till it be day.
      [*Thay put Veritie in the stocks and returne to Spiritualitie.*

DISSAIT.

My Lord, wee have, with diligence,
   Bucklit up weill yon bledrand baird.

SPIRITUALITIE.

I think ye serve gude recompence :
   Tak thir ten crowns, for your rewaird.   10

VERITIE.

The Prophesie of the Propheit Esay
Is practickit, alace ! on mee this day ;
Quha said, the Veritie sould be trampit doun
Amid the streit, and put in strang presoun :
His fyve and fyftie chapter, quha list luik,   15
Sall find thir wordis, writtin in his buik.
Richt sa, Sanct Paull wrytis to Timothie,
That men sall turne thair earis from veritie.
Bot in my Lord God, I have esperance,
He will provide for my deliverance.   20

Bot, ye Princes of Spiritualitie,
Quha sould defend the sinceir veritie,
I dreid the plagues of Johnes Revelatioun
Sall fall upon your generatioun.
I counsall yow this misse to amend,   5
Sa that ye may eschaip that fatall end.
    [*Heir sall Chastitie entir, and say,*

CHAISTITIE.

How lang sall this inconstant warld indure,
 That I sould baneist be, sa lang, alace!
Few creatures, or nane, takis on me cure,
 Quhilk gars me monie nicht ly harbrieles,   10
 Thocht I have past all yeir, fra place to place,
Amang the Temporall, and Spirituall Staits;
 Nor, amang Princes, I can get na grace;
Bot boustuouslie am halden at the yetis.

DILIGENCE.

Ladie, I pray yow schaw me your name,   15
 It dois me noy your lamentatioun.

CHASTITIE.

My freind, thairof I neid not to think shame,
 Dame Chastitie, baneist from town to town.

DILIGENCE.

 Then, pas to Ladeis of Religioun,
Quhilk maks thair vow, to observe chastitie,   20
 Lo! quhair thair sits ane Priores of renown,
Amangs the rest of Spiritualitie.

CHASTITIE.

I grant, yon Ladie hes vowit chastitie,
   For hir professioun thairto sould accord:
Scho maid that vow, for ane Abesie,
   Bot nocht for Christ Jesus, our Lord.
   Fra tyme, that thay get thair vows, I stand for'd,
Thay banische hir out of thair companie;   [5
   With Chastitie, thay can mak na concord,
Bot leids thair lyfis in sensualitie.
   I sall observe your counsall, gif I may,
   Cum on, and heir quhat yon Ladie will say?
      [*Chastitie passis to the Ladie Priores, and sayis*,
My prudent lustie Ladie Priores,   10
   Remember how ye did vow chastitie:
Madame, I pray yow of your gentilnes,
   That ye wald pleis to haif of me pitie,
   And, this ane nicht, to gif me harberie;
For this I mak yow supplicatioun,   15
   Do ye nocht sa, Madame, I dreid perdie,
It will be caus of depravatioun.

PRIORES.

Pas hynd, Madame, be Christ, ye cum nocht heir,
   Ye ar contrair to my complexioun:
Gang seik ludging at sum auld monk, or freir,   20
   Perchance, thay will be your protectioun;
   Or to Prelats, mak your progressioun,
Quhilkis ar obleist to yow, als weill as I:
   Dame Sensuall hes gevin directioun,
Yow till exclude out of my cumpany.   25

CHASTITIE.

Gif ye wald wit mair of the veritie,
  I sall schaw yow, be sure experience,
How that the Lords of Spiritualitie
  Hes baneist me, alace! fra thair presence.
      [Chastitie passis to the Lords of Spiritualitie.
My Lords! laud, gloir, triumph, and reverence,   5
  Mot be unto your halie Sprituall Stait:
I yow beseik, of your benevolence,
  To harbry mee, that am sa desolait.
Lords, I have past throw mony uncouth schyre,
  Bot in this Land, I can get na ludgeing: 10
  Of my name, gif ye wald haif knawledging,
Forsuith, my Lords, they call me Chastitie:
  I yow beseik, of your graces bening,
Gif me ludging this nicht for charitie?

SPIRITUALITIE.

Pas on, Madame, we knaw yow nocht,   15
Or, be Him that the warld wrocht,
Your cumming sall be richt deir coft,
  Gif ye mak langer tarie.

ABBOT.

But dout, wee will baith leif and die,
With our luif Sensualitie,   20
Wee will haif na mair deall with thee,
  Then with the Queene of Farie.

PERSONE.

Pas hame amang the Nunnis, and dwell,
Quhilks ar of chastitie the well:

I traist thay will, with buik and bell,
    Ressave yow in thair closter.

CHASTITIE.

Sir, quhen I was the Nunnis amang,
Out of thair dortour thay mee dang,
And wald nocht let me bide sa lang,   5
    To say my Pater Noster.
I se na grace, thairfoir to get,
I hauld it best, or it be lait,
For till go prove the Temporall Stait,
    Gif thay will mee resaif.   10

Gud-day, my lord Temporalitie,
And yow merchant of gravitie,
Ful faine wald I haif harberie,
    To ludge among the laif.

TEMPORALITIE.

Forsuith, wee wald be weill content,   15
To harbrie yow with gude intent,
War nocht, we haif impediment
    For quhy, we twa ar maryit
Bot wist our wyfis that ye war heir,
Thay wald mak all this town on steir,   20
Thairfoir, we reid yow reid rin areir,
    In dreid ye be miscaryit.

AN INTERLUDE OF CHASTITIE, THE SOWTAR, AND TAYLOR.

[*Heir sall Dame Chastitie pas, and seik luging athort all the Spirituall Estait, and Temporall Estait, quhill scho cum to the Sowttar, and Tailyeour, and say:*

CHASTITIE.

Ye men of craft of greit ingyne,
Gif me harbrie, for Christis pyne,
And win God's bennesone and myne,
    And help my hungrie hart.

SOWTAR.

Welcum, be him that maid the Mone,   5
Till dwell with us, till it be June:
We sall mend baith your hois and schone,
    And plainlie tak your part.

TAYLOUR.

Is this fair ladie Chastitie?
Now, welcum, be the Trinitie: 10
I think it war ane gret pitie,
    That thow sould ly thair out:
Your great displeasour, I forthink,
Sit doun, Madame, and tak ane drink;
And let na sorrow in yow sink,   20
    Bot let us play cap'out.

SOWTAR.

Fill in, and play cap'out,
   For, I am wonder dry :
The Devill snyp aff thair snout,
   That haits this company.
[*Heir sall thay gar Chastitie sit doun and drink.*

JENNIE.

Hoaw! mynnie, mynnie, mynnie!   5

TAYLOUR'S WYFE.

Quhat wald thow, my deir dochter Jennie?
Jennie, my joy, quhair is thy dadie?

JENNIE.

Mary, drinkand with ane lustie Ladie,
Ane fair young mayden cled in quhyte,
Of quhom my dadie taks delyte,   10
Scho hes the fairest forme of face,
Furnischit with all kynd of grace :
I traist gif I can reckon richt,
Scho schaips to ludge with him all nicht.

SOWTAR'S WYFE.

Quhat dois the Sowtar, my gudman?   15

JENNIE.

Mary, fillis the cap and turnes the can,
Or he cum hame, be God, I trow,
He will be drunkin lyke ane sow.

TAYLOUR'S WYFE.

This is ane greit dispyte, I think,

For to resave sic ane kow-clink :
Quhat is your counsell, that wee do ?

SOWTAR'S WYFE.

Cummer, this is my counsall, lo !
Ding ye the tane, and I the uther.

TAYLOUR'S WYFE.

I am content, be God's Mother,   5
I think for mee thay huirsome smaiks ;
Thay serve richt weill, to get thair paiks.
Quhat maister feind neids all this haist ?

SOWTAR'S WYFE.

God, nor my trewker mence ane tedder,

And now thay will sit doun, and drink,   10
In company, with ane kow-clink,
Gif thay haif done us this dispyte,
Let us go ding thame till thay dryte.
    [*Heir the Wyfis shall chase away Chastitie.*

TAYLOUR'S WYFE.

Go hence, harlot, how durst thow be sa bauld,
  To ludge with our gudemen, but our licence :   15
I mak ane vow to Him that Judas sauld,
  This rock of myne sall be thy recompence ;
Schaw me thy name, dudroun, with diligence ?

CHASTITIE.

Marie, Chastitie is my name, be Sanct Blais.

TAYLOUR'S WYFE.

I pray God, nor he work on thee vengeance;
For I luifit never Chastitie all my dayes.

SOWTAR'S WYFE.

Bot, my gudeman, the treuth I sall thé tell,
Gars me keip chastitie sair aganis my will:
Becaus that monstour hes maid sic ane mint,   5
With my bedstaf, that dastard beirs ane dint,
And als I vow, cum thow this gate againe,
Thy buttoks sall be beltit be Sanct Blaine.
> [*Heir sall thay speik to thair Gudemen and ding them.*

TAYLOUR'S WYFE.

Fals horson carle, bot dout thou sall forthink,
That ever thow eat 'or drink with yon kow-clink.   10

SOWTER'S WYFE.

I mak ane vow to Sanct Crispine,
Ise be revengit on that graceles grume:
And to begin the play, tak thair ane flap.

SOWTAR.

The Feind ressave the hands that gaif mee that.

SOWTAR'S WYFE.

Quhat now, huirsun, begins thow for till ban?   15
Tak thair ane uther upon thy peil'd harne pan.
Quhat now, cummer, will thow nocht tak my part?

TAYLOUR'S WYFE.

That sall I do, cummer, with all my hart.
> [*Heir sall thay ding thair Gudemen, with silence.*

TAYLOUR.

Alace! gossop, alace! how stands with yow?
Yon cankart carling, alace! hes brokin my brow.
Now, weill's yow preistis, now weill's yow all your lyfes,
That ar nocht weddit with sic wickit wyfes.

SOWTAR.

Gossop, alace, that blak bánd we may wary,　　5
That ordanit sic puir men as us to mary.
Quhat may be done bot tak in patience?
And on all wyfis we'ill cry ane loud vengence.

　　　　[*Heir sall the Wyfis stand be the watter syde
　　　　　and say,*

SOWTAR'S WYFE.

Sen, of our Cairls, we have the victorie,
Quhat is your counsell, cummer, that be done?　　10

TAYLOUR'S WYFE.

Send for gude wine, and hald our selfis merie,
I hauld this ay best, cummer, be Sanct Clone.

SOWTAR'S WYFE.

Cummer, will ye draw aff my hois, and schone,
To fill the quart, I sall rin to the toun.

TAYLOUR'S WYFE.

That sall I do, be him that made the Mone,　　15
With all my hart, thairfoir, cummer sit doun.
　　Kilt up your claithis, abone your waist,
　　And speid yow hame againe in haist,

And I sall provide for ane paist,
   Our corsses to comfort.

SOWTAR'S WYFE.

Then help me, for to kilt my clais,
Quhat gif the padoks nip my tais,
I dreid to droun heir, be Sanct Blais,   5
   Without I get support.
       [*Scho lifts up hir clais above hir waist, and
         enters in the water.*
Cummer, I will nocht droun my sell;
   Go East about the Nether mill.

TAYLOUR'S WYFE.

I am content, be Bryd's bell,
   To gang with yow, quhair ever ye will.
      [*Heir sall thay depairt, and pas to the palzeoun.*

DILIGENCE *to* CHASTITIE.

Madame, quhat gars yow gang sa lait?   10
Tell me, how ye have done debait,
With the Temporal, and Spirituall Stait;
   Quha did yow maist kyndnes?

CHASTITIE.

In faith, I fand bot ill and war;
Thay gart mee stand fra thame askar,   15
Evin lyk ane begger, at the bar,
   And fleimit mair and lesse.

DILIGENCE.

I counsall yow, but tarying,
Gang tell Humanitie, the King,

Perchance, heè of his grace bening,
  Will mak to yow support.

CHASTITIE.

Of your counsell, I am content,
To pas to him incontinent,
And my service till him present,   5
  In hope of sum comfort.
          [*Heir sall thay pass to the King.*

[END OF THE INTERLUDE.]

DILIGENCE.

Hoaw! Solace, gentil Solace declair unto the King,
  How thair is heir ane Ladie fair of face,
That in this cuntrie can get na ludging,
  Bot pitifullie flemit from place to place,   10
  Without the King, of his speciall grace,
As ane sarvand, hir in his Court ressaif.
  Brother Solace, tell the King all the cace.
That scho may be resavit amang the laif.

SOLACE.

Soverane, get up, and se ane hevenlie sicht;   15
  Ane fair Ladie, in quhyt abuilzement:
Scho may be peir unto ane king or knicht,
  Most lyk ane angell, be my judgment.

REX HUMANITAS.

I sall gang se that sicht, incontinent:
Madame, behauld, gif ye have knawledging
  Of yon Ladie, or quhat is hir intent;
Thairefter, wee sall turne but tarying.

SENSUALITIE.

Sir, let me se quhat yon mater may meine,   5
  Perchance, that I may knaw hir be hir face:
But doubt, this is Dame Chastitie, I weine;
  Sir, I and scho cannot byde in ane place,
  But, gif it be the pleasour of your Grace,
That I remaine, into your cumpany,   10
  This woman richt haistelie gar chace,
That scho na mair be sene in this cuntrie.

REX HUMANITAS.

As ever ye pleis, Sweit hart, sa sall it be;
  Dispone hir, as ye think expedient:
Evin as ye list, to let hir live or die,   15
  I will refer that thing to your judgement.

SENSUALITIE.

I will that scho be flemit incontinent,
And never to cum againe in this cuntrie:
  And gif scho dois, but doubt scho sall repent,
As als perchance, a duilfull deid sall die.   20

Pas on, sir Sapience, and Discretioun,
  And banische hir out of the King's presence.

DISSAIT.

That sall we do, Madame, be God's passioun,
  Wee sall do your command with diligence;
  And at your hand, serve gudely recompence:
Dame Chastitie, cum on, be not agast;
  Wee sall rycht sone upon your awin expence,   5
Into the stocks your bony fute mak fast.
        [Heir sall thay harll Chastitie to the stocks,
            and scho sall say,

I pray yow, Sirs, be patient,
For I sall be obedient
    Till do quhat ye command;
Sen I se thair is na remeid.   10
Howbeit, it war to suffer deid,
    Or flemit furth of the land.
I wyte the Empreour Constantine,
That I am put to sic ruine,
    And baneist from the Kirk: 15
For, sen he maid the Paip ane king,
In Rome I could get na ludging;
    Bot, heidlangs, in the mirk.
Bot Ladie Sensualitie,
Sensyne hes gydit this cuntrie,   20
    And monie of the rest:
And now, scho reulis all this land,
And hes decryit, and hir command,
    That I suld be supprest.
Bot all comes for the best,   25
  Til him that lovis the Lord:
Thocht I be now molest,
  I traist to be restorde.
        [Heir sall thay put hir in the stocks.

Sister, alace! this is ane cairfull cace,
  That wee, with Princes, sould be sa abhorde.

VERITIE.

Be blyth, Sister, I trust, within schort space,
  That we sall be richt honorablie restorde,
  And with the Kyng wee sall be at concorde;   5
For I heir tell, Divyne Correctioun
  Is new landit, thankit be Christ our Lord!
I wait hee will be our protectioun.
      [*Heir sall enter Correctiouns Varlet.*

VARLET.

  Sirs, stand abak, and hauld yow coy,
  I am the King Correctioun's boy;   10
      Cum heir to dres his place:
  Se that ye mak obedience,
  Untill his nobill excellence,
  Fra tyme ye se his face.
  For, he maks reformatiouns,   15
  Out-throw all Christin Natiouns,
      Quhair he finds gret debaits:
  And sa far as I understand,
  He sall reforme into this Land,
      Evin all the Thrie Estaits.   20
  God, furth of heavin, hes him send,
  To punische all that dois offend
      Against his Majestie;
  As lyks him best, to tak vengeance,
  Sumtyme, with sword, and pestilence,   25

With derth, and povertie.
Bot, quhen the pepill dois repent.
And beis to God obedient,
    Then will he gif them grace :
Bot, thay that will nocht be correctit,
Rycht sudanlie will be dejectit,
    And flemit from his face.

Sirs, thocht wee speik in generall.
Let na man, into speciall,
    Tak our wordis at the warst :
Quhat ever wee do, quhat ever wee say,
I pray yow tak it all in play,
    And judge ay to the best :
    For silence, I protest,
Baith of Lord, Laird, and Ladie :
    Now, I will rin, but rest,
And tell that all is ready.

DISSAIT.

Brother, heir ye yon proclamatioun ;
I dreid full sair of reformatioun,
    Yon message maks me mangit :
Quhat is your counsell, to me tell,
Remaine wee heir, be God himsell,
    Wee will be all thrie hangit.

FLATTERIE.

I'le gang to Spiritualitie,
And preich out-throw his dyosie,
    Quhair I wald be unknawin :

Or keip me closse into sum closter,
With mony piteous Pater Noster,
 Till all thir blasts be blawin.

DISSAIT.

I'le be weill treitit, as ye ken,
With my masteris, the Merchand men,   5
 Quhilk can mak small debait:
Ye ken richt few of them that thryfes,
Or can begyll the landwart wyfes,
 But me thair man, Dissait.

Now, Falset, quhat sall be thy schift?   10

FALSET.

Na cuir thow nocht, man, for my thrift,
 Trows thou, that I be daft?
Na, I will leif ane lustye lyfe,
Withouttin ony sturt and stryfe,
 Amang the men of craft.   15

FLATTERIE.

I na mair will remaine besyd yow;
Bot counsell yow, rycht weill to gyde yow,
 Byde nocht on Correctioun:
Fair-weils, I will na langer tarie,
I pray the alrich Queene of Farie,   20
 To be your protectioun.

DISSAIT.

Falset, I wald wee maid ane band,

Now, quhill the King is yit sleipand,
    Quhat rack to steill his box?

FALSET.

Now, weill said, be the Sacrament,
I sall it steill incontinent,
    Thocht it had twentie lox.   5
[*Heir sall Falset steill the King's Box, with silence.*

Lo! heir the Box, now let us ga,
    This may suffice, for our rewairds.

DISSAIT.

Yea, that it may, man, be this day
    It may weill mak of landwart lairds:
Now, let us cast away our clais,   10
    In dreid, sum follow on the chase.

FALSET.

Richt weill devysit, man, be Sanct Blais,
    Wald God! wee war out of this place.

DISSAIT.

Now, sen thair is na man to wrang us,
    I pray yow, brother, with my hart,   15
Let us ga part this pelf amang us.
    Syne, haistelye, we sall depart.

FALSET.

Trows thou, to get als mekill as I?
    That sall thow nocht I staw the box,

Thou did nathing bot luikit by,
  Ay lurkeand, lyke ane wylie fox.

DISSAIT.

Thy heid sall beir ane cuppill of knox,
  Pellour, without I get my part:
Swyith, huirsun smaik, ryfe up the lox,   5
  Or, I sall stick thé throuch the hart.
        [*Heir sall thay fecht, with silence.*

FALSET.

Alace! for ever, my eye is out,
  Walloway! will na man red the men?

DISSAIT.

Upon thy craig, tak thair ane clout,
  To be courtesse, I sall thé ken.   10
Fare-weill! for I am at the flicht,
  I will nocht byde on ma demands;
And wee twa meit againe this nicht,
  Thy feit salbe worth fourtie hands.
        [*Heir sal Dissait rin away, with the Box,
        through the water.*

DIVYNE CORRECTIOUN.

"*Beati qui esuriunt et sitiunt Justitiam:*"
Thir ar the wordis of the redoutit Roy,   15
  The Prince of peace, above all kings, King:
Quhilk hes me sent all cuntreis to convoye,
  And all misdoars dourlie to doun thring.
I will do nocht, without the conveining

Ane Parliament of the Estaits all ;
   In their presence, I sall, but feinzeing,
Iniquitie, under my sword, doun thrall.

Thair may no Prince do acts honorabill,
   Bot gif, his Counsall thairto will assist :   5
How may he knaw the thing maist profitabil,
   To follow vertew, and vycis to resist,
   Without he be instructit, and solist ?
And quhen the King standis at his Counsell sound,
   Then welth sall wax, and plentie, as he list,   10
And policie sall in his Realme abound.

Gif ony list my name for till inquyre,
   I am callit Divyne Correctioun.
I fled throch mony uncouth land, and schyre,
   To the greit profit of ilk Natioun :   15
   Now am I cum into this Regioun,
To teill the ground, that hes bene lang unsawin.
   To punische tyrants, for thair transgressioun,
And to caus leill men live upon thair awin.

Na realme, nor land but my support may stand ;   20
   For I gar kings live into royaltie :
To rich, and puir, I beir ane equall band,
   That thay may live into thair awin degrie :
   Quhair I am nocht, is no tranquilitie.
Be me, tratours, and tyrants, ar put doun ;   25
   Quha thinks na schame of thair iniquitie,
Till thay be punisched be mee Correctioun.

Quhat is ane king? nocht bot ane officiar,
  To caus his leiges live in equitie:
And, under God, to be ane punischer
  Of trespassouris against His Majestie.
But, quhen the king dois law in tyrannie, 5
Breakand justice for feare or affectioun;
  Then, is his realme in weir, and povertie,
With schamefull slauchter, but correctioun.

I am ane Juge richt potent, and seveir,
  Cum, to do justice, monie thowsand myle: 10
I am sa constant baith in peace and weir,
  Na bud, nor favour, may my sicht ouersyle,
  Thair is thairfoir richt monie in this Ile,
Of my repair, but doubt, that dois repent:
  Bot verteous men, I traist, sall on me smyle, 15
And of my cumming sall be richt weill content.

[GUDE COUNSALL.]

Welcum, my Lord, welcum ten thousand tymes
  Till all faithfull men of this regioun;
Welcum, for till correct all falts, and crymes,
  Amang this cankerd congregatioun. 20
  Lowse Chastitie, I mak supplicatioun;
Put till fredome fair Ladie Veritie,
  Quha, be unfaithfull folk of this Natioun,
Lyis bund full fast into captivitie.

DIVYNE CORRECTIOUN.

I mervel, Gude Counsell, how that may be, 25
  Ar ye nocht with the King familiar?

GUDE COUNSALL.

That I am nocht, my Lord, full wa is me,
    Bot, lyke ane begger, am halden at the bar :
    Thay play Bo-keik, evin as I war ane skar :
Thair came thrie knaves, in cleithing counterfeit,
    And, fra the King, thay gart me stand affar ;   5
Quhais names war Flatterie, Falset, and Dissait :

Bot, quhen thay knavis hard tell of your cumming,
    Thay staw away, ilk ane ane sindrie gait ;
And cuist fra them thair counterfit cleithing,
    For thair leving full weill thay can debait :   10
    The merchandmen, thay haif resavit Dissait.
As for Falset, my Lord, full weill I ken,
    He will be richt weill treitit, air and lait,
Among the maist part of the craftis men.

Flattrie has taine the habite of ane Freir,   15
    Thinkand to begyll Spiritualitie.

DIVYNE CORRECTIOUN.

But dout, my freind, and I live half ane yeir,
    I sall search out that great iniquitie.
        Quhair lyis yon Ladyes in captivitie ?
How now, Sisters, quha hes yow sa disgysit ?   20

VERITIE.

Unfaithfull members of iniquitie.
Dispytfullie, my Lord, hes us supprysit.

DIVYNE CORRECTIOUN.

Gang, put yon Ladyis to thair libertie
   Incontinent, and break doun all the stocks:
But dout, thay ar full deir welcum to mee;
   Mak diligence, me think ye do bot mocks;   [5
Speid hand, and spair nocht for to break the locks,
And tenderlie, tak thame up be the hand;
   Had I thame heir, thay knaves suld ken my knocks,
That them opprest, and baneist aff the land.
        [*Thay tak the Ladyis furth of the stocks;
         and Veritie sall say:*

VERITIE.

Wee thank you, Sir, of your benignitie,
   Bot, I beseik your Majestie royall,   10
That ye wald pas to King Humanitie,
   And fleime from him, yon Ladie Sensuall,
   And enter in his service Gude Counsall:
For ye will find him verie counsalabill.

DIVYNE CORRECTIOUN.

Cum on, Sisters, as ye haif said, I sall,   15
And gar him stand with yow thrie, firme and stabill.
      [*Divyne Correctioun passis towards the King, with
       Veritie, Chastitie, and Gude Counsell.*

WANTONNES.

Solace, knawis thou not quhat I se?
Ane knicht, or ellis ane king, thinks me,
With wantoun wings as he wald flie;
   Brother, quhat may this meine?   20

I understand nocht, be this day
Quhidder that he be freind or fay,
Stand still, and heare quhat he will say,
    Sic ane I haif nocht seine.

SOLACE.

Yon is ane stranger, I stand forde,   5
He semes to be ane lustie lord,
Be his heir-cumming, for concorde,
    And be kinde till our King:
He sall be welcome to this place,
And treatit with the King's grace;   10
Be it nocht sa, we sall him chace,
    And to the Divell him ding.

PLACEBO.

I reid us put upon the King,
And walkin him of his sleiping.
Sir, rise, and se ane uncouth thing: 15
    Get up, ye ly too lang?

SENSUALITIE.

Put on your hude, John Fule, ye raif,
    How dar ye be so pert, Sir knaif,
    To tuich the King! sa Christ me saif,
        Fals huirsone, thow sall hang.   20

DIVYNE CORRECTIOUN.

Get up, Sir King! ye haif sleipit aneuch
Into the armis of Ladie Sensual;

Be suir, that mair belangis to the pleuch,
  As efterwards perchance, rehears I sall
  Remember how the king Sardanapall,
Amang fair ladyes tuke his lust sa lang;
  Sa that, the maist pairt of his leiges all   5
Rebeld, and syne him duilfully doun thrang.

Remember how into the tyme of Noy,
  For the foull stinckand sin of lechery,
God, be my wande, did al the Warld destroy.
  Sodome and Gomore, richt sa full rigorously,   10
  For that vyld sin, war brunt maist cruelly:
Thairfoir, I thé command incontinent,
  Banische from thé that huir Sensualitie,
Or els, but dout, rudlie thow sall repent.

REX HUMANITAS.

Be quhom, haif ye sa greit authoritie?   15
  Quha dois presume, for till correct ane King?
Knaw ye nocht me, greit King Humanitie!
  That in my Regioun royally dois ring.

DIVYNE CORRECTIOUN.

I have power greit Princes to doun thring,
That lives contrair the Majestie Divyne,   20
  Against the treuth quhilk plainlie dois maling,
Repent thay nocht, I put thame to ruyne.

I will begin at thee, quhilk is the head,
  And mak on thee first reformatioun,
Thy leiges than, will follow thee but pleid,   25
  Swyith, harlot! hence without dilatioun.

SENSUALITIE.

My Lord, I mak yow supplicatioun,
Gif me licence, to pas againe to Rome;
Amang the princes of that natioun,
I lat yow wit, my fresche beautie will blume.
Adew, Sir King, I may na langer tary, 5
I cair nocht that, als gude luife cumis as gais;
I recommend yow to the Queene of Farie,
I see ye will be gydit, with my fais.
As for this King, I cure him nocht twa strais:
War I amang bischops, and cardinals, 10
I wald get gould, silver, and precious clais:
Na earthlie joy, but my presence, availis.
[Heir sall scho pas to Spiritualitie.

My Lords of the Spirituall Stait;
Venus preserve yow, air and lait;
For, I can mak na mair debait, 15
I am partit with your King;
And am baneischt this regioun,
Be counsell of Correctioun;
Be ye nocht my protectioun,
I may seik my ludgeing. 20

SPIRITUALITIE.

Welcum, our dayis darling,
Welcum, with all our hart:
Wee all, but feinzeing,
Sall plainly tak your part.
[Heir sall the Bischops, Abbots, and Persons, kiss the Ladies.

DIVYNE CORRECTIOUN.

Sen ye ar quyte of Sensualitie,
    Resave into your service Gude Counsall,
And richt sa this fair ladie Chastitie,
    Till ye mary sum Queene of blude royall;
    Observe then Chastitie matrimoniall;   5
Richt sa, resave Veritie be the hand;
    Use thair counsell, your fame sall never fall:
With thame, thairfoir, mak ane perpetuall band.
    [*Heir sall the King resave Gude Counsall,*
        Veritie, and Chastitie.

    Now, Sir, tak tent, quhat I will say,
    Observe thir same baith nicht and day,   10
    And let thame never part yow fray,
        Or els, withoutin doubt,
Turne ye to Sensualitie,
To vicious lyfe, and rebaldrie,
    Out of your Realme richt schamefullie,   15
        Ye sall be ruttit out;
As was Tarquine, the Romane king,
Quha was, for his vicious living,
And for the schamefull ravisching
    Of the fair chaist Lucres: 20
He was degraidit of his croun,
And baneist aff his regioun;
I maid on him correctioun,
    As storeis dois expres.

REX HUMANITAS.

I am content to your counsall to inclyne,   25
    Ye beand of gude conditioun.

At your command sall be all that is myne,
  And heir I gif you full commissioun,
  To punische faults, and gif remissioun.
To all vertew, I sal be consociabill,
  With yow, I sall confirme ane unioun,   5
And, at your counsall, stand ay firme and stabill.
      [*The King imbraces Correctioun with a humbill countenance.*

DIVYNE CORRECTIOUN.

I counsall yow, incontinent,
To gar proclame ane Parliament,
  Of all the Thrie Estaits:
That thay be heir, with diligence,   10
To mak to yow obedience,
  And syne dres all debaits.

REX HUMANITAS.

That salbe done, but mair demand.
Hoaw! Diligence, cum heir fra hand,
  And tak your informatioun;   15
Gang warne the Spiritualitie,
Rycht sa the Temporalitie,
  Be oppin proclamatioun,
In gudlie haist, for to compeir,
In thair maist honorabill maneir,   20
  To gif us thair counsails:
Quha that beis absent to them schaw,
That thay sall underly the law,
  And punischt be, that fails.

DILIGENCE.

Sir, I sall baith in bruch and land,
With diligence, do your command,
    Upon my awin expens :
Sir, I have servit yow all this yeir,
Bot, I gat never ane denneir
    Yit, for my recompence.

REX HUMANITAS.

Pas on, and thou sall be regairdit,
And, for thy service, weill rewairdit;
    For quhy, with my consent,
Thou sall haif yeirly, for thy hyre,
The teind mussellis of the Ferrie myre,
    Confirmit in Parliament.

DILIGENCE.

I will get riches throw that rent,
    Efter the day of Dume,
Quhen in the colpots of Tranent,
    Butter will grow on brume !
Or I proclame ocht with my mouth,
    I micht nocht sleip ane wink ;
All nicht, I had sa mekill drouth,
    But doubt, I man haif drink.

DIVYNE CORRECTIOUN.

Cum heir Placebo, and Solace,
With your companzeoun, Wantonnes,

I knaw weill your conditioun:
For tysting King Humanitie,
To resave Sensualitie,
    Ye man suffer punitioun.

WANTONNES.

We grant, my Lord, we have done ill;   5
Thairfoir, wee put us in your will,
    Bot, wee haife bene abusit;
For, in gude faith, Sir, wee beleifit
That lecherie had na man greifit,
    Becaus it is sa usit.   10

PLACEBO.

Ye sé how Sensualitie,
With Principals of ilk cuntrie,
    Bene glaidlie lettin in,
And, with our Prelatis, mair and les:
Speir at my ladie Priores,   15
    Gif lechery be sin?

SOLACE.

Sir, wee sall mend our conditioun,
Sa ye give us remissioun,
    Bot, give us leave to sing?
To dance, to play at chesse, and tabills,   20
To reid stories, and mirrie fabils,
    For pleasure of our King.

DIVYNE CORRECTIOUN.

Sa that ye do na uther cryme,

Ye sall be pardonit, at this tyme,
    For quhy ? as I suppois,
Princes may sumtyme seik solace,
With mirth, and lawful mirrines,
    Thair spirits to rejoyis.   5
And richt sa, halking and hunting,
Ar honest pastymes, for ane king,
    Into the tyme of peace :
And leirne to rin ane heavie spear,
That he into the tyme of wear,   10
    May follow at the cheace.

REX HUMANITAS.

Quhair is Sapience, and Discretioun !
    And quhy cums nocht Devotioun nar ?

VERITIE.

Sapience, Sir, was ane verie loun,
    And Discretioun was nathing war :   15
The suith, Sir, gif I wald report,
    Thay did begyle your Excellence ;
And wald not suffer to resort
    Ane of us thrie to your presence.

CHASTITIE.

Thay thrie war Flattrie, and Dissait,   20
    And Falset, that unhappie loun,
Against us thrie quhilk maid debait,
    And baneischt us from town to town,
Thay gart us twa fall into sowne,

Quhen thay us lockit in the stocks:
That dastart knave, Discretioun,
Full thifteouslie did steill your box.

REX HUMANITAS.

The Devill tak them, sen thay ar gane,
   Me thocht them ay thrie verie smaiks,   5
I mak ane vow to Sanct Mavane,
   Quhen I them finde thay bear thair paiks:
I se thay haif playit me the glaiks.
Gude Counsall, now schaw me the best;
   Quhen I fix on yow thrie my staiks,   10
How I sall keip my Realme in rest.
   Initium sapientiæ est timor Domini.

GUDE COUNSALL.

Sir, gif your Hienes yearnis lang to ring,
First dread your God abuif all uther thing:
For ye ar bot ane mortall instrument,
To that great God and King Omnipotent: 15
Preordinat be his Divine Majestie,
To reull his peopill intill unitie.
The principall point, Sir, of ane King's office,
Is for to do to everilk man justice;
And for to mix his justice with mercie,   20
But rigour, favour, or parcialitie.
Forsuith, it is na littill observance,
Great regions to have in governance:
Quha ever takis on him that kinglie cuir,
To get ane of thir twa, he suld be suir,   25

Greit paine, and labour, and that continuall,
Or ellis till have defame perpetuall:
Quha guydis weill they win immortall fame,
Quha the contrair, they get perpetuall schame;
Efter quhais deith, but doubt, ane thousand yeir,   5
Thair life, at lenth, rehearst sall be, perqueir.
The Chroniklis to knaw, I yow exhort,
Thair sall ye finde baith gude and evill report:
For everie Prince, efter his qualitie,
Thocht he be deid, his deidis sall never die.   10
Sir, gif ye please, for to use my counsall,
Your fame and name sall be perpetuall.

    [*Heir sall the messinger Diligence returne; and cry a Hoyzes, a Hoyses, a Hoyzes, and say:*

At the command of King Humanitie,
    I wairne, and charge, all members of Parliament,
Baith Spirituall Stait, and Temporalitie,   15
    That till his Grace, thay be obedient,
    And speid them to the Court incontinent,
In gude ordour arrayit royally;
    Quha beis absent, or inobedient,
The King's displeasure they sall underly.   20
And als I mak yow exhortatioun,
    Sen ye haif heard the FIRST PAIRT of our Play,
Go tak ane drink, and mak collatioun;
    Ilk man drink till his marrow, I yow pray,
    Tarie nocht lang, it is lait in the day;   25
Let sum drink ayle, and sum drink claret wine,
    Be gret Doctors of Physick, I heare say,
That michtie drink comforts the dull ingine.

And ye Ladies, that list to pisch,
Lift up your taill, plat in ane disch;
And gif that your mawkine cryis quhisch,
    Stop in ane wusp of stray.
Let nocht your bladder burst, I pray yow,   5
For that war evin aneuch to slay yow:
For yit thair is to cum, I say yow,
    The best pairt of our Play.

THE END OF THE FIRST PART OF THE SATYRE.

[*Now sall the Pepill mak collatioun: then beginnis the Interlude; the Kings, Bischops, and principall Players, being out of their seats.*

[AN INTERLUDE OF THE PUIR MAN AND THE PARDONER.]

[Heir sall entir Pauper the puir man.

PAUPER.

Of your almis, gude folks, for God's luife of heavin,
For I have motherles bairns either sax, or seavin:
Gif ye'ill gif me na gude, for the luife of Jesus,
Wische me the richt way till Sanct-Androes.

DILIGENCE.

Quhair haif wee gottin this gudly companzeoun? 5
Swyith! out of the feild, [thow] fals raggit loun.
God wait, gif heir be ane weill keipit place,
Quhen sic ane vilde begger Carle may get entres.
Fy! on yow officiars! that mends nocht thir failyies,
I gif yow all till the Devill baith Provost, and Bailȝies!
Without ye cum, and chase this Carle away,   [10
The devill a word ye'is get mair of our Play.

 Fals huirsun, raggit Carle, quhat Devil is that thou
  rugs?

PAUPER.

Quha Devill, maid thee ane gentill man, that wald cut
  not thy lugs?

DILIGENCE.

Quhat now! me thinks the Carle begins to crack,
Swyith! Carle away, or be this day, Is'e break thy back.

   [*Heir sall the Carle clim up and sit in the King's tchyre.*

Cum doun, or be God's croun, fals loun, I sall slay thee.

PAUPER.

Now sweir be thy brunt schinnis, the Devill ding thame fra thee.
Quhat say ye till thir court dastards? be thay get [5
 hail clais,
Sa sune as thay leir to sweir, and trip on thair tais.

DILIGENCE.

Me thocht, the Carle callit me knave, evin in my face.
Be Sanct Fillane! thou sal be slane, bot gif thou ask grace:
Loup doun, or be the gude Lord, thow sall lose thy heid.

PAUPER.

I sall anis drink or I ga, thocht thou had sworne my deid.   10

   [*Heir Diligence castis away the ledder.*

DILIGENCE.

Loup now, gif thou list, for thou hes lost the ledder:
It is full weill thy kind, to loup, and licht in a tedder.

PAUPER.

Thou sall be faine, to fetch agane the ledder, or I loup;
I sall sit heir, into this tcheir, till I have tumde the stoup.

[*Heir sall the Carle loup aff the scaffald.*

DILIGENCE.

Swyith! beggar, bogill, haist thee away;
Thow art over pert to spill our Play.

PAUPER.

I will not gif, for al your Play, worth an sowis fart: 5
For, thair is richt lytill play, at my hungrie hart.

DILIGENCE.

Quhat devill ails this cruckit Carle?

PAUPER.

Marie! meikill sorrow:
I can not get, thocht I gasp, to beg, nor to borrow.

DILIGENCE.

Quhair devill is this thou dwels? or quhat's thy intent? 10

PAUPER.

I dwell into Lawthiane, ane myle fra Tranent.

DILIGENCE.

Quhair wald thou be, Carle? the suth to me schaw.

PAUPER.

Sir, evin to Sanct-Androes, for to seik law.

DILIGENCE.

For to seik law, in Edinburgh was the neirest way.

PAUPER.

Sir, I socht law thair this monie deir day:
Bot, I culd get nane at Sessioun, nor Seinzie;
Thairfor, the meikill din Devill droun all the meinzie.

DILIGENCE.

Schaw me thy mater, man, with all the circumstances, 5
How that thou hes happinit on thir unhappie chances.

PAUPER.

Gude man, will ye gif me of your charitie,
And I sall declair yow the black veritie.
My Father was ane auld man, and ane hoir,
And was of age fourscoir of yeirs and moir. 10
And Mald, my mother, was fourscoir and fyfteine,
And with my labour I did thame baith susteine.
Wee had ane meir, that caryit salt and coill,
And everie ilk yeir, scho brocht us hame ane foill.
Wee had thrie ky, that was baith fat and fair, 15
Nane tydier into the toun of Air.
My Father was sa waik of blude, and bane,
That he deit, quhairfoir my Mother maid great maine:
Then scho deit, within ane day or two;
And thair began my povertie, and wo. 20
Our gude gray meir was baittand on the feild,
And our Land's laird tuik hir, for his hyreild,
The Vickar tuik the best cow be the heid,
Incontinent, quhen my father was deid.

And quhen the Vickar hard tel how that my mother
Was deid, fra hand, he tuke to him ane uther:
Then Meg, my wife, did murne baith evin, and morrow,
Till at the last scho deit for verie sorrow:
And quhen the Vickar hard tell my wyfe was dead,   5
The thrid cow he cleikit be the heid.
Thair umest clayis, that was of rapploch gray,
The Vickar gart his Clark bear them away.
Quhen all was gane, I micht mak na debeat,
Bot with my bairns past for till beg my meat.   10
   Now, haif I tald yow the blak veritie,
   How I am brocht into this miserie.

DILIGENCE.

How did the Person? was he not thy gude freind?

PAUPER.

The Devil stick him! he curst me for my teind:
And halds me yit under that same proces,   15
That gart me want the Sacrament at Pasche.
In gude faith, Sir, thocht he wald cut my throt,
I have na geir, except ane Inglis grot,
Quhilk I purpois to gif ane man of law.

DILIGENCE.

Thou art the daftest fuill, that ever I saw;   20
Trows thou, man, be the law, to get remeid
Of men of Kirk! Na, nocht till thou be deid.

PAUPER.

Sir, be quhat law, tell me, quhairfoir, or quhy
That ane Vickar suld tak fra me thrie ky?

DILIGENCE.

Thay have na law, exceptand consuetude,
Quhilk law, to them, is sufficient and gude.

PAUPER.

Ane consuetude against the common weill,
Suld be na law, I think, be sweit Sanct Geill.
Quhair will ye find that law, tell gif ye can, 5
To tak thrie ky, fra ane pure husband man?
Ane for my father, and for my wyfe ane uther,
And the third cow, he tuke fra Mald my mother.

DILIGENCE.

It is thair law, all that thay have in use,
Thocht it be cow, sow, gauer, gryse, or guse. 10

PAUPER.

Sir, I wald speir at yow ane questioun:
Behauld sum Prelats of this regioun,
Manifestlie, during thair lusty lyfis,
. . . .
Quhidder say ye, that law is evill, or gude?

DILIGENCE.

Hald thy toung, man, it seims that thou war
    mangit. 15
Speik thou of Preists, but doubt, thou will be hangit.

PAUPER.

Be Him, that buir the cruell croun of thorne,
I cair nocht to be hangit, evin the morne.

DILIGENCE.

Be sure, of Preistis thou will get na support.

PAUPER.

Gif that be trew, the Feind resave the sort?
Sa, sen I se, I get na uther grace,
I will ly down, and rest me in this place.
    [*Heir sall the Puirman ly doun in the feild;
    and the Pardoner sall cum in and say:*

PARDONER.

Bona dies! Bona dies!   5
Devoit pepill, gude day, I say yow,
Now tarie ane lytill quhyll, I pray yow,
    Till I be with yow knawin:
Wat ye weill how I am namit?
Ane nobill man, and undefamit,   10
    Gif all the suith war schawin.
I am Sir Robert Rome-raker,
Ane perfyte publike Pardoner,
    Admittit be the Paip:
Sirs, I sall schaw yow, for my wage,   15
My pardons, and my pilgramage,
    Quhilk ye sall se, and graip;
I give to the Devill, with gude intent,
This unsell wickit New Testament,
    With thame that it translaitit: 20
Sen layik men knew the veritie,
Pardoners gets no charitie,
    Without that thay debait it.
Amang the wives with wrinks and wyles,

As all my marrowis, men begyles,
    With our fair fals flattrie:
Yea, all the crafts I ken perqueir,
As I was teichit, be ane Freir,
    Callit Hypocrisie.   5
Bot now, allace! our greit abusioun
Is cleirlye knawin till our confusioun,
    That we may sair repent:
Of all credence, now I am quyte,
For, ilk man halds me at dispyte,   10
    That reids the New Test'ment,
Duill fell the braine, that hes it wrocht,
Sa fall them that the Buik hame brocht:
    Als I pray to the Rude,
That Martin Luther, that fals loun,   15
Black Bullinger, and Melancthoun,
    Had bene smorde in their cude.
Be Him, that buir the crowne of thorne,
I wald Sanct Paull had never bene borne,
    And als, I wald his buiks,   20
War never red in the kirk,
Bot amangs friers, into the mirk,
    Or riven amang ruiks.
          [*Heir sall he lay doun his geir upon ane
                buird, and say,*
My patent Pardouns, ye may se,
Cum fra the Cane of Tartarie,   25
    Weill seald with oster-schellis.
Thocht ye have na contritioun,
Ye sall have full remissioun,
    With help of buiks, and bellis.

Heir is ane relict, lang and braid
Of Fine Macoull the richt chaft blaid,
  With teith, and al togidder :
Of Colling's cow, heir is ane horne,
For eating of Makconnal's corne,   5
  Was slane into Balquhidder.
Heir is ane coird, baith great and lang,
Quhilk hangit Johne the Armistrang :
  Of gude hemp soft, and sound :
Gude, halie peopill I stand for'd   10
Quha ever beis hangit with this cord,
  Neids never to be dround.
The culum of Sanct Bryd's kow,
The gruntill of Sanct Antonis sow,
  Quhilk buir his haly bell ;   15
Quha ever he be heiris this bell clinck,
Gif me ane ducat for till drink,
  He sall never gang to hell,
Without he be of Baliell borne :
Maisters, trow ye, that this be scorne !   20
  Cum win this Pardoun, cum.
Quha luifis thair wyfis nocht, with thair hart,
I have power thame for till part,
  Me think yow deif and dum.
Hes naine of yow curst wickit wyfis,   25
That halds yow intill start and stryfis,
  Cum tak my dispensatioun :
Of that cummer, I sall mak yow quhyte,
Howbeit your selfis be in the wyte,
  And mak ane fals narratioun.   30
Cum win the Pardoun, now let se,

For meill, for malt, or for monie,
    For cok, hen, guse, or gryse.
Of relicts, heir I haif ane hunder;
Quhy cum ye nocht? this is ane wounder:
    I trow ye be nocht wyse.   5

SOWTAR.

Welcum hame, Robert Rome-raker,
Our halie patent pardoner.:
    Gif ye haif dispensatioun,
To pairt me, and my wickit wyfe,
And me deliver from sturt and stryfe,   10
    I mak yow supplicatioun.

PARDONER.

I sall yow pairt, but mair demand,
Sa, I get mony in my hand;
    Thairfoir let se sum cunzie.

SOWTAR.

I have na silver, be my lyfe,   15
Bot fyve schillings, and my schaipping knyfe,
    That sall ye have, but sunzie.

PARDONER.

Quhat kynd of woman is thy wyfe?

SOWTAR.

Ane quick devill, Sir, ane storme of stryfe,
    Ane frog, that fyles the winde;   20
Ane fistand flag, a flagartie fuffe,

At ilk ane pant, scho lets ane puffe,
    And hes na ho behind.
All the lang day, scho me dispyts,
And all the nicht, scho flingis, and flyts,
    Thus sleip I never ane wink :   5
That cockatrice, that commoun huir,
The mekill Devill may nocht induir
    Hir stuburness, and stink.

SOWTAR'S WYFE.

Theif Carle, thy wordis I hard rycht weill,
In faith, my friendschip, ye sall feill,   10
    And I thee fang.

SOWTAR.

Gif I said ocht, Dame, be the Rude,
Except ye war baith fair and gude,
    God nor I hang.

PARDONER.

Fair dame, gif ye wald be ane wower,   15
To part yow twa, I have ane power,
    Tell on, ar ye content ?

SOWTAR'S WYFE.

Ye, that I am, with all my hart,
Fra that fals huirsone till depart,
    Gif this theif will consent.   20
Causses to part I haif anew ;
Becaus I gat na chamber-glew,
    I tell yow verely ;

I mervell nocht, sa mot I lyfe,
Howbeit that swingeour can not swyfe,
   He is baith cauld and dry.

PARDONER.
Quhat will ye giff me, for your part?

SOWTAR'S WYFE.
Ane cuppill of sarks, with all my hart,   5
   The best claith, in the land.

PARDONER.
To part, sen ye ar baith content,
I sall yow part incontinent,
   Bot, ye mon do command:
My will, and finall sentence is,   10
Ilk ane of yow uthers arsse kiss.
Slip doun your hois! me thinkis the carle is glaikit,
Set thow not by, howbeit scho kisse, and slaik it.
    [*Heir sall scho kis hiss arsse, with silence.*
Lift up hir clais, kiss hir hoill with your hart.

SOWTAR.
I pray yow, Sir, forbid hir for to fart.   15
    [*Heir sall the Carle kiss hir arsse, with silence.*

PARDONER.
Dame, pas ye to the east end of the toun:
And pas ye west, evin lyke ane cuckald loun;
Go hence ye baith, with Baliel's braid blissing!
Schirs, saw ye ever mair sorrowles pairting?
    [*Heir sall the Boy cry aff the hill, and say:*

WILKIN.

Hoaw! Maister, hoaw! quhair ar ye now?

PARDONER.

I am heir, Wilkin widdiefow.

WILKIN.

 Sir, I have done your bidding;
For, I have fund ane greit hors bane,
Ane fairer saw ye never nane,   5
 Upon dame Flescher's midding.
Sir, ye may gar the wyfis trow,
It is ane bane of Sanct Bryd's cow;
 Gude for the fever quartane:
Sir, will ye reull this relict weill,   10
All the wyfis will baith kiss, and kneill,
 Betuixt this and Dumbartane.

PARDONER.

Quhat say thay of me, in the Toun?

WILKIN.

Some sayis, ye ar ane verie loun,   15
 Sum sayis, *Legatus Natus;*
Sum sayis ye ar ane fals Saracene;
And sum sayis, ye ar for certaine
 Diabolus Incarnatus.
Bot keip yow fra subjectioun   20
Of the curst King Correctioun;
 For be ye with him fangit

Becaus ye ar ane Rome-raker,
Ane common publick cawsay-paker,
   But doubt ye will be hangit.

PARDONER.

Quhair sall I ludge into the toun?

WILKIN.

With gude kynde Cristiane Anderson,   5
   Quhair ye will be weill treatit.
Gif ony limmer yow demands,
Scho will defend yow with hir hands,
   And womanlie debait it.
Bawburdie sayis, be the Trinitie,   10
That scho sall beir yow cumpanie,
   Howbeit ye byde ane yeir.

PARDONER.

Thou hes done weill, be God's mother,
Tak ye the taine, and I the tother,
   Sa sall we mak greit cheir.   15

WILKIN.

I reid yow, speid yow heir,
   And mak na langer tarie;
Byde ye lang thair, but weir,
   I dreid your weird yow warie.
         [*Heir sall Pauper rise, and rax him.*

PAUPER.

Quhat thing was yon that I heard crak and cry?   20
I have bene dreamand, and dreveland of my ky,

With my richt hand my haill bodie I saine,
Sanct Bryd, Sanct Bryd, send me my ky againe!
I se standand yonder ane halie man,
To mak me help, let me se gif he can.
Halie Maister, God speid yow! and gude morne.   5

PARDONER.

Welcum to me, thocht thou war at the horne,
Cum win the pardoun, and syne I sall thé saine.

PAUPER.

Will that pardon get me my ky againe?

PARDONER.

Carle, of thy ky, I have nathing ado:
Cum, win my pardon, and kis my relicts to.   10
        [*Heir sall he saine him with his relictis*:
Now lowse thy purse, and lay doun thy offrand,
And thou sall have my pardoun evin fra hand.
With raipis, and relicts, I sall thé saine againe;
Of gut, or gravell, thou sall never have paine;
Now, win the pardoun, limmer, or thou art lost.   15

PAUPER.

My haly Father, quhat wil that pardon cost?

PARDONER.

Let se quhat mony thou bearest in thy bag.

PAUPER.

I haif ane grot heir, bund into ane rag.

PARDONER.

Hes thou na uther silver bot ane groat

PAUPER.
Gif I have mair, Sir, cum and rype my coat.

PARDONER.
Gif me that groat, man, gif thou hest na mair.

PAUPER.
With all my hart, Maister, lo tak it thair:
Now let me se your pardon, with your leif.

PARDONER.
Ane thousand yeir of pardons, I thee geif. 5

PAUPER.
Ane thousand yeir ! I will nocht live sa lang ;
Delyver me it, Maister, and let me gang,

PARDONER.
Ane thousand yeir, I lay upon thy head,
With *totiens quotiens:* now, mak me na mair plead :
Thou hast resaifit thy pardon now already. 10

PAUPER.
Bot, I can se na thing, Sir, be Our Lady :
Forsuith, Maister, I trow I be nocht wyse,
To pay ere I have sene my marchandryse.
That ye have gottin my groat full sair I rew ;
Sir, quhidder is your pardon black, or blew ? 15
Maister, sen ye have tain fra me my cunzie,
My marchandryse schaw me, withouttin sunzie ;
Or, to the Bischop I sall pas, and pleinzie,

In Sanct-Androis, and summond yow to the Seinzie.

PARDONER.

Quhat craifis the Carle ? me thinks thou art not wise.

PAUPER.

I craif my groat, or ellis my marchandrise.

PARDONER.

I gaif thee pardon for ane thowsand yeir.

PAUPER.

How sall I get that pardon, let me heir. 5

PARDONER.

Stand still, and I sall tell the haill storie :
Quhen thow art deid, and gais to Purgatorie,
Being condempnit to paine a thowsand yeir,
Then sall thy pardoun thee releif but weir :
Now be content, ye ar ane mervelous man. 10

PAUPER.

Sall I get nathing, for my groat, quhill than ?

PARDONER.

That sall thou not, I mak it to yow plaine.

PAUPER.

Na than, gossop, gif me my groat againe,
Quhat say ye, Maisters ? call ye this gude resoun,
That he suld promeis me ane gay pardoun, 15
And he resave my mony, in his stead ;

Syne mak me na payment till I be dead?
Quhen I am deid, I wait full sikkerlie,
My sillie saull will pas to Purgatorie;
Declair me this, now God, nor Baliell, bind thee,
Quhen I am thair, curst Carle, quhair sall I find thee? 5
Not into heavin, but rather into hell:
Quhen thow art thair, thou cannot help thy sell.
Quhen will thou cum my dolours till abait?
Or I thee find, my hippis will get ane hait.
Trowis thou, butchour, that I will buy blind lambis? 10
Gif me my groat, the Devill dryte in thy gambis.

PARDONER.

Swyith! stand abak! I trow this man be mangit:
Thou gets not this, Carle, thocht thou suld be hangit.

PAUPER.

Gif me my groat, weill bund into ane clout,
Or, be Goddis breid, Robin sall beir ane rout. 15
      [*Heir sall thay fecht with silence; and
        Pauper sal cast down the buird, and
        cast the relicts in the water.*

DILIGENCE.

Quhat kind of daffing is this al day?
Swyith, smaiks! out of the feild, away:
Intill ane presoun put them sone,
Syne hang them, quhen the PLAY is done.

[ANE PLEASANT SATYRE OF THE THRIE ESTAITIS, &c. PART THE SECOND.]

[Heir sall Diligence mak his Proclamatioun.

DILIGENCE.

Famous Peopill, tak tent, and ye sall se
   The Thrie Estaits of this Natioun
Cum to the Court, with ane strange gravitie;
   Thairfoir, I mak yow supplicatioun,
   Till ye have heard our haill narratioun,   5
To keip silence, and be patient, I pray yow,
   Howbeit we speik be adulatioun,
Wee sall say nathing bot the suith, I say yow:

Gude, verteous men, that luifis the veritie,
   I wait thay will excuse our negligence: 10
Bot vicious men, denude of charitie,
   As fenzeit, fals, flattrand Saracens;
   Howbeit thay cry on us ane loud vengence,
And of our pastyme mak ane fals report:
   Quhat may wee do, bot tak in patience?   15
And us refer unto the faithfull sort.

Our Lord Jesus, Peter, nor Paull,
Culd nocht compleis the peopill all,
   Bot sum war miscontent:

Howbeit thay schew the veritie,
Sum said that it war heresie,
   Be thair maist fals judgement.
      [*Heir sall The Thrie Estaits cum fra
       the palzeoun, gangand backwart, led
       be thair Vyces.*

WANTONNES.

Now braid Benedicite !
Quhat thing is yon that I se ?   5
   Luke, Solace, my hart.

SOLACE.

Brother Wantonnes, quhat thinkis thow ?
Yon ar The Thrie Estaits, I trow,   10
   Gangand backwart.

WANTONNES.

Backwart, backwart! out wallaway !
It is gret schame for them, I say,
   Backwart to gang ;
I trow the King Correctioun,   15
Man mak ane reformatioun.
   Or it be lang.
Now let us go, and tell the King.   [*Pausa.*

Sir, we have sene ane mervelous thing,
   Be our judgement :   20
The Thrie Estaits of this Regioun
Ar cummand backwart, throw this toun,
   To the Parliament.

REX HUMANITAS.

Backwart, backwart! how may that be?
Gar speid them haistelie to me;
   In dreid, that thay ga wrang.

PLACEBO.

Sir, I se them yonder cummand,
Thay will be heir evin fra hand   5
   Als fast as thay may gang.

GUDE COUNSEL.

Sir, hald you stil, and skar them nocht,
Till ye persave quhat be thair thocht,
   And se quhat men them leids:
And let the King Correctioun,   10
Mak ane scharp inquisitioun,
   And mark thame be the heids.
Quhen ye ken the occasioun,
That makis them sic persuasioun,
   Ye may expell the caus: 15
Syne them reforme, as ye think best,
Sua that the Realme may live in rest,
   According to God's lawis.
   [*Heir sall The Thrie Estaits cum and turne
   thair faces to the King.*

SPIRITUALITIE.

Gloir, honour, laud, triumph, and victorie,
   Be to your michtie, prudent, Excellence!   20
Heir ar we cum, all The Estaits Thrie,
   Readie to mak our dew obedience,

At your command, with humbill observance,
   As may pertene to Spiritualitie,
With counsell of the Temporalitie.

TEMPORALITIE.

Sir, wee with michtie curage, at command
   Of your superexcellent Majestie,   5
Sall mak service, baith with our hart and hand,
   And sall not dreid in thy defence to die :
   Wee ar content, but dout, that wee may se
That nobyll heavenlie King Correctioun.
Sa he, with mercie, mak punitioun.   10

MERCHAND.

Sir, wee ar heir, your burgessis, and merchands,
   Thanks be to God, that we may se your face :
Traistand wee may now, into divers lands,
   Convoy our geir, with support of your Grace :
   For now, I traist, wee sall get rest, and peace,   15
Quhen misdoars ar, with your sword, overthrawin ;
Then, may leil merchandis live upon thair awin.

REX HUMANITAS.

Welcom to me, my prudent Lordis all.
   Ye ar my members, suppois I be your head :
Sit doun, that wee may, with your just counsall,   20
   Aganis misdoars find soveraine remeid :
   Wee sall nocht spair, for favour nor for feid,
With your avice to mak punitioun,
And put my sword to executioun.

CORRECTIOUN.

My tender friends, I pray yow, with my hart,
 Declair to me the thing that I wald speir,
Quhat is the caus, that ye gang all backwart?
 The veritie thairof faine wald I heir.

SPIRITUALITIE.

 Soveraine, wee have gaine sa, this mony a yeir;   5
Howbeit ye think we go undecently,
Wee think wee gang richt wonder pleasantly.

DILIGENCE.

Sit doun, my Lords, into your proper places:
Syne let the King consider all sic caces.
Sit doun, sir Scribe; and sit doun Dampster to,   10
And fence the Court, as ye war wont to do.
> [*Thay ar set doun, and Gud Counsell sal pas to his seat.*

> [*Heir sall The Thrie Estaitis compeir to the Parliament; and the King sall say.*

REX HUMANITAS.

My prudent Lords of The Thrie Estaits,
 It is our will abuife all uther thing,
For to reforme all thame that maks debaits
 Contrair the richt, quhilk daylie dois maling;   15
 And thay, that dois the Common-weil doun thring,
With help, and counsell, of King Correctioun,
 It is our will, for to mak punisching;
And plaine oppressours put to subjectioun.

SPIRITUALITIE.

Quhat thing is this, Sir, that ye have devysit?
Schirs, ye have neid, for till be weill advysit:
Be nocht haistie into your executioun.
And be nocht ouer extreime in your punitioun.
And gif ye please to do, Sir, as wee say,　　　　5
Postpone this Parlament till ane uther day:
For quhy! the peopill of this Regioun
May nocht indure extreme correctioun.

CORRECTIOUN.

Is this the part, my Lords, that ye will tak?
To mak us supportatioun to correct:　　　　10
It dois appeir, that ye ar culpabill,
That ar nocht to Correctioun applyabill.
Swyith, Diligence, ga schaw it is our will,
That everilk man opprest, geif in his bill.

DILIGENCE.

All maneir of men, I wairne, that be opprest,　　　　15
Cum and complaine, and thay sall be redrest.
For quhy, it is the nobill Prince's will,
That ilk compleiner sall gif in his bill.

JOHNE THE COMMON-WEILL.

Out of my gait, for God's saik let me ga:
Tell me againe, gude Maister, quhat ye say.　　　　20

DILIGENCE.

I warne al that be wrangouslie offendit,
Cum, and complaine, and thay sall be amendit.

JOHNE.

Thankit be Christ, that buir the croun of thorne,
For I was never sa blyth, sen I was borne.

DILIGENCE.

Quhat is thy name, fallow, that wald I feill?

JOHNE.

Forsuith, thay call me Johne the Common-weill.
Gude maister, I wald speir at you ane thing,   5
Quhair, traist ye, I sall find yon new-cumde King?

DILIGENCE.

Cum over, and I sall schaw thee to his Grace.

JOHNE.

God's bennesone licht on that luckie face!
Stand by the gait: let se, gif I can loup,
I man rin fast, in cace I get ane coup.   10
   [*Heir sall Johne loup the stank, or els fall in it.*

DILIGENCE.

Speid thee away, thou taryis all to lang.

JOHNE.

Now, be this day, I may na faster gang.
                   [*Johne to the King*
Gude day, gude day! greit God saif baith your Graces
Wallie, wallie, fall thay twa weill fairde faces.

REX HUMANITAS.

Shaw me thy name, gude man, I thee command.   15

JOHNE.

Marie, Johne the Common-weill of fair Scotland.

REX HUMANITAS.

The Commoun-weill hes bene amang his fais.

JOHNE.

Yea, Sir, that gars the Commoun-weill want clais.

REX HUMANITAS.

Quhat is the caus the Common-weill is crukit?

JOHNE.

Becaus the Common-weill hes bene ouerlukit.

REX HUMANITAS.

Quhat gars thee luke sa, with ane dreirie hart?   5

JOHNE.

Becaus The Thrie Estaitis gangs all backwart.

REX HUMANITAS.

Sir Common-weill, knaw ye the limmers, that them leids?

JOHNE.

Thair canker cullours, I ken them be the heads:
As for our reverent fathers of Spiritualitie,
They ar led be Covetice, and cairles Sensualitie.   10
And as ye se Temporalitie hes neid of correctioun,
Quhilk hes lang tyme bene led be Publick Oppressioun:
Loe! quhair the loun lyis lurkand, at his back;
Get up, I think to se thy craig gar ane raip crack.
Loe! heir is Falset and Dissait, weill I ken,   15
Leiders of the Merchants, and sillie crafts-men.
Quhat mervell thocht The Thrie Estaits backwart gang?

Quhen sic an vyle cumpanie dwels them amang;
Quhilk hes reulit this rout monie deir dayis,
Quhilk gars Johne the Common-weill want his warme
  clais :
Sir, call them befoir yow, and put them in ordour,
Or els Johne the Common-weill man beg on the Bor-
  dour.   5
Thou feinzeit Flattrie, the Feind fart in thy face,
Quhen ye was guyder of the Court we gat litill grace;
Ryse up Falset, and Dissait, without ony sunzie,
I pray God! nor the Devil's dame dryte on thy grunzie.
Behauld, as the loun lukis evin lyke a theif,   10
Monie wicht warkman, thow brocht to mischeif.
My soveraine Lord Correctioun, I mak yow supplica-
  tion.
Put thir tryit truikers from Christis congregation.

CORRECTIOUN.

As ye have devysit, but doubt, it sal be done :
Cum heir, my Sergeants, and do your debt sone :   15
Put thir thrie pellours into pressoun strang,
Howbeit ye sould hang thame, ye do them na wrang.

FIRST SERGEANT.

Soverane Lordis, wee sall obey your commands.
Brother, upon thir limmers, lay on thy hands ;
Ryse up sone, loun, thou luiks evin lyke ane lurden, 20
Your mouth war meit to drink an wesche jurden.

SECUND SERGEANT.

Cum heir, gossop, cum heir, cum heir,
  Your rackles lyfe ye sall repent :

Quhen was ye wont to be sa sweir!
Stand still and be obedient.

FIRST SERGEANT.

Thare is nocht in all this toun,
   (Bot, I wald nocht this taill war tald,)
Bot I wald hang him for his goun,   5
   Quhidder that it war laird, or laid.
I trow this pellour be spur-gaid
   Put in thy hand into this cord,
Howbeit, I se thy skap skyre skaid;
   Thou art ane stewat I stand foir'd.   10
      [*Heir sall the Vycis be led to the stocks.*

SECUND SERGEANT.

Put in your leggis into the stocks,
   For, ye had never ane meiter hois:
Thir stewats stinks as thay war broks,
   Now ar ye sikker, I suppois.   [*Pausa.*

My Lordis, wee have done your commands;   15
   Sall we put Covetice in captivitie?

CORRECTIOUN.

Yea, hardlie lay on them your hands;
   Richt sa upon Sensualitie.

SPIRITUALITIE.

This is my graniter and my chalmerlaine;
   And hes my gould, and geir, under hir curis: 20
I mak ane vow to God, I sall complaine
   Unto the Paip, how ye do me injuris.

COVETICE.

My reverent Fathers, tak in patience,
I sall nocht lang remaine from your presence,
Thocht for ane quhyll, I man from yow depairt,
I wait my spreit sall remaine in your hart : 5
And quhen this King Correctioun beis absent,
Then sall we twa returne incontinent ;
Thairfoir adew !—

SPIRITUALITIE.

Adew, be Sanct Mavene !
Pas quhair ye will, we ar twa naturall men.

SENSUALITIE.

Adew, my Lord ! 10

SPIRITUALITIE.

Adew, my awin sweit hart !
Now, duill fell me that wee twa man depart.

SENSUALITIE.

My Lord, howbeit this parting dois me paine,
I traist in God, we sal meit sone againe.

SPIRITUALITIE.

To cum againe, I pray yow, do your cure, 15
Want I yow twa, I may nocht lang indure.
      [*Heir sal the Sergeants chase them away, and
        they sall gang to the seat of Sensualitie.*

TEMPORALITIE.

My Lords, ye knaw The Thrie Estaits

For Common-weill suld mak debaits :
Let now, amang us, be devysit,
Sic Actis that with gude men be praysit,
Conformyng to the common law,
For of na man we sould stand aw : 5
And, for till saif us fra murmell,
Schone, Diligence fetch us Gude Counsell ;
For quhy, he is ane man that knawis
Baith the Cannon, and Civill Lawis.

DILIGENCE.

Father, ye man incontinent 10
Pass to the Lordis of Parliament :
For quhy, thay ar determinat all,
To do na thing bot be your counsall.

GUDE COUNSELL.

That sall I do within schort space,
Praying the Lord, to send us grace, 15
For till conclude, or wee depart ;
That thay may profeit efterwart,
Baith to the Kirk, and to the King,
I sall desyre na uther thing.   [*Pausa*

My Lords, God glaid the cumpanie ! 20
Quhat is the caus, ye send for me ?

MERCHAND.

Sit doun, and gif us your counsell,
How we sall slaik the greit murmell
Of pure peopill, that is weill knawin,
And as the Common-weill hes schawin : 25

And als, we knaw, it is the Kingis will,
That gude remeid be put thairtill.
Sir Common-weill, keip ye the bar,
Let nane except yourself cum nar.

JOHNE.

That salll I do, as I best can, 5
I sall hauld out baith wyfe and man.
Ye man let this puir creature,
Support me, for till keip the dure :
I knaw his name, full sickerly,
He will complaine, als weill as I. 10

GUDE COUNSELL.

My worthy Lords, sen ye have taine on hand,
Sum reformatioun to mak into this land :
And als ye knaw, it is the King's mynd,
Quha to the Common-weill hes ay bene kynd :
Thocht reif, and thift, wer stanchit weill aneuch, 15
Yit sumthing mair belangis to the pleuch.
Now, into peace, ye sould provyde for weirs,
And be sure of how mony thowsand speirs,
The King may be, quhen he hes ocht ado ;
For quhy, my Lords, this is my ressoun to : 20
The husband-men, and commons, thay war wont,
Go, in the battell, formest in the front,
Bot I have tint all my experience,
Without ye mak sum better diligence :
The Common-weill mon uther wayis be styllit, 25
Or, be my faith, the King will be begyllit.
Thir pure commouns, daylie, as ye may se,

Declynis doun till extreme povertie :
For, sum ar hichtit sa into thair maill,
Thair winning will nocht find them water kaill.
How Prelats heichtis thair teinds, it is weill knawin,
That husband-men may not weill hald thair awin : 5
And, now begins ane plague, amang them new,
That gentill men thair steadings taks in few :
Thus man thay pay greit ferme, or lay thair steid.
And sum ar plainlie harlit out be the heid,
And ar distroyit, without God on thame rew. 10

PAUPER.

Sir, be God's breid, that taill is verie trew.
It is weill kend, I had baith nolt, and hors ;
Now, all my geir ye se upon my cors.

CORRECTIOUN.

Or I depairt, I think till mak ane ordour.

JOHNE.

I pray you, Sir, begin first at [the] Bordour : 15
For, how can we fend us aganis Ingland,
Quhen we can nocht, within our native land,
Destroy our awin Scots, common trator theifis,
Quha, to leill laborers, daylie dois mischeifis ?
War I ane king, my Lord, be God's wounds, 20
Quha ever held common theifis within thir bounds,
Quhairthrow, that dayly leil men micht be wrangit,
Without remeid, thair chiftanis suld be hangit,
Quhidder he war ane Knicht, ane Lord, or Laird,
The Devill draw me to hell, and he war spaird. 25

TEMPORALITIE.

Quhat uther enemies hes thou, let us ken?

JOHNE.

Sir, I compleine upon the idill men:
For quhy, Sir, it is God's awin bidding,
All Christian men to wirk for thair living,
Sanct Paull, that pillar of the kirk, 5
Sayis to the wretchis, that will not wirk,
And bene to vertews laith,
Qui non laborat non manducet,
This is in Inglische toung, or leit,
QUHA LABOURIS NOCHT HE SALL NOT EIT. 10
This bene against the strang beggers,
Fidlers, pypers, and pardoners:
Thir jugglars, jestars, and idill cuitchours,
Thir carriers, and thir quintacensours;
Thir babil-beirers and thir bairds, 15
Thir sweir swyngeours with lords, and lairds:
Ma, than thair rents may susteine,
Or to thair profeit neidfull bene,
Quhilk bene ay blythest of discords,
And deidly feid amang thair lords: 20
For then, they sleutchers man be treatit,
Or els, thair querrels undebaitit.
This bene against thir great fat Freiris,
Augustenes, Carmleits, and Cordeleirs;
And all uthers, that in cowls bene cled, 25
Quhilk labours nocht; and bene weill fed
I mein, nocht laborand spirituallie,
Nor, for thair living, corporallie:

Lyand, in dennis, lyke idill doggis,
I thame compair to weil-fed hoggis.
I think thay do thame selfis abuse,
Seing that thay the warld refuse :
Haifing profest sic povertie, 5
Syne fleis fast fra necessitie.
Quhat, gif thay povertie wald professe?
And do, as did Diogenes,
That great famous philosophour ;
Seing, in earth, bot vaine labour, 10
Alutterlie, the warld refusit,
And in ane tumbe, him self inclusit,
And leifit on herbs, and water cauld,
Of corporall fude, na mair he wald :
He trottit nocht, from toun to toun, 15
Beggand to fed his carioun :
Fra tyme that lyfe he did profes,
The warld of him was cummerles.
Richt sa of Marie Magdalene,
And of Mary th' Egyptiane, 20
And of auld Paull, the first hermeit ;
All thir had povertie compleit.
Ane hundreth ma, I micht declair,
Bot, to my purpois I will fair,
Concluding sleuthfull idilness, 25
Against the Common-weill expresse.

CORRECTIOUN.
Quhom upon ma, will ye compleine ?

JOHNE.
Marie ! on ma, and ma againe :

For, the pure peopill cryis with cairis,
The infetching of Justice Airis,
Exercit mair, for covetice,
Than, for the punisching of vyce.
Ane peggrell theif, that steillis ane kow,
Is hangit; bot he, that steillis ane bow,
With als meikill geir as he may turs,
That theif is hangit be the purs :
Sic pykand peggrell theifis ar hangit;
Bot, he that all the warld hes wrangit,
Ane cruell tyrane, ane strang transgressour,
Ane common publick plaine oppressour,
By buds may he obteine favours
Of Treasurers and Compositours,
Thocht he serve greit punitioun,
Gets easie compositioun :
And, throch laws Consistoriall,
Prolixt, corrupt, and perpetuall,
The common peopill ar put sa under.
Thocht thay be puir, it is na wonder,

CORRECTIOUN.

Gude Johne, I grant all that is trew,
Your infortoun full sair I rew :
Or I pairt aff this Natioun,
I sall mak reformatioun.
And als, my Lord Temporalitie,
I yow command, in tyme, that ye
Expell oppressioun aff your lands :
And als, I say to yow, Merchands,
Gif ever I find, be land, or sie,

Dissait be in your cumpanie,
Quhilk ar to Common-weill contrair,
I vow to God, I sall nocht spair,
To put my sword to executioun,
And mak on yow extreme punitioun,   5
Mairover, my Lord Spiritualitie,
In gudelie haist, I will, that ye
Set into few your temporall lands,
To men that labours with thair hands ;
Bot nocht to ane gearking gentill man,   10
That nether will he wirk, nor can :
Quhairthroch the policy may incresse.

TEMPORALITIE.

I am content, Sir, be the Messe ;
Swa, that the Spiritualitie
Sets thairs in few, als weill as wee.   15

CORRECTIOUN.

My Spirituall Lords, ar ye content?

SPIRITUALITIE

Na, na! wee man tak advysement
In sic maters, for to conclude
Ouir haistelie, wee think nocht gude.

CORRECTIOUN.

Conclude ye nocht with the Common-weill,   20
Ye salbe punischit, be Sanct Geill.

[*Heir sall the Bischops cum with the Freir.*

SPIRITUALITIE.

Schir, we can schaw exemptioun,
Fra your temporall punitioun;
The quhilk we purpois till debait.

CORRECTIOUN.

Wa! than, ye think to stryve for stait.
My Lords, quhat say ye to this play? 5

TEMPORALITIE.

My soverane Lords, we will obay,
And tak your part, with hart and hand,
Quhat ever ye pleis us to command.
    [*Heir sal the Temporall Stait sit doun on
        thair kneis, and say:*
Bot, wee beseik yow, Soveraine!
Of all our cryms, that ar bygaine, 10
To gif us ane remissioun;
And heir, wee mak to yow conditioun
The Common-weill for till defend,
From hence-forth, till our lives end.

CORRECTIOUN.

On that conditioun, I am content 15
Till pardon yow, sen ye repent,
The Common-weill tak be the hand,
And mak with him perpetuall band.
    [*Heir sall the Temporall Staitis, to wit,
        the Lords and Merchands, imbrasse
        Johne the Commonweill.*
Johne, haif ye ony ma debaits,
Aganis the Lords of Spirituall Staits? 20

JOHNE.

Na, Sir, I dar nocht speik ane word;
To plaint on Preistis, it is na bourd.

CORRECTIOUN.

Flyt on thy fow fill I desyre thé;
Swa, that thou schaw bot the veritie.

JOHNE.

Grandmerces, then, I sall nocht spair,   5
First, to compleine on the Vickair:
The pure Cottar, lykand to die,
Haifand young infants, twa, or thrie;
And hes twa ky, but ony ma,
The Vickar must haif ane of thay,   10
With the gray frugge, that covers the bed,
Howbeit, the wyfe be purelie cled;
And gif the wyfe die on the morne,
Thocht all the bairns sould be forlorne,
The uther kow, he cleiks away,   15
With the pure cot of raploch gray:
Wald God! this custome war put doun,
Quhilk never was foundit be ressoun.

TEMPORALITIE.

Ar all thay tails trew, that thou telles?

PAUPER.

Trew, Sir, the Divill stick me elles: 20
For, be the Halie Trinitie,
That same was practeisit on me;

For our Vickar, God give him pyne,
Hes yit thrie tydie kye of myne :
Ane, for my father, and for my wyfe, ane uther,
And the thrid cow, he tuke, for Mald my mother.

JOHNE.

Our Persone, heir, he takis na uther pyne, 5
Bot, to ressave his teinds, and spend them syne :
Howbeit, he be obleist, be gude ressoun,
To preich the Evangell to his parochoun.
Howbeit thay suld want preiching sevintin yeir,
Our Persoun will not want ane scheif of beir. 10

PAUPER.

Our Bischops, with thair lustie rokats quhyte,
Thay flow in riches, royallie, and delyte,
Lyke paradice, bene thair palices, and places,
And wants na plesour of the fairest faces.
Als, thir Prelates hes great prerogatyves ; 15
For quhy, thay may depairt ay with thair wyves,
Without ony correctioun, or damnage ;
Syne tak ane uther wantoner, but mariage.
But doubt, I wald think it ane pleasant lyfe,
Ay on, quhen I list, to part with my wyfe ; 20
Syne, tak ane uther of far greater bewtie :
Bot ever alace ! my Lords, that may not be,
For I am bund, alace ! in mariage ;
Bot thay lyke rams, rudlie in thair rage.
Unpysalt, rinnis amang the sillie yowis, 25
Sa lang, as kynde of nature, in them growis.

PERSON.

Thou lies, fals huirson, raggit loun !
Thair is na preists, in all this toun,
That ever usit sic vicious crafts.

JOHNE.

The Feind ressave thay flattrants chafts :
Sir Domine, I trowit, ye had be[ne] dum,   5
Quhair Devil, gat we this ill-fairde blaitie bum ?

PERSON.

To speik of Priests be sure it is na bourds ;
Thay will burne men, now, for rakles words,
And, all thay words ar heresie in deid.

JOHNE.

The mekil Feind resave the saul that leid ;   10
All that I say is trew, thocht thou be greifit,
And that, I offer, on thy pallet, to preif it.

SPIRITUALITIE.

My Lords, quhy do ye thoil that lurdun loun,
Of kirk-men, to speik sic detractioun :
I let yow wit, my Lords, it is na bourds,   15
Of Prelats, for till speik sic wantoun words.
        [*Heir Spiritualitie fames and rages.*
Yon villaine puttis me out of charitie.

TEMPORALITIE.

Quhy, my Lord, sayis he ocht bot verity ;

Ye can nocht stop ane pure man, for till pleinze,
Gif he hes faltit summond him to your seinze.

SPIRITUALITIE.

Yea, that I sall, I mak greit God a vow!
He sall repent, that he spak of the kow;
I will nocht suffer sic words of yon villaine.   5

PAUPER.

Than, gar gif me my thrie fat ky againe.

SPIRITUALITIE.

Fals Carle, to speik to me, stands thou not aw?

PAUPER.

The Feind resave them, that first devysit that law!
Within an houre, efter my dade was deid,
The Vickar had my kow hard be the heid.   10

PERSON.

Fals huirson Carle! I say that law is gude,
Becaus, it hes bene lang our consuetude.

PAUPER.

Quhen I am Paip, that law I sall put doun;
It is ane sair law, for the pure commoun.

SPIRITUALITIE.

I mak an vow, thay wordis thou sal repent.   15

GUDE COUNSELL.

I yow requyre, my Lords, be patient:
Wee came nocht heir, for disputatiouns;
Wee came to mak gude reformatiouns.

Heirfoir, of this your propositioun,
Conclude, and put to executioun.

MERCHAND.

My Lords, conclud that al the Temporal lands
Be set, in few, to laboreris, with thair hands,
With sic restrictiouns as sall be devysit;   5
That thay may live, and nocht to be supprysit,
With ane ressonabill augmentatioun:
And, quhen thay heir ane proclamatioun,
That the King's Grace dois mak him, for the weir,
That thay be reddie, with harneis, bow, and speir. 10
As for my self, my Lord, this I conclude.

GUDE COUNSELL.

Sa, say we all, your ressoun be sa gude:
To mak ane Act on this we ar content.

JOHNE.

On that, sir Scribe, I tak ane instrument:
Quhat do ye of the corspresent, and kow?   15

GUDE COUNSELL.

I wil conclude nathing of that, as now,
Without my Lord of Spiritualitie
Thairto consent, with all this haill cleargie.
My Lord Bischop, will ye thairto consent?

SPIRITUALITIE.

Na, na! never, till the day of Judgement: 20
Wee will want nathing, that wee have in use,
Kirtil nor kow, teind lambe, teind grysc, nor guse.

TEMPORALITIE.

Forsuith, my Lord, I think we suld conclude ;
Seing this kow, ye have in consuetude:
We will decerne heir, that the King's grace
Sall wryte unto the Paipis Holines :
With his consent, be proclamatioun, 5
Baith corspresent, and cow, wee sall cry doun.

SPIRITUALITIE.

To that, my Lords, wee plainlie disassent,
Noter, thairof I tak ane instrument.

TEMPORALITIE.

My Lord, be Him that all the warld hes wrocht,
Wee set nocht by, quhider ye consent, or nocht :
Ye ar bot ane Estait, and we ar twa,
Et ubi major pars, ibi tota. 10

JOHNE.

My Lords, ye haif richt prudentlie concludit ;
Tak tent, now, how the land is clein denudit,
Of gould, and silver, quhilk daylie gais to Rome, 15
For buds, mair than the rest of Christindome.
War I ane king, Sir, be cok's passioun,
I sould gar mak ane proclamatioun,
That never ane penny sould go to Rome at all,
Na mair than did to Peter, nor to Paull. 20
Do ye nocht sa, heir, for conclusioun,
I gif yow all my braid black malesoun.

MERCHAND.

It is of treuth, Sirs, be my christindome,
That mekil of our money gais to Rome :

For, we Merchants, I wait, within our bounds,
Hes furneist Preists ten hundreth thowsand pounds,
For thair finnance, nane knawis sa weill as wee :
Thairfoir, my Lords, devyse sum remedie ;
For throw thir playis, and thir promotioun,　　5
Mair for denners, nor for devotioun,
Sir Symonie hes maid with them ane band,
The gould of weicht, thay leid out of the land ;
The Common-weill thairthroch bein sair opprest ;
Thairfoir, devyse remeid, as ye think best.　　10

GUDE COUNSELL.

It is schort tyme, sen ony benefice,
Was sped in Rome, except greit bischopries.
Bot, now for ane unworthie vickarage,
Ane preist will rin to Rome, in pilgramage.
Ane cavell, quhilk was never at the scule,　　15
Will rin to Rome, and keip ane bischop's mule ;
And syne cum hame, with mony colorit crack,
With ane buirdin of beneficee on his back ;
Quhilk bene against the law, ane man alane,
For till posses ma benefices nor ane :　　20
Thir greit Commends, I say, withouttin faill,
Sould nocht be given, bot to the blude Royall :
Sa, I conclude, my Lords, and sayis for me,
Ye sould annull all this pluralitie.

SPIRITUALITIE.

The Paip hes given us dispensatiouns.　　25

GUDE COUNSELL.

Yea, that is, be your fals narratiouns :

Thocht the Paip, for your plesour, will dispence,
I trow, that can nocht cleir your conscience:
Advyse, my Lords, quhat ye think to conclude.

TEMPORALITIE.

Sir, be my faith, I think it verie gude,
That, fra hence furth, na Priestis sall pas to Rome; 5
Becaus our substance thay do still consume,
For pleyis, and for thair profeit singulair,
Thay haif of money maid this realme bair:
And als, I think it best, be my advyse,
That ilk priest sall haif bot ane benefice: 10
And gif thay keip nocht that fundation,
It sall be caus of deprivatioun.

MERCHAND.

As ye haif said, my Lord, we will consent:
Scribe, mak ane Act on this incontinent.

GUDE COUNSELL.

My Lords, thair is ane thing yit unproponit: 15
How Prelats, and Preistis, aucht to be disponit:
This beand done, wee have the les ado;
Quhat say ye, Sirs? This is my counsall, lo!
That, or wee end this present Parliament,
Of this mater, to tak rype advysement. 20
Mark weill, my Lords, thair is na benefice,
Given to ane man, bot for ane gude office.
Quha taks office, and syne thay can nocht use it,
Giver and taker, I say, ar baith abusit.
Ane bischop's office is for to be ane preichour, 25
And of the Law of God ane publick techour.

Richt sa, the Persone unto his parochoun,
Of the Evangell sould leir thame ane lessoun.
Thair sould na man desyre sic dignities,
Without he be abill for that office :
And for that caus, I say, without leising,   5
Thay have thair teinds, and for na uther thing.

SPIRITUALITIE.

Freind, quhair find ye, that we suld precheours be?

GUDE COUNSELL.

Luik quhat Sanct Paul wryts unto Timothie :
Tak thair the Buik, let se, gif ye can spell.

SPIRITUALITIE.

I never red that, thairfoir reid it yoursell.   10

[*Gude Counsell sall reid thir words on ane Buik :*
"*Fidelis sermo, Si quis Episcopatum desiderat, bonum opus desiderat. Oportet eum irreprehensibilem esse, unius uxoris virum, sobrium, prudentum, ornatum, pudicum, hospitalem, doctorem : Non vinolentum, non percussorem : sed modestum. That is :*

"This is a true saying, If any man desire the office of a bishop, he desireth a worthie worke : A bishop therefore must be unreproveable, the husband of one wife, &c."

SPIRITUALITIE.

Ye temporall men, be Him that heryit hell,
Ye ar ouir peart, with sik maters to mell.

TEMPORALITIE.

Sit still, my Lord, ye neid not for til braull,
Thir ar the verie words of th' Apostill Paull.

SPIRITUALITIE.

Sum sayis, be Him that wore the croun of thorne,
It had bene gude that Paull had neir bene borne.

GUDE COUNSALL.

Bot ye may knaw, my Lord, Sanct Paul's intent,
Schir, red ye never the New Testament?

SPIRITUALITIE.

Na, Sir, be him that our Lord Jesus sauld,   5
I red never the New Testament, nor Auld;
Nor ever thinks to do, Sir, be the Rude;
I heir Freiris say, that reiding dois na gude.

GUDE CQUNSELL.

Till yow, to reid them, I think it is na lack,
For anis, I saw them baith, bund on your back: 10
That samin day, that ye was consecrat,
Schir, quhat meinis that?

SPIRITUALITIE.

The Feind stick them that wat.

MERCHANT.

Then, befoir God, how can ye be excusit?
To haif ane office, and waits not how to use it: 15
Quhairfoir, war gifin yow all the temporal landis?
And all thir teinds, ye haif amang your handis:
Thay war givin yow, for uther causses, I weine,
Nor mummill matins and hald your clayis clene.
Ye say, till the Appostils that ye succeid,   20
Bot ye schaw nocht that, into word nor deid.
The law is plaine, our teinds suld furnisch teichours.

GUDE COUNSELL.
Yea, that it sould, or susteine prudent preichours.

PAUPER.
Sir, God, nor I be stickit with ane knyfe,
Gif ever our Persoun preichit in all his lyfe.

PARSON.
Quhat Devil raks thee of our preiching undocht?

PAUPER.
Think ye, that ye suld haif the teinds for nocht? 5

PARSON.
Trowis thou, to get remeid, Carle, of that thing?

PAUPER.
Yea, be God's breid, richt sone, war I ane King.

PARSON.
Wald thou, of Prelats mak deprivatioun?

PAUPER.
Na, I suld gar them keip thair fundatioun: [10
Quhat devill is this, of quhom sould kings stand aw?
To do the thing, that thay sould be the law.
War I ane King, be cok's deir passioun,
I sould richt sone mak reformatioun.
Failzeand thairof, your Grace sould richt sone finde,
That Preists sall leid yow, lyke ane bellie blinde. 15

JOHNE.

Quhat, gif King David war leivand in thir dayis?
The quhilk did found sa mony gay Abayis:
Or out of heavin, quhat gif he luikit doun?
And saw the great abominatioun,
Amang thir Abesses, and thir Nunries,   5
Thair publick huirdomes, and thair harlotries:
He wald repent, he narrowit sa his bounds,
Of yeirlie rent, thriescoir of thowsand pounds;
His successours maks litill ruisse, I ges,
Of his devotioun, or of his holines.   10

ABBASSE.

How dar thou, Carle, presume, for to declair,
Or, for to mell thé, with sa heich a mater?
For, in Scotland, thair did yit never ring,
I let the wit, ane mair excellent King.
Of holines he was the verie plant,   15
And now, in heavin, he is ane michtfull Sanct;
Becaus, that fyftein Abbasies he did found;
Quhair throw, great riches hes ay done abound
Into our Kirk, and daylie yit abunds,
Bot, kings now, I trow, few abbasies founds,   20
I dar weill say, thou art condempnit in hell,
That dois presume, with sic maters, to mell.
Fals hureson Carle, thou art ovir arrogant,
To juge the deids of sic ane halie Sanct.

JOHNE.

King James the first, roy of this regioun,   25
Said that he was ane sair Sanct to the croun.

I heir men say, that he was sumthing blind,
That gave away mair nor he left behind.
His successours that halines did repent,
Quhilk gart thame do great inconvenient.

ABBASSE.

My Lord Bishop, I mervel how that ye 5
Suffer this Carle for to speik heresie.
For, be my faith, my Lord, will ye tak tent,
He servis for to be brunt incontinent.
Ye can nocht say, bot it is heresie,
To speik against our law and libertie. 10

SPIRITUALITIE.

Sancte Pater, I mak yow supplicatioun,
Exame yon Carle, syne mak his dilatioun:
I mak ane vow to God Omnipotent,
That bystour sall be brunt incontinent.
Venerabill Father, I sall do your command, 15
Gif he servis deid I sall sune understand. [*Pausa.*
Fals huirsun Carle, schaw furth thy faith!

JOHNE.

Me think ye speik as ye war wraith.
To yow I will nathing declair;
For ye ar nocht my Ordinair. 20

FLATTERIE.

Quhom in trowis thou, fals monster mangit?

JOHNE.

I trow to God, to see thé hangit:

War I ane King, be cok's passioun,
I sould gar mak ane congregatioun,
Of all the Freiris of the four Ordouris,
And mak yow vagers, on the Bordours.
Schir, will ye give me audience, 5
And I sal schaw your Excellence;
Sa that your grace will give me leife,
How into God that I beleife.

CORRECTIOUN.

Schaw furth your faith, and fenzie nocht.

JOHNE.

I beleife in God, that all hes wrocht, 10
And creat everie thing of nocht,
And, in his Son, our Lord Jesu,
Incarnat of the Virgin trew;
Quha under Pilat tholit passioun,
And deit for our salvatioun; 15
And, on the thrid day, rais againe,
As halie Scriptour schawis plane:
And als my Lord, it is weill kend,
How he did to the heavin ascend;
And set him doun at the richt hand 20
Of God the Father, I understand;
And sall cum judge on Dumisday:
Quhat will ye mair, Sir, that I say?

CORRECTIOUN.

Schaw furth the rest, this is na game.

JOHNE.

I trow *Sanctam Ecclesiam,*
Bot nocht in thir Bishops nor thir Freirs,
Quhilk will, for purging of thir neirs :
Sard up the ta raw, and doun the uther.
The mekill Devill resave the fidder.   5

CORRECTIOUN.

Say quhat ye will, Sirs, be Sanct Tan,
Me think Johne ane gude Christian man.

TEMPORALITIE.

My Lordis, let be your disputatioun,
Conclude, with firme deliberatioun,
How Prelatis, fra thyne, sall be disponit.   10

MERCHAND.

I think, for me, evin as ye first proponit,
That the King's grace sall gif na benefice,
Bot till ane preichour, that can use that office :
The sillie sauls, that bene Christis scheip,
Sould nocht be givin to gormand wolfis to keip.   15
Quhat bene the caus of all the heresies,
Bot the abusioun of the Prelacies ?
Thay will correct, and will nocht be correctit :
Thinkand to na prince thay will be subjectit :
Quhairfoir, I can find na better remeid,   20
Bot that thir kings man tak it in thair heid,
That thair be given to na man bischopries,
Except thay preich out throch thair diosies ;
And ilk persone preich in his parochon :
And this, I say, for finall conclusioun.   25

TEMPORALITIE.

Wee think your counsall is verie gude:
As ye have said, wee all conclude.
Of this conclusioun, Noter, wee mak ane Act.

SCRYBE.

I wryte all day, bot gets never ane plack.

PAUPER.

Och! my Lords, for the Halie Trinitie,   5
Remember to reforme the Consistorie:
It hes mair neid of reformatioun,
Nor Ploutois court, Sir, by cok's passioun.

PARSON.

Quhat caus hes thow, fals pellour, for to pleinze,
Quhair was ye ever summond to thair senze?   10

PAUPER.

Marie! I lent my gossop my mear, to fetch hame coills,
And he hir drounit into the Querrell hollis:
And I ran to the Consistorie, for to pleinze,
And thair I happinit amang ane greidie meinze.
Thay gave me first ane thing, thay call *Citendum*,   15
Within aucht dayis, I gat bot *Lybellandum*,
Within ane moneth, I gat *ad Opponendum*,
In half ane yeir, I gat *Interloquendum*,
And syne, I gat, how call ye it? *ad Replicandum*:
Bot, I could never ane word yit understand him;   20
And than, thay gart me cast out many plackis,
And gart me pay for four-and-twentie actis:

Bot, or thay came half gait to *Concludendum*,
The Feind ane plack was left for to defend him:
Thus, thay postponit me twa yeir, with thair traine,
Syne, *Hodie ad octo*, bad me cum againe:
And than, thir ruiks, thay roupit wonder fast, 5
For sentence silver, thay cryit at the last.
Of *Pronunciandum*, thay maid me wonder faine;
Bot I got never my gude gray meir againe.

TEMPORALITIE.

My Lords, we man reforme thir Consistory lawis,
Quhais great defame, above the heavins blawis. 10
I wist ane man, in persewing ane kow,
Or he had done, he spendit half ane bow:
Sa that the King's honour wee may avance;
Wee will conclude, as thay have done in France,
Let Spirituall maters pas to Spiritualitie, 15
And Temporall maters to Temporalitie.
Quha failzeis of this sall cost them of their gude.
Scribe, mak ane Act, for sa wee will conclude.

SPIRITUALITIE.

That Act, my Lords, plainlie I will declair,
It is againis our profeit singulair: 20
Wee will nocht want our profeit, be Sanct Geill.

TEMPORALITIE.

Your profeit is aganis the Common-weill.
It sal be done, my Lordis, as ye have wrocht,
We cure nocht, quhidder ye consent, or nocht:
Quhairfoir servis, then, all thir Temporall Judges? 25

Gif temporall maters sould seik, at yow, refuges,
My Lord, ye say that ye are Spirituall;
Quhairfoir mell ye, than, with things temporall?
As we have done conclude, sa sall it stand.
Scribe, put our Acts in ordour, evin fra hand.   5

SPIRITUALITIE.

Till all your·Acts, plainlie, I disassent:
Notar, thairof, I tak ane instrument.
  [*Heir sall Veritie and Chastitie mak thair
  complaint at the bar.*

VERITIE.

My Soverane, I beseik your excellence,
  Use justice on Spiritualitie:
The quhilk to us hes done great violence;   10
  Becaus we did rehers the veritie.
Thay put us close into captivitie,
And sa remanit into subjectioun:
  Into great langour, and calamitie,
Till we war fred be king Correctioun.   15

CHASTITIE.

My Lord, I haif gret caus for to complaine,
  I could get na ludging intill this land;
The Spiritual Stait had me sa at disdane,
  With dame Sensuall, thay have maid sic ane band,
  Amang them all na freindschip, Sirs, I fand;   20
And quhen I came the nobill innis amang,
  My lustie Ladie Priores, fra hand
Out of hir dortour, durlie, scho me dang.

VERITIE.

With the advyse, Sir, of the Parliament,
   Hairtlie we mak yow supplicatioun:
Cause King Correctioun tak incontinent,
   Of all this sort examinatioun.
     Gif thay be digne of deprivatioun,   5
Ye have power for till correct sic cases:
   Chease the maist cunning Clerks of this natioun,
And put mair prudent Pastours in thair places.
My prudent Lords, I say, that pure craftsmen,
   Abufe sum Prelats, are mair for to commend: 10
Gar exame them, and sa ye sall sune ken
   How thay, in vertew, Bischops dois transcend.

SCRYBE.

Thy life, and craft, mak to thir Kings kend:
Quhat craft hes thow, declair that to me plaine;

TAILZOUR.

Ane Tailzour, sir, that can baith mak and mend;
I wait nane better into Dumbartane.   [15

SCRYBE.

Quhairfoir of Tailzeours beirs thou the styll?

TAILZOUR.

Becaus I wait is nane within ane myll
Can better use that craft, as I suppois:
For I can mak baith doublit, coat, and hois.   20

SCRYBE.

How call thay you, sir, with the schaiping knife?

SOWTAR.

Ane Sowtar, sir, nane better in Fyfe.

SCRYBE.

Tel me, quhairfoir ane Sowtar ye are namit?

SOWTAR.

Of that surname I neid nocht be aschamit:
For I can mak schone, brotekins, and buittis:
Gif me the coppie of the King's cuittis.   5
And ye sall se, richt sune, quhat I can do:
Heir is my lasts, and weill wrocht ledder lo.

GUDE COUNSELL.

O Lord, my God, this is an mervelous thing,
How sic misordour in this realme sould ring.
Sowtars and Tailzeours, thay ar far mair expert   10
In thair pure craft, and in thair handie art,
Nor ar our Prelatis in thair vocatioun :
I pray yow, Sirs, mak reformatioun.

VERITIE.

Alace! alace! quhat gars thir temporal kings
Into the kirk of Christ admit sic doings?   15
My Lords, for lufe of Christ's passioun,.
Of thir ignorants, mak deprivatioun,
Quhilk in the court can do bot flatter and fleich,
And put into thair places that can preich :
Send furth, and seik sum devoit cunning Clarks,   20
That can steir up the peopill to gude warks.

CORRECTIOUN.

As ye have done, Madame, I am content,
Hoaw! Diligence, pas hynd, incontinent,
And seik out throw all towns and cities;
And visie all the Universities.
Bring us sum Doctours of Divinitie, 5
With Licents in the Law and Theologie,
With the maist cunning Clarks in all this land;
Speid sune your way, and bring them heir fra hand.

DILIGENCE.

Quhat, gif I find sum halie Provinciall?
Or minister of the Gray Freiris all? 10
Or ony Freir, that can preich prudentlie,
Sall I bring them with me in cumpanie?

CORRECTIOUN.

Cair thou nocht quhat estait sa ever he be,
Sa thay can teich, and preich the veritie.
Maist cunning Clarks with us is best beluifit, 15
To dignitie thay sall be first promuifit;
Quhidder thay be munk, channon, preist or freir,
Sa thay can preich, faill nocht to bring them heir,

DILIGENCE.

Then fair-weill, Sir, for I am at the flicht,
I pray the Lord to send yow all gude nicht. 20
    [*Heir sall Diligence pas to the palzeoun.*

TEMPORALITIE.

Schir, we beseik your soverane celsitude,
  Of our dochtours to have compassioun;

Quhom wee may na way marie, be the Rude,
   Without we mak sum alienatioun
   Of our land for thair supportatioun;
For quhy? the markit raisit bene sa hie,
   That Prelats dochtours of this natioun   5
Ar maryit with sic superfluitie:
Thay will nocht spair to gif twa thowsand pound,
   With thair dochtours, to ane nobill man;
In riches, sa thay do superabound:
   Bot we may nocht do sa, be Sanct Allane: 10
Thir proud Prelats our dochtours sair may ban;
That thay remaine at hame sa lang unmaryit:
   Schir, let your barrouns do the best thay can,
Some of our dochtours, I dreid, sal be miscaryit.

CORRECTIOUN.

My Lord, your complaint is richt ressonabill,   15
And richt sa to our dochtours profitabill:
I think, or I pas aff this Natioun,
Of this mater till mak reformatioun.
            [*Heir sall enter Commoun Thift.*

COMMOUN THIFT.

Ga by the gait, man, let me gang,
How Devill came I into this thrang?   20
With sorrow I may sing ane sang,
   And I be taine:
For I have run baith nicht and day,
Throw speid of fut, I gat away:
Gif I be kend heir, wallaway!   25
   I will be slaine.

PAUPER.

Quhat is thy name, man be thy thrift?

COMMOUN THIFT.

Huirson, thay call me Commoun thift.
For quhy? I had na uther schift
    Sene I was borne:
In Ewisdaill was my dwelling place,   5
Mony ane wyfe gart I cry, Alace!
At my hand thay gat never grace,
    Bot aye forlorne.
Sum sayis ane King is cum amang us,
That purposis to head and hang us: 10
Thair is na grace, gif he may fang us,
    Bot on ane pin.
Ring he, we theifis will get na gude,
I pray God, and the halie Rude,
He had bene smoird into his cude,   15
    And all his kin.
Get this curst King me in his grippis,
My craig will wit quhat weyis my hippis:
The Devill, I gif his toung and lippis,
    That of me tellis: 20
Adew! I dar na langer tarie;
For be I kend, thay will me carie,
And put me in ane fierie farie,
    I se nocht ellis.
I raife, be Him that herryit hell,   25
I had almaist foryet my sell:
Will na gude fallow to me tell,
    Quhair I may finde

The Erle of Rothus best haiknay?
That was my earand, heir-away:
He is richt starck, as I heir say,
  And swift as winde.
Heir is my brydill and my spurris,   5
To gar him lance ouir land and furris
Micht I him get to Ewis durris,
  I tak na cuir.
Of that hors, micht I get ane sicht,
I haife na doubt, yit or midnicht,   10
That he and I sould tak the flicht
  Throch Dysert Mure.
Of cumpanarie, tell me, brother,
Quhilk is the richt way to the Strother?
I wald be welcum to my mother,   15
  Gif I micht speid:
I wald gif baith my coat and bonet
To get my Lord Lindesayis broun jouet,
War he beyond the watter of Annet,
  We sould nocht dreid.   20

Quhat now, Oppressioun, my maister deir!
Quhat mekill devill hes brocht yow heir?
Maister, tell me the caus, perqueir,
  Quhat is, that ye have done?

   OPPRESSIOUN.

Forsuith, the King's majestie   25
Hes set me heir, as ye may se:
Micht I speik Temporalitie,
  He wald me releife sone.

I beseik yow, my brother deir,
Bot halfe ane houre for to sit heir;
Ye knaw, that I was never sweir
    Yow to defend;
Put in your leg in to my place,   5
And heir, I sweir be God's grace,
Yow to reliefe within schort space,
    Syne let yow wend.

COMMOUN THIFT.

Than maister deir, gif me your hand,
And mak to me ane faithfull band,   10
That ye sall cum agane, fra hand,
    Withoutin faill.

OPPRESSIOUN.

Tak thair my hand, richt faithfullie,
Als I promit thee, verelie,
To gif to thee ane cuppill of kye,   15
    In Liddisdaill.

    [*Heir sall Commoun Thift put his feit in
        the stokkis; and Oppressioun sall steill
        away and betray him.*

[Bruder, tak patience in thy pane,
For I sweir thee be Sanct Fillane,
We twa sall nevir meit agane,
    In land nor toun.   20

COMMOUN THIFT.

Maister, will ye not keip conditioun,
And put me furth of this suspitioun;

OPPRESSIOUN.

Na, nevir, quhill I get remissioun.
    Adew! my companyeoun;
I sall commend thee to thy dame.

COMMOUN THIFT.

Adew! than, in the Devillis name!
For to be fals thinkis thow na schame?   5
    To leif me in this pane,
Thow art ane loun, and that ane liddir.

OPPRESSIOUN.

Bo, man! I will go to Balquhiddir;
It sall be Pasche, be Goddis moder,
    Or evir we meit agane.]   10
Haif I nocht maid ane honest schift,
That has betrasit Commoun Thift?
For thair is nocht under the lift,
    Ane curster cors
I am richt sure, that he and I,   15
Within this half-yeir, craftely
Hes stolne ane thowsand scheip and ky,
    By meiris and hors.
Wald God! I war baith sound and haill
Now liftit into Liddisdaill,   20
The Mers sould find me beif and kaill,
    Quhat rak of bread:
War I thair liftit, with my lyfe,
The Devill sould stick me with ane knyfe,
And ever I come againe to Fyfe,   25
    Quhyll I war dead.

Adew! I leife the Devill amang yow,
That in his fingers he may fang yow,
With all leill men that dois belang yow:
    For I may rew
That ever I came into this land.   5
For quhy? ye may weill understand,
I gat na geir to turne my hand;
    Yit anis adew!
    [*Heir sall Diligence convoy the thrie Clarks.*

DILIGENCE.

Schir, I have brocht unto your Excellence
Thir famous Clarks of greit intelligence;   10
For to the common peopill thay can preich,
And in the scuilis, in Latine toung, can teich.
This is ane Doctour of Divinitie,
And thir twa Licents, men of gravitie.
I heare men say, thair conversatioun   15
Is maist in Divine Contemplatioun.

DOCTOUR.

Grace, peace, and rest, from the hie Trinitie,
Mot rest amang this godlie cumpanie;
Heir ar we cumde, as your obedients,
For to fulfill your just commandements.   20
Quhat evir it please your Grace us to command,
Sir, it sall be obeyit, evin fra hand.

REX.

Gude freinds, ye ar richt welcome to us all;
Sit doun all thrie, and geif us your counsall

DIVYNE CORRECTIOUN.

Sir, I give yow baith counsal and command,
    In your office, use exercitioun;
First, that ye gar search out throch all your land,
    Quha can nocht put to executioun
      Thair office, efter the institution,   5
Of godlie lawis, conforme to thair vocatioun:
    Put in thair places men of gude conditioun,
And this ye do without dilatioun.

Ye ar the head, Sir, of this congregatioun,
    Preordinat be God Omnipotent;   10
Quhilk hes me send, to mak yow supportatioun,
    Into the quhilk I salbe diligent:
      And quhasaever beis inobedient,
And will nocht suffer for to be correctit,
    They sal be all deposit incontinent,   15
And from your presence thay sall be dejectit.

GUDE COUNSALL.

Begin first, at the Spiritualitie;
    And tak of them examinatioun,
Gif they can use thair divyne dewetie;
    And, als, I mak yow supplication,   20
All thay that hes thair offices misusit,
    Of them mak haistie deprivatioun:
Sa that the peopill be na mair abusit.

DIVYNE CORRECTIOUN.

Ye ar ane Prince of Spiritualitie:
How have ye usit your office, now let se?   25

SPIRITUALITIE.

My Lords, quhen was thair ony Prelatis wont
Of thair office till ony King mak count?
Bot of my office, gif ye wald have the feill,
I let yow wit, I have it usit weill:
For I tak in my count twyse in the yeir,   5
Wanting nocht of my teind ane boll of beir.
I gat gude payment of my Temporall lands,
My buttock-maill, my coattis, and my offrands,
With all that dois perteine my benefice,
Consider now, my Lord, gif I be wyse.   10
I dar nocht marie, contrair the common law,
Ane thing thair is, my Lord, that ye may knaw.
Howbeit, I dar nocht plainlie spouse ane wyfe,
Yit concubeins I have had four or fyfe.
And to my sons I have givin rich rewairds,   15
And all my dochters maryit upon lairds.
I let yow wit, my Lord, I am na fuill,
For quhy! I ryde upon ane amland muill.
Thare is na temporall lord in all this land,
That maks sic cheir, I let yow understand.   20
And als, my Lord, I gif with gude intentioun,
To divers temporall lords ane yeirlie pensioun
To that intent, that thay, with all thair hart,
In richt, and wrang, sal plainlie tak my part.
Now, have I tald yow, Sir, on my best ways,   25
How that I have exercit my office.

DIVYNE CORRECTIOUN.

I wein'd your office had bene for till preich,
And God's law to the peopill teich;

Quhairfoir weir ye that mytour? ye me tell.

SPIRITUALITIE.
I wat nocht, man, be Him that herryit hell.

DIVYNE CORRECTIOUN.
That dois betakin, that ye, with gude intent,
Sould teich, and preich, the Auld and New Testament.

SPIRITUALITIE.
I have ane Freir to preiche into my place, 5
Of my office, ye heare na mair quhyll Pasche.

CHASTITIE.
My Lords, this Abbot, and this Priores,
   Thay scorne thair Gods, this is my reason quhy:
Thay beare ane habit of fenziet halines,
   And in thair deid, thay do the contrary: 10
   For to live chaist, thay vow solemnitly.
Bot, fra that thay be sikker of thair bowis,
   Thay live in huirdome, and in harlotry:
Examine them, Sir, how thay observe thair vowis.

DIVYNE CORRECTIOUN.
Sir Scribe, ye sall, at Chastitie's requeist, 15
Pas, and exame yon thrie, in gudlie haist.

SCRYBE.
Father Abbot, this Counsall bids me speir
How ye have usit your Abbay, thay wald heir:
And als, thir Kings hes given to me commissioun
Of your office, for to mak inquisitioun. 20

ABBOT.

Tuiching my office, I say to yow plainlie,
My Monks and I, we leif richt easelie:
Thare is na monks, from Carrick to Carraill,
That fairs better, and drinks mair helsum aill.
My Prior is ane man of great devotioun:
Thairfor, daylie, he gets ane double portioun.

SCRYBE.

My Lords, how have ye keipt your thrie vows?

ABBOT.

Indeid richt weill, till I gat hame my bows,
In my Abbay, quhen I was sure professour
Then did I leife, as did my predecessour.
My paramours is baith als fat and fair,
As ony wench, intill the toun of Air.
I send my sons to Pareis, to the scuillis,
I traist in God that thay sall be na fuillis.
And all my douchters, I have weill provydit,
Now, judge ye, gif my office be weill gydit.

SCRYBE.

Maister Person, schaw us gif ye can preich;

PERSON.

Thocht I preich not, I can play at the caiche:
I wait thair is nocht ane amang yow all,
Mair ferilie can play at the fut-ball;
And for the carts, the tabils, and the dyse,
Above all persouns, I may beir the pryse.

Our round bonats, we mak thame now four nuickit;
Of richt fyne stuiff, gif yow list, cum and luikit.
Of my office, I have declarit to thee;
Speir quhat ye pleis, ye get na mair of me.

SCRYBE.

Quhat say you now, my Ladie Priores? 5
How have ye usit your office, can ye ges?
Quhat was the caus ye refusit harbrie:
To this young, lustie, Ladie Chastitie?

PRIORES.

I wald have harborit hir, with gude intent,
Bot, my complexioun thairto wald not assent: 10
I do my office, efter auld use and wount,
To your Parliament, I will mak na mair count.

VERITIE.

Now, caus sum of your cunning clarks,
Quhilk ar expert in heavenlie warkis,
And men fulfillit with charitie, 15
That can weill preiche the veritie,
My Lord, gif sum of them command,
Ane sermon for to mak, fra-hand.

DIVYNE CORRECTIOUN.

As ye have said, I am content, [20
To gar sum preich incontinent. [*Pausa*

Magister Noster, I ken how ye can teiche,
  Into the scuillis, and that richt ornatlie:
I pray yow, now, that ye wald please to prieche,
  In Inglisch toung, land folk to edifie.

DOCTOUR.

Soverane, I sall obey yow humbillie,
With ane schort sermon, presentlie, in this place :
And schaw the word of God unfeinzeitlie,
And sinceirlie, as God will give me grace.

[Heir sall the Doctour pas to the pulpit, and say,

Si vis ad vitam ingredi, serva mandata.

Devoit peopill, Sanct Paull, the preichour sayis, 5
   The fervent luife, and fatherlie pitie,
Quhilk God Almichtie hes schawin mony ways,
   To man in his corrupt fragilitie,
Exceids all luife, in earth, sa far, that we
May never to God mak˙ recompence conding ; 10
   As quha sa lists to reid the veritie,
In halie Scripture, he may find this thing :

Sic Deus dilexit mundum.

Tuiching nathing, the great prerogative,
   Quhilk God, to man, in his creatioun, lent :
How man, of nocht creat, superlative, 15
   Was to the image of God, Omnipotent :
   Let us consider that speciall luife ingent,
God had to man, quhen our foir-father fell ;
   Drawing us all, in his loynis immanent,
Captive from gloir, in thirlage to the hell. 20

Quhen angels fell, thair miserabil ruyne
   Was never restorit, bot for our miserie,
The Sun of God, secund persone divyne,
   In ane pure Virgin tuke humanitie :
   Syne, for our saik, great harmis suffered he, 25

In fasting, walking, in preiching, cauld and heit,
   And at the last, ane schamefull death deit he,
Betwix twa theifis, on croce, he yeild the spreit:

And, quhair an drop of his maist precious blude
   Was recompence sufficient, and conding,   5
Ane thowsand warlds to ransoum, from that wod,
   Infernall feind, Sathan ; nochtwithstanding,
He luifit us sa, that for [our] ransoning,
He sched furth all the blude of his bodie,   [10
   Riven, rent, and sair woundit, quhair he did hing,
Naild on the croce, on the Mont Calvary :

    Et copiosa apud eum redemptio.

O cruell death, be thee, the venemous
   Dragon, the devill infernall, lost his pray :
Be thee, the stinkand, mirk, contageous,
   Deip pit of hell, mankynd escaipit fray :   15
Be thee, the port of paradice alsway
Was patent maid unto the heavin sa hie :
   Opinnit to man and maid ane reddie way,
To gloir eternall, with th' haly Trinitie.

And yit, for all this luife incomparabill,   20
   God askis na rewaird, fra us againe,
Bot, luife for luife, in his command, but fabill,
   Conteinit ar all haill the lawis ten ;
   Baith ald, and new, and commandements ilk ane,
Luife bene the ledder, quhilk hes bot steppis twa : 25
   By quhilk, we may clim up to lyfe againe,
Out of this vaill of miserie, and wa.

*Diliges Dominum Deum tuum ex toto corde tuo,
et proximum tuum sicut teipsum ; in his
duobus mandatis, &c..*

The first step suithlie of this ledder is,
   To luife thy God, as the fontane and well
Of luif, and grace ; and the secund, I wis,
   To luife thy nichtbour as thou luiffis thy sell.
   Quha tynis ane step of thir twa, gais to hell,   5
But he repent, and turne to Christ anone.
   Hald this na fabill, the Halie Evangell
Bears, in effect, thir words, everie one :

Si vis ad vitam ingredi, serva mandata Dei.

That tyne thir steps, all they quha ever did sin,
   In pryde, invy, in ire, and lecherie ;   10
In covetice, or ony extreme win,
   Into sweirnes, or into gluttonye :
   Or quha dois nocht the deids of mercie,
Gif hungrie meit, and gif the naikit clayis.

PERSON.

Now, walloway ! thinkis thou na schame to lie ? 15
I trow, the devill a word is trew, thou sayis :

Thow sayis, thair is bot twa steppis to the hevin,
 . Quha failzeis them man backwarts fall in hell :
I wait it is ten thowsand mylis, and sevin,
   Gif it be na mair, I do it upon thy sell.   20
   Schort leggit men, I se, be Bryd's bell,
Will nevir cum thair, thay steppis bene sa wyde :
   Gif thay be the words of the Evangell ;
The Spirituall men hes mister of ane gyde.

ABBOT.

And I beleif, that cruikit men, and blinde,
   Sall never get up upon sa hich ane ledder :
By my gude faith, I dreid to ly behinde,
   Without, God draw me up into ane tedder ;
   Quhat and I fal, then I will break my bledder :   5
And I cum thair this day, the devill speid me ;
   Except, God made me lichter nor ane fedder,
Or send me doun gude widcok wingis to flie.

PERSONE.

Cum doun, dastard, and gang sell draiff,
   I understand nocht quhat thow said ;   10
Thy wordis war nather corne, nor caiff ;
   I wald thy toung againe war laide.
Quhair, thow sayis pryde is deidlie sin :
   I say pryde is bot honestie,
And covetice of warldlie win   15
   Is bot wisdome, I say for me :
Ire, hardines, and gluttonie,
   Is nathing ellis, bot lyfis fude :
The naturall sin of lecherie
Is bot trew luife ; all thir ar gude.   20

DOCTOUR.

God, and the Kirk, hes gevin command,
   That all gude Christian men refuse them.

PERSONE.

Bot, war thay sin, I understand,
   We men of Kirk wald never use them.

DOCTOUR.

Brother, I pray the Trinitie,
   Your faith, and charitie, to support:
Causand you knaw the veritie,
   That ye your subjects may comfort.
To your prayers, peopill, I recommend,   5
   The rewlars of this nobill regioun:
That our Lord God his grace mot to them send,
   On trespassours, to mak punitioun:
Prayand to God, from feinds yow defend,
   And of your sins, to gif yow full remissioun: 10
I say na mair, to God, I yow commend!
     [*Heir Diligence spyis the Freir roundand
      to the Prelate.*

DILIGENCE.

My Lords, I persave, that the Spirituall Stait,
Be way of deid, purpois to mak debait:
For, be the counsall of yon flattrand Freir,
Thay purpois, till mak all this toun on steir.   15

FIRST LICENTIATE.

Traist ye, that thay wil be inobedient,
To that, quhilk is decreitit in Parliament?

DILIGENCE.

Thay se the Paip, with awfull ordinance,
Makis weir aganis the michtie king of France:
Richt sa, thay think, that Prelats suld nocht sunzie, 20
Be way of deid, defend thair patrimonie.

FIRST LICENTIATE.

I pray thee, brother, gar me understand,
Quhair ever Christ possessit ane fut of land.

DILIGENCE.

Yea, that he did, Father, withouttin fail:
For Christ Jesus was King of Israell.

FIRST LICENTIATE.

I grant that Christ was king abufe al kings: 5
Bot he mellit never with temporall things;
As he hes plainlie done declair himsell,
As thou may reid, in his halie Evangell:
Birds hes thair nest, and tods hes thair den,
Bot Christ Jesus, the Saviour of men, 10
In all this warld, hes nocht ane penny braid,
Quhairon he may repois his heavinlie head.

DILIGENCE.

And is that trew?

BATCHELOR.

    Yea, brother, be Alhallows:
Christ Jesus had na propertie but the gallows: 15
And left not quhen he yeildit up the spreit,
To by himself ane simpill winding scheit.

DILIGENCE.

Christ's successours, I understand,
Thinks na schame to have temporall land.
Father, thay have na will, I yow assure, 20
In this warld, to be indigent, and pure:

Bot, Sir, sen ye ar callit sapient,
Declair to me the caus, with trew intent,
Quhy that my lustie ladie Veritie,
Hes nocht bene weill treatit in this cuntrie?   5

BATCHELOR.

Forsuith, quhair Prelats uses the counsall
    Of beggand Freirs, in monie regioun,
And thay Prelats, with Princes principall,
    The veritie, but doubt, is trampit doun;
    And Common-weill put to confusioun.   10
Gif this be trew, to yow, I me report:
    Tharfoir, My Lords, mak reformatioun
Or ye depairt, hartlie, I yow exhort.

Sirs, Freirs wald never, I yow assure,
    That ony prelats usit preiching: 15
And Prelats tuke on them that cure,
    Freirs wald get nathing for thair fleiching.

    Thairfoir, I counsall yow fra hand,
    Banische yon Freir out of this land,
        And that incontinent: 20
    Do ye nocht sa, withoutin weir,
    He will mak all this toun on steir,
        I knaw his fals intent.
    Yon Priores, withoutin fabill,
    I think scho is nocht profitabill,   25
        For Christis regioun.
    To begin reformatioun,
    Mak of them deprivatioun,
        This is my opinioun.

FIRST SERGEANT.

Sir, pleis ye, that we twa invaid thame,
And ye sall se us sone degraid thame
    Of cowll, and skaplarie ?

DIVYNE CORRECTIOUN.

Pas on, I am richt weill content :
Syne banische thame incontinent,   5
    Out of this cuntrie.

FIRST SERGEANT.

Cum on, Sir Freir, and be nocht fleyit,
The King our maister mon be obeyit,
    Bot ye sall have na harme :
Gif ye wald travell, fra toun to toun,   10
I think this hude, and habbie goun,
    Will hald your wambe ouir warme.

FLATTRIE (the Frier).

Now, quhat is this, that thir monster meins ?
I am exemptit fra Kings, and Queens,
    And fra all humane law.   15

SECUND SERGEANT.

Tak ye the hude, and I the gown,
This limmer luiks als lyke ane lown,
    As any that ever I saw.

FIRST SERGEANT.

Thir Freiris, to chaip punitioun,
Haulds them at thair exemptioun,   20

And na man will obey:
Thay ar exempt, I yow assure,
Baith fra Paip, King, and Empreour,
And that maks all the pley.

SECUND SERGEANT.

On Dumisday, quhen Christ sall say,   5
   Venite, Benedicti:
The Freirs will say, without delay,
   Nos sumus exempti.
    [*Heir sall thay spoilze Flattrie of the Freirs habite.*

GUDE COUNSALL.

Sir, be the Halie Trinitie,
This same is feinzeit Flattrie,
   I ken him, be his face:
Beleivand for to get promotioun,   10
He said that his name was Devotioun;
   And sa begylit your Grace.

FIRST SERGEANT.

Cum on, my ladie Priores,
   We sall leir yow to dance;
And that, within ane lytill space,   15
   Ane new pavin of France,
    [*Heir sall thay spuilze the Priores, and scho sall have ane kirtill of silk under hir habite.*

Now brother, be the Masse,
   Be my judgement, I think,
This halie Priores
   Is turnit in ane cowclink.   20

PRIORES.

I gif my freinds my malisoun,
That me compellit till be ane nun,
    And wald nocht let me marie :
It was my freinds greadines,
That gart me be ane Priores,   5
    Now hartlie them I warie.
Howbeit, that nunnis sing nichts and dayis,
Thair hart waitis nocht quhat thair mouth sayis,
    The suith, I yow declair :
Makand yow intimatioun,   10
To Christis congregatioun,
    Nunnis are nocht necessair.
Bot I sall do the best I can,
And marie sum gude honest man,
    And brew gude aill and tun :   15
Mariage, be my opinioun,
It is better religioun,
    As to be freir, or nun.

FLATTRIE (the Freir).

My Lords, for God's saik, let not hang me,
Howbeit, that widdiefows wald wrang me,   20
    I can mak na debait,
To win my meat, at pleuch, nor harrowis,
Bot, I sall help to hang my marrowis,
    Baith Falset, and Dissait.

DIVYNE CORRECTIOUN.

Than pas thy way, and greath the gallowis,   25

Syne help for to hang up thy fellowis,
Thou gets na uther grace.

FLATTRIE.

Of that office, I am content,
Bot our Prelatis, I dreid, repent,
 Be I fleinnde from thair face.   5
  [*Heir sall Flattrie pas to the stokkis, and
  sit besyd his marrowis.*

DISSAIT.

Now Flattrie, my auld companzeoun,
Quhat dois yon King Correctioun?
 Knawis thou nocht his intent?
Declair to us of thy novellis.

[FLATTRIE.]

Ye'ile all be hangit, I se nocht ellis;   10
 And that incontinent.

DISSAIT.

Now, walloway! will ye gar hang us?
The Devill brocht yon curst King amang us,
 For mekill sturt and stryfe.

FLATTRIE.

I had bene put to deid amang yow,   15
War nocht I tuk on hand till hang yow;
 And sa I saifit my lyfe:
I heir them say, thay will cry doun
All Freirs, and Nunnis, in this regioun,
 Sa far as I can feill: 20

Becaus, thay ar nocht necessair,
And als, thay think thay ar contrair,
    To Johne the Common-weill.
        [*Heir sal the Kings and the Temporal
        Stait round togider.*

DIVYNE CORRECTIOUN.

With the advice of King Humanitie,
    Heir I determine, with rype advysement,   5
That all thir Prelats sall deprivit be ;
    And be decreit of this present Parliament,
    That thir thrie cunning Clarks sapient,
Immediatlie thair places sall posses ;
    Becaus, that thay have bene sa negligent,   10
Suffring the word of God for till decres.

REX HUMANITAS.

As ye have said, but dout, it salbe done,
Pas to, and mak this interchainging sone.
        [*The King's servants lay hands on the
        thrie Prelats and says :*

WANTONNES.

My Lordis, we pray yow to be patient,
For, we will do the King's commandement.   15

SPIRITUALITIE.

I mak ane vow to God, and ye us handill,
Ye sallbe curst, and gragit, with buik and candill :
Syne, we sall pas unto the Paip, and pleinzie ;
And to the Devill of hell condemne this meinze ;

For quhy? sic reformatioun, as I weine,
Into Scotland was never hard, nor seine.
    [*Heir sal they spuilze them with silence,
    and put thair habite on the thrie Clarks.*

MERCHAND.

We mervell of yow, paintit sepulturis,
That was sa bauld, for to accept sic cuiris.
With glorious habite, rydand upon your muillis,   5
Now men may se, ye ar bot verie fuillis.

SPIRITUALITIE.

We say, the Kings war greiter fuillis, nor we,
That us promovit to sa greit dignitie.

ABBOT.

Thair is ane thowsand, in the Kirk, but doubt,
Sic fuillis as we, gif thay war weill socht out;   10
Now, brother, sen it may na better be,
Let us ga soup with Sensualitie.
    [*Heir sall they pas to Sensualitie.*

SPIRITUALITIE.

Madame, I pray yow, mak us thrie gude cheir;
We cure nocht to remaine with yow all yeir.

SENSUALITIE.

Pas fra us, fuillis, be Him that hes us wrocht,   15
Ye ludge nocht heir, becaus I knaw yow nocht.

SPIRITUALITIE.

Sir Covetice, will ye also misken me?

I wat richt weill, ye wil baith gif, and len me:
Speid hand, my freind, spair nocht to break the lockis:
Gif me ane thowsand crouns out of my box.

COVETYCE.

Quhairfoir, Sir Fuill, gif yow ane thowsand crouns?
Ga hence, ye seme to be thrie verie lowns.   5

SPIRITUALITIE.

I se nocht els, brother, withouttin faill,
Bot, this fals warld is turnit top ouir taill:
Sen, all is vaine, that is under the lift,
To win our meat, we man make uther schift.
With our labour, except we mak debait,   10
I dreid full sair, we want baith drink and meat.

PARSON.

Gif, with our labour, we man us defend,
Then let us gang, quhair we war never kend.

SPIRITUALITIE.

I wyte thir Freirs, that I am thus abusit;
For, by thair counsall, I have bene confusit: 15
Thay gart me trow, it suffysit, allace!
To gar thame plainlie preich, into my place.

ABBOT.

Allace! this reformatioun, I may warie;
For I have yit twa dochteris for to marie;
And thay ar baith contractit, be the Rude,   20
And waits nocht how to pay thair tocher-gude.

PARSON.

The Devill mak cair, for this unhappie chance,
For I am young, and thinks to pas to France;
And tak wages, amang the men of weir,
And win my living, with my sword and speir.
> [*The Bischop, Abbot, Persone, and Priores depairts altogidder.*

GUDE COUNSALL.

Or ye depairt, Sir, aff this regioun,   5
Gif Johne the Common-weill ane gay garmoun;
Becaus the Common-weill hes bene overluikit,
That is the caus, that Common-weill is cruikit.
With Singular Profeit, he hes bene sa supprysit,
That he is baith cauld, naikit, and disgysit.   10

DIVYNE CORRECTIOUN.

As ye have said, Father, I am content:
Sergeants, gif Johne ane new abuilzement.
Of sating damais, or of the velvot fyne;
And gif him place in our Parliament syne.
> [*Heir sal thay cleith Johne the Common-weill gorgeouslie, and set him doun among them in the Parliament.*

All verteous Peopil, now, may be rejoysit,   15
  Sen, Common-weill hes gotten ane gay garmoun:
And ignorants, out of the Kirk, deposit,
  Devoit Doctours, and Clarks of renoun,
  Now, in the Kirk, sall have dominioun:
And Gude Counsall, with ladie Veritie,   20
Ar profest with our King's Majestie.

Blist is that realme, that hes' ane prudent King,
    Quhilk dois delyte to heir the veritie ;
Punisching thame, that plainlie dois maling,
    Contrair the common-weill, and equitie.
Thair may na peopill have prosperitie,   5
Quhair ignorance hes the dominioun,
And Common-weill, be tirants, trampit doun. [*Pausa*

Now Maisters ye sall heir incontinent,
    At great leysour, in your presence, proclamit
The nobill Acts of our Parliament ;   10
    Of quhilks, we neid nocht for to be aschamit.
Cum heir Trumpet, and sound your warning tone,
That every man may knaw quhat we have done.
    [*Heir sall Diligence with the Scribe and the Trumpet
    pas to the pulpit, and proclame the Actis.*

THE FIRST ACT.

I. IT IS DEVYSIT, be thir prudent Kings,
    Correctioun, and King Humanitie,   15
That thair leigis, induring all thair ringis,
    With the avyce of the Estaits Thrie,
    Sall manfullie defend and fortifie
The Kirk of Christ, and his religioun,
    Without dissimulance, or hypocrisie ;   20
Under the paine of thair punitioun.

II. ALS thay will, that the Actis honorabill,
    Maid be our prince, in the last Parliament,
Becaus thay ar baith gude, and profitabill ;
    Thay will, that everie man be diligent   25

Thame til observe, with unfenzeit intent:
Quha disobeyis, inobedientlye,
  Be thair lawis, but doubt, they sall repent,
And painis contenit thairin sall underly.

III. AND als the Common-weill, for til advance,   5
  It is statute, that all the temporall landis,
Be set in few, efter the forme of France,
  Til verteous men, that labours, with thair hands;
  Resonabillie restrictit, with sic bands,
That thay do service, nevertheles,   10
  And to be subject ay under the wands;
That riches may, with policie, incres.

IV. ITEM, this prudent Parliament hes devysit,
  Gif lords halds under thair dominioun
Theifis, quhair throch puir pepil bein supprisit: 15
  For them thay sall mak answeir to the croun,
  And to the pure mak restitutioun:
Without thay put them in the judges hands;
  For thair default to suffer punitioun;
Sa that na theifis remaine within thair lands.   20

V. To that intent, that justice sould incres,
  It is concludit, in this Parliament,
That into Elgin, or into Innernesse,
  Sall be ane sute of Clarks sapient,
  Togidder with ane prudent President;   25
To do justice, in all the Norther airtis,
  Sa equallie, without impediment,
That thay neid nocht seik justice in thir pairts.

THE THRIE ESTAITIS.

VI. WITH licence of the Kirks halines,
   That justice may be done continuallie,
All the maters of Scotland, mair and les,
   To thir twa famous saits, perpetuallie,
   Salbe directit, becaus men seis plainlie,   5
Thir wantoun Nunnis ar na way necessair,
   Till Common-weill, nor yit to the glorie
Of Christ's Kirk, thocht thay be fat and fair.

And als, that fragill ordour feminine
   Will nocht be missit in Christ's religioun,   19
Thair rents usit till ane better fyne,
   For Common-weill of all this regioun,
   Ilk Senature, for that erectioun,
For the uphalding of thair gravitie,
   Sall have fyve hundredth mark of pensioun,   15
And also bot twa sall thair nummer be.

Into the North, saxteine sall thair remaine,
   Saxtein richt sa, in our maist famous Toun
Of Edinburgh, to serve our Soveraine;
   Chosen without partiall affectioun   20
   Of the maist cunning clarks of this regioun:
Thair Chancellar chosen of ane famous clark,
   Ane cunning man of great perfectioun,
And for his pensioun have ane thowsand mark.

VII. IT is devysit, in this Parliament,   25
   From this day furth, na mater temporall,
Our new Prelats thairto hes done consent,
   Cum befoir judges Consistoriall,

Quhilk has bene sa prolixt, and partiall;
To the great hurt of the communitie;
   Let Temporall men seik Judges temporall,
And Spirituall men to spiritualitie.

VIII. Na benefice beis giffin, in tyme cumming,   5
   Bot to men of good eruditioun;
Expert in the halie Scripture, and cunning,
   And that thay be of good conditioun,
Of publick vices but suspitioun;
And qualifeit richt prudentlie to preich,   10
   To thair awin folk baith into land and toun,
Or ellis, in famous scuillis, for to teich.

IX. Als becaus of the great pluralitie
   Of ignorant Preists, ma than ane legioun,
Quhairthroch, of teicheouris the heich dignitie   15
   Is vilipendit, in ilk regioun :
Thairfoir, our Court hes maid ane provisioun,
That na Bischops mak teichours, in tyme cumming,
   Except men of gude eruditioun,
And for preistheid qualifeit and cunning.   20

Siclyke as ye se, in the Borrows toun,
   Ane tailzeour is nocht sufferit to remaine,
Without he can mak doublet, coat, and gown,
   He man gang till his prenteischip againe :
Bischops sould nocht ressave, me think certaine   25
Into the Kirk, except ane cunning Clark :
   Ane idiot preist, Esay compaireth, plaine,
Till ane dum dogge, that can nocht byte nor bark.

X. Fra this day furth, se na prelats pretend,
  Under the paine of inobedience,
At Prince, or Paip, to purchase ane Commend
  Againe the kow, becaus it dois offence:
    Till ony preist, we think sufficience   5
Ane benefice, for to serve God withall;
  Twa prelacies sall na man have, from thence,
Without that he be of the blude royall.

XI. Item, this prudent counsall hes concludit,
  Sa that our haly vickars be nocht wraith,   10
From this day furth, thay salbe cleane denudit,
  Baith of corspresent, cow, and umest claith,
    To pure commons, becaus it hath done skaith:
And mairover, we think it lytill force,
  Howbeit, the Barronns thairto will be laith, 15
From thine-furth, thay sall want thair hyrald hors.

XII. It is decreit, that in this Parliament,
  Ilk Bischop, Minister, Priour, and Persoun;
To the effect thay may tak better tent,
  To saulis, under thair dominioun,   20
    Efter the forme of thair foundatioun,
Ilk Bischop, in his diosie sall remaine:
  And everilk Persoun, in his parochoun,
Teiching thair folk, from vices to refraine.

XIII. Becaus that Clarks our substance dois consume,
  For bils, and proces, of thair prelacies: [25
Thairfoir thair sall na money ga to Rome,
  From this day furth, or any benefice:

Bot gif, it be for gret archbischopries;
As for the rest, na money gais at all :
  For the incressing of thair dignities,
Na mair, nor did to Peter, nor to Paull.

XIV. CONSIDERING that our Preistis, for the maist
    part,   5
  Thay want the gift of Chastitie, we se;
Cupido hes sa perst thame throch the hart;
  We grant them licence, and frie libertie,
That thay may have fair virgins to thair wyfis;
  And sa keip matrimoniall chastitie,   10
And nocht in huirdome, for to leid thair lyfis.

XV. THIS Parliament, richt sa, hes done conclude :
  From this day forth, our Barrouns temporall
Sall na mair mix thair nobil ancient blude
  With bastard bairns of stait Spirituall :   15
  Ilk stait amang thair awin selfis marie sall
Gif Nobils marie with the Spiritualitie,
  From thyne, subject thay sal be, and all
Sal be degraidit of thair Nobilitie.

And from amang the Nobils cancellit,   20
  Untill the tyme thay by thair lybertie,
Rehabilit, be the Civill magistrate :
  And sa sall marie the Spiritualitie;
  Bischops with bischops sall mak affinitie,
Abbots, and prioris, with the priores :   25
  As bischop Annas, in Scripture, we may se,
Maryat his dochter on bischop Caiphas.

Now, have ye heard the ACTIS honorabill,
   Devysit in this present Parliament,
To Common-weill we think agreabil :
   All faithfull folk sould heirof be content,
   Thame till observe, with hartlie trew intent ;   5
I wait nane will against our acts rebell,
   Nor till our law be inobedient,
Bot Plutois band, the potent Prince of hell.
   [*Heir sall Pauper cum befoir the King, and say* :

PAUPER.

I gif yow my braid bennesoun,
That hes givin Common-weill a goun :   10
I wald nocht, for ane pair of plackis,
Ye had nocht maid thir nobill Actis.
I pray to God ! and sweit Sanct Geill !
To gif yow grace to use them weill :
Wer thay weill keipit, I understand,   15
It war great honour to Scotland.
It had bene als gude, ye had sleipit,
As to mak Acts, and be nocht keipit :
Bot, I beseik yow, for Allhallows,
To heid Dissait, and hang his fellows ;   20
And banische Flattrie aff the Toun,
For thair was never sic ane loun.
That beand done, I hauld it best,
That everie man ga to his rest.

DIVYNE CORRECTIOUN.

As thou hes said, it salbe done :   25
Suyith ! Sergeants, hang yon swingeours sone.

[*Heir sall the Sergeants lous the presoners out of the stocks, and leid them to the gallows.*

FIRST SERGEANT.

Cum heir, Sir Theif, cum heir, cum heir:
Quhen war ye wont to be sa sweir?
To hunt cattell ye war ay spedie,
Thairfoir ye sall waive in ane widdie.

COMMOUN THIFT.

Man I be hangit? allace! allace!   5
Is thair nane heir, may get me grace?
Yit, or I die, gif me ane drink.

FIRST SERGEANT.

Fy! huirsun Carle, I feil ane stink.

COMMOUN THIFT.

Thocht I wald nocht, that it war wittin,
Sir, in gude faith, I am bedirtin: 10
To wit the veritie, gif ye pleis,
Lous doun my hois, put in your neis,

FIRST SERGEANT.

Thou art ane limmer, I stand foir'd,
Slip in thy heid into this coird,
For thou had never ane meiter tippit.   .15

COMMOUN THIFT.

Allace! this is ane felloun rippit.   [*Pausa*
The widdifow Wairdanis tuke my geir,
And left me nether hors, nor meir:

Nor erthlie gude, that me belangit,
Now, walloway! I man be hangit.
Repent your lyfis, ye plaine oppressouris,
All ye misdoars, and transgressours:
Or ellis, gar chuse yow gude confessours,   5
    And mak yow forde:
For gif ye tarie in this land,
And cum under Correctioun's hand:
Your grace salbe, I understand,
    Ane guid scharp coird.   10

Adew! my Bretheren, common theifis,
That helpit me, in my mischeifis:
Adew! Grosars, Nicksons, and Bellis,
Oft have we run out-thoart the fellis.
Adew! Robsonis, Hansles, and Pylis,   15
That in our craft hes mony wyllis:
Lytils, Trumbels, and Armestrangs,
Adew! all theifis that me belangs;
Tailzeours, Eurwings, and Elwands,
Speidie of fut and wicht of hands.   20
The Scottis of Ewisdaill, and the Graimis,
I have na tyme, to tell your namis.
With King Correctioun, and ye be fangit,
Beleif richt weill, ye wilbe hangit.

FIRST SERGEANT.

Speid hand, man, with thy clitter clatter.   25

COMMOUN THIFT,

For God's saik, sir, let me mak watter;

Howbeit, I have bene cattel-gredie,
It schamis to pische into ane widdie.
> [*Heir sal Commoun Thift be drawin up,
> or his figour.*

SECUND SERGEANT.

Cum heir, Dissait, my companzeoun,
Saw ever ane man, lyker ane loun,
   To hing upon ane gallows ?   5

DISSAIT.

This is aneuch to mak me mangit,
Duill fell me, that I man be hangit,
   Let me speik with my fallows.
I trow wan-fortune brocht me heir ;
   Quhat mekill feind maid me sa speidie ?   10
Sen it was said, it is sevin yeir,
   That I sould weave into ane widdie,
I leirit my maisters to be gredie.
Adew ! for I se na remeid :
   Luke quhat it is to be evil-deidie !   15

SECUND SERGEANT.

Now, in this halter slip thy heid.
   Stand still, me think ye draw aback.

DISSAIT.

Allace ! maister, ye hurt my crag.

SECUND SERGEANT.

It will hurt better, I woid ane plak,
   Richt now, quhen ye hing on ane knag.   20

DISSAIT.

Adew! my Maisters, merchant men,
I have yow servit, as ye ken,
    Truelie, baith air and lait:
I say to yow, for conclusioun,
I dreid, ye gang to confusioun,   5
    Fra tyme ye want Dissait.
I leirit yow, merchants, mony ane wyle,
Upalands wyfis, for to begyle,
    Upon ane market day:
And gar them trow your stuffe was gude,   10
Quhen it was rottin, be the Rude,
    And sweir it was nocht sway,
I was ay roundand in your ear,
And leirit yow for to ban and sweir,
    Quhat your geir cost in France: 15
Howbeit, the devill ane word was trew,
Your craft, gif King Correctioun knew,
    Wald turne yow to mischance.
I leirit yow wyllis monyfauld,
To mix the new wyne, and the auld,   20
    That faschioun was na follie:
To sell richt deir, and by gude-chaip,
And mix ry-meill amang the saip.
    And saiffrone with oyl-dolie.
Forzet nocht ocker, I counsall yow,   25
Mair than the Vicker dois the kow,
    Or Lords thair doubill maill:
Howbeit, your elwand be too skant,
Or your pound wecht thrie unces want,
    Think that bot lytill faill.   30

Adew! the greit clan Jamesone,
The blude royall of Clappertoun,
 I was ay to yow trew:
Baith Andersone, and Patersone,
Above them all, Thome Williamsone,   5
 My absence ye will rew.
Thome Williamsone, it is your pairt,
To pray for me, with all your hairt,
 And think upon my warks :
How I leirit yow ane gude lessoun,   10
For to begyle, in Edinburgh toun,
 The Bischop and his Clarks.
Ye young merchants may cry Allace,
For wanting of your wonted grace,
 Yon curst King ye may ban :   15
Had I leifit bot half ane yeir.
I sould have leirit yow craftis, perqueir,
 To begyle wyfe, and man.
How may ye merchants mak debait?
Fra tyme ye want your man, Dissait,   20
 For yow, I mak greit cair :
Without I ryse fra deid to lyfe,
I wait weill, ye will never thryfe,
 Farther nor the fourth air.
  [*Heir sal Dissait be drawin up, or
  ellis his fygure.*

FIRST SERGEANT.

Cum heir, Falset, and mence the gallows,   25
Ye man hing up amang your fallows,
 For your cankart conditioun ;

Monie ane trew man have ye wrangit;
Thairfoir, but dout, ye sal be hangit
    But mercie, or remissioun.

FALSET.

Allace! man I be hangit to?
Quhat mekill devill is this ado;
    How came I to this cummer?   5
My gude maisters, ye Crafts men,
Want ye Falset, full weill I ken,
    Ye will all die for hunger.
Ye men of craft may cry Allace!
Quhen ye want me, ye want your grace;   10
    Thairfoir, put into wryte
My lessouns that I did yow leir,
Howbeit, the commons eyne ye bleir,
    Count ye nocht that ane myte.
Find me ane wobster, that is leill,   15
Or ane walker, that will nocht steill,
    Thair craftines, I ken:
Or ane millair, that is na falt,
That will nather steill meall, nor malt;
    Hald them for halie men.   20
At our fleschers tak ye na greife,
Thocht thay blaw leane mutton, and beife,
    That thay seime fat, and fair:
Thay think that practick bot ane mow,
Howbeit, the devill a thing it dow;   25
    To thame I leirit that lair.
I leirit tailzeours, in everie toun,
To schaip fyve quarters in ane goun,

In Angus, and in Fyfe:
To uplands tailzeours, I gave gude leife,
To steill ane sillie stump, or sleife,
    Unto Kittok, his wyfe.
My gude maister, Andro Fortoun,
Of tailzeours, that may weir the croun,   5
    For me, he will be mangit:
Tailzeour Baberage, my sone and air,
I wait for me, will rudlie rair,
    Fra tyme he se me hangit.
The barfit deacon Jamie Ralfe,   10
Quha never yit bocht kow, nor calfe;
    Becaus he can nocht steall:
Willie Cadzeoch will mak na plead,
Howbeit, his wyfe want beife, and bread,
    Get he gude barmie aill.   15
To the brousters of Cowper toun,
I leife my braid black malesoun,
    Als hartlie, as I may:
To mak thinne aill, thay think na falt,
Of mekill barme, and lytill malt,   20
    Agane the market day.
And thay can mak, withouttin doubt,
Ane kynde of aill, thay call Harns-out,
    Wait ye how thay mak that?
Ane curtill queine, ane laidlie lurdane,   25
Of strang wesche scho will tak ane jurdane,
    And settis in the gyle-fat:
Quha drinkis of that aill, man or page,
It will gar all his harnis rage,
    That jurdane I may rew;   30

It gart my heid rin hiddie giddie,
Sirs, God! nor I die in ane widdie,
    Gif this taill be nocht trew.
Speir at the sowtar, Geordie Sillie,
Fra tyme that he had fil'd his bellie,
    With this unhelthsum aill: 5
Than all the baxters will I ban,
That mixes bread with dust and bran,
    And fyne flour with beir maill.
Adew! my maisters, wrichts, and maissouns,
I have neid to leir yow few lessouns,   10
    Ye knaw my craft, perqueir:
Adew! blak-smythis, and lorimers,
Adew! ye craftie cordiners,
    That sellis the schone over deir.
Goldsmythis, fair-weill, abuve thame all!   15
Remember my memoriall,
    With mony ane sittill cast:
To mix, set ye nocht by twa preinis,
Fyne ducat gold with hard gudlingis,
    Lyke as I leirnit yow last.   20
Quhen I was ludgit upaland,
The schiphirds maid with me ane band,
    Richt craftelie to steill:
Than, did I gif ane confirmatioun
To all the schiphirdis of this natioun,   25
    That thay sould nevir be leill:
And ilk ane to reset ane uther,
I knaw fals schiphirds fyftie fidder,
    War thair carteleinis kend:
How thay mak, in thair conventiouns,   30

> On montans, far fra ony touns,
> God let them never mend.
> Amang crafts men, it is ane wonder,
> To find ten leill amang ane hunder,
> The treuth I to yow tell:
> Adew! I may na langar tarie, 5
> I man pass to the King of Farie,
> Or ellis the rycht to hell.
>> [*Heir sall he luke up to his fallows hingand,
>> and say,*
>
> Wais me! for thee gude Common Thift,
> Was never man maid ane mair honest schift,
> His leifing for to win: 10
> Thare was nocht ane, in all Liddisdaill,
> That ky mair craftelie culd staill,
> Quhare thou hings on that pin.
> Sathan ressave thy saull, Dissait,
> Thou was to me ane faithfull mait, 15
> And als my father brother;
> Duill fell the sillie merchant men,
> To mak thame service weill I ken,
> Tha'ill never get sic ane uther.
>> [*Heir sall thay festin the cord to his neck,
>> with ane dum countenance: thairefter
>> he sall say:*
>
> Gif any man list, for to be my mait, 20
> Cum follow me, for I am at the gait:
> Cum follow me all catyfe covetous kings,
> Reavers, but richt, of utheris realmis, and rings;
> Togiddir with all wrangous conquerours,

And bring with yow all publick oppressours;
With Pharao, king of Egiptians,
With him, in hell, salbe your recompence,
All creuell schedders of blude innocent,
Cum follow me, or ellis rin, and repent.   5
Prelats that hes ma benefeits nor thrie,
And will nocht teich, nor preiche, the veritie:
Without at God, in tyme, thay cry for grace,
In hiddeous hell, I sall prepair thair place.
Cum follow me all fals corruptit judges,   10
With Pontius Pilat, I sall prepair your ludges:
All ye officials, that parts men with thair wyfis,
Cum follow me, or els gang mend your lyfis:
With all fals leidars of the Coustrie law,
With wanton scribes, and clarks, intill ane raw;   15
That to the puir, maks mony partiall traine,
Syne, *hodie ad octo* bids thame cum againe,
And ye, that taks rewairds at baith the hands,
Ye sall, with me, be bund in Baliel's bands.
Cum follow me all curst unhappy wyfis,   20
That, with your gudemen, dayly flytis, and stryfis,
And quyetlie with rybalds maks repair;
And taks na cure to mak ane wrangous air:
Ye sall in hell rewairdit be, I wein.
With Jesabell, of Israell the queine,   25
I have ane curst, unhappy wyfe my sell,
Wald God! scho war, befoir me, into hell:
That bismair, war scho thair, withoutin doubt,
Out of hell, the Devill scho wald ding our.
Ye maryit men, evin as ye luife your lyfis,   30
Let never preists be hamelie with your wyfis.

My wyfe, with preists, scho doith me greit unricht:
And maid me nine tymes cuckald, on ane nicht.
Fairweill! for I am to the widdie wend,
For quhy, Falset maid never ane better end.
  [*Heir sall he be heisit up, and not his figure,*
   and an Craw, or ane Ke, salbe castin
   up, as it war his saull.

FLATTRIE

Have I nocht chaipit the widdie weill?   5
Yea, that I have, be sweit Sanct Geill;
 For I had nocht bene wrangit;
Becaus I servit, be Alhallows,
Till have bene merchellit amang my fallowis,
 And heich above them hangit.   10
I maid far ma faltis, nor my maits,
I begylde all The Thrie Estaits,
 With my hypocrisie:
Quhen I had on my Freir's hude,
All men beleifit that I was gude;   15
 Now, judge ye gif I be.
Tak me, ane rakles rubiatour,
Ane theif, ane tyrane, or ane tratour,
 Of everie vyce the plant:
Gif him the habite of ane freir,   20
The wyfis will trow, withoutin weir,
 He be ane verie Saint.
I knaw that cowle and skaplarie
Genners mair hait, nor charitie,
 Thocht thay be blak, or blew: 25
Quhat halines is thair within,

THE THRIE ESTAITIS.

Ane wolfe cled in ane wedder's skin,
 Judge ye, gif this be trew.
Sen, I have chaipit this firie farie,
Adew! I will na langer tarie,
 To cumber yow, with my clatter: 5
Bot, I will, with ane humbill spreit,
Gang serve the Hermeit of Lareit:
 And leir him, for till flatter.

[THE SERMON OF FOLY:

AN INTERLUDE.]

       [*Heir sall enter Folie.*

FOLIE.

Gude day, my Lords, and als God saine!
Dois na man bid, Gude day, againe?   10
Quhen fuillis are fow, then are thay faine,
 Ken ye nocht me?
How call thay me, can ye nocht tell?
Now, be Him that herryit hell,
I wait nocht how thay call my sell,   15
 Bot gif I lie.

DILIGENCE.

Quhat brybour is this, that maks sic beiris?

FOLIE.

The Feind ressave that mouth, that speiris:

Gude man, ga play yow, with your feiris,
With muck upon your mow.

DILIGENCE.

Fond Fuill, quhair hes thou bene sa lait?

FOLIE.

Marie! cummand throw the Schogait,
Bot, thair hes bene ane great debait, 5
    Betwix me, and ane sow.
The sow cryit guff, and I to ga,
Throw speid of fute, I gat awa,
Bot, in the midst of the cawsa,
    I fell into ane midding: 10
Scho lap upon me, with ane bend,
Quha ever the middings sould amend,
God send them ane mischevous end!
    For, that is bot God's bidding.
As I was pudlit thair, God wait, 15
But with my club I maid debait;
Ise never cum againe that gait,
    I sweir yow, be Alhallows.
I wald the officiars of the toun,
That suffers sic confusioun, 20
That thay war harbreit with Mahown,
    Or hangit on ane gallows.
Fy! fy! that sic ane fair cuntrie
Sould stand sa lang but policie:
I gif thame to the Devill, hartlie, 25
    That hes the wyte:
I wald the Provost wald tak in heid;

Of yon midding, to make remeid,
Quhilk pat me and the sow at feid,
Quhat may I do, bot flyte?

REX HUMANITAS.

Pas on my servant, Diligence,
And bring yon Fuill to our presence.   5

DILIGENCE.

That sall be done, but tarying:
Foly, ye man ga to the King.

FOLIE.

The King? quhat kynde of thing is that?
Is yon he, with the goldin hat?

DILIGENCE.

Yon same is he: cum on thy way.   10

FOLIE.

Gif ye be king, God [gif] yow gude day!
I have ane plaint, to make to yow.

REX HUMANITAS.

Quhom on, Folie?

FOLIE.

Marie! on ane sow.

. . . .
Gif ye be King, be Sanct Allan,   15
Ye sould do justice to ilk man.

Had I nocht keipit me with my club,
The sow had drawin me in ane dub.
I heir them say, thair is cum to the Toun,
Ane King, callit Correctioun :
I pray yow, tell me, quhilk is he ?   5

DILIGENCE.
Yon, with the wings; may [thow] nocht se ?

FOLIE.
Now, wallie fall that weill-fairde mow,
Sir, I pray yow, correct yon sow :
Quhilk with hir teith, but sword or knyfe,
Had maist have reft me of my lyfe :   10
Gif ye will nocht mak correctioun,
Than gif me your protectioun,
Of all swyne for to be skaithles,
Betuix this toun and Innernes.

DILIGENCE.
Folie, hes thou ane wyfe, at hame ?   15

FOLIE.
Yea, that I have, God send hir schame !
I trow be this scho is neir deid,
I left ane wyfe bindand hir heid ;
To schaw hir seiknes, I think schame,
Scho hes sic rumbling in hir wambe,   20

*That all the nicht my hart overcasts
with boking, with thunder-blasts.*

DILIGENCE.
Recoverit scho nocht at the last ?

FOLIE.

Yea, bot wit ye weil, scho fartit fast;
Bot, quhen scho sichis, my hart is sarie,

DILIGENCE.

Bot drinkis scho ocht?

FOLIE.

   Yea, be Sanct Marie!
Ane quart at anis, it will nocht tarie,   5
 And leif the devill a drap:
Than sic flobbage, scho layis fra hir,
About the wallis, God wait sic wair,
Quhen it was drunkin, I gat to skair
 The lickings of the cap.   10

DILIGENCE.

Quhat is in that creill, I pray thee tell?

FOLIE.

Marie! I have Folie Hats, to sell.

DILIGENCE.

I pray thee, sell me ane, or tway.

FOLIE.

Na, tarie quhill the market day.
I will sit doun heir, be Sanct Clune,   15
And gif my babies thair disjune.
Cum heir gude Glaiks, my dochter deir,
Thou sal be maryit, within ane yeir,

Upon ane freir of Tillilum;
Na, thou art nather deaf nor dum :
Cum hidder, Stult, my sone and air,
My joy, thou art baith gude and fair,
Now, sall I fend yow, as I may, 5
Thocht ye cry lyke ane Ke, all day.
    [*Heir sal the bairns cry Keck, lyke ane Ke, and*
        he sal put meat in thair mouth.

DILIGENCE.

Get up, Folie, but tarying,
And speid yow haistelie to the King;
Get up! me think, the Carle is dum.

FOLIE.

Now, bum, baleriebum, bum. 10

DILIGENCE.

I trow the trucour lyis, in ane trance;
Get up, man, with ane mirrie mischance!
Or be Sanct Dyonis of France,
    Ise gar thee want thy wallet;
It's schame to se, man, how thow lyis. 15

FOLIE.

Wa, yit againe, now this is thryis:
The Devill wirrie me, and I ryse,
    Bot, I sall break thy pallet.

· · · · · · · · ·

Suyith! harlot, haist thee to the King,
And let allane thy trattilling. 20

Lo! heir is Folie, Sir, alreadie,
Ane richt sweir swingeour, be our Ladie!

FOLIE.

Thou art nocht half sa sweir thy sell;
Quhat meins this pulpit, I pray thee tell?

DILIGENCE.

Our New Bischops hes maid ane preiching,   5
Bot thou heard never sic pleasant teiching;
Yon Bischop will preich throch the coast.

FOLIE.

Than stryk ane hag into the poast,
For, I hard never, in all my lyfe,
Ane Bischop cum to preich in Fyfe.   10
Gif Bischops to be preichours leiris,
Wallaway! quhat sall word of Freiris!
Gif prelats preich, in brugh, and land,
The sillie freirs, I understand,
Thay will get na mair meall, nor malt: 15
Sa I dreid freirs sall die for falt.
Sen, sa is, that yon nobill King
Will mak men bischops for preiching:
Quhat say you, Sirs, hauld ye nocht best,
That I gang preich amang the rest?   20
Quhen, I have preichit on my best wyis,
Then, will I sell my merchandise,
To my bretherin, and tendir maits,
That dwellis amang The Thrie Estaits:

VOL. II.   U

For I haif heir gude chaifery.
Till any Fuill that lists to by.
> [*Heir sall Folie hing up his Hattis on the pulpet, and say:*]

God sen, I had ane Doctours hude.

REX HUMANITAS.

Quhy, Folie, wald thou mak ane preiching?

FOLIE.

Yea, that I wald, Sir, be the Rude,   5
  But eyther flattering, or fleiching.

REX HUMANITAS.

Now, brother, let us heir this teiching,
  To pas our tyme, and heir him raife.

DILIGENCE.

He war far meiter for the kitching,
  Amang the pottis, sa Christ me saife.   10
Fond Folie, sall I be thy Clark?
  And answeir thee ay, with Amen.

FOLIE.

Now, at the beginning of my wark,
  The Feind ressave that graceles grim.
> [*Heir sall Folie begin his Sermon as followis:*]

STULTORUM NUMERUS INFINITUS:

Salomon, the maist Sapient king,   15

In Israell quhan he did ring,
Thir words, in effect, did write,
THE NUMBER OF FUILLIS AR INFINITE.
I think na schame, sa Christ me saife,
To be ane Fuill, amang the laife,   5
Howbeit, ane hundreth stands heir by,
Perventure, als great fuillis as I.

STULTORUM.

I have of my geneologic,
Dwelland in everie cuntrie,
Erles, Duiks, Kings, and Empriours,   10
With mony guckit conquerours :
Quhilk dois in folie perseveir,
And hes done sa this monie yeir;
And seiks to warldlie dignities,
And sum to sensuall vanities :   15
Quhat vails all thir vaine honouris,
Nocht being sure to leife twa houris?
Sum greidie fuill dois fill ane box,
Ane uther fuill cummis, and breaks the lox;
And spends that uther fuillis hes spair'd.   20
Quhilk never thocht on them to wairde,
Sum dois as thay sould never die,
Is nocht this Folie, quhat say ye?

SAPIENTA HUJUS MUNDI, STULTITIA EST APUD DEUM.

Becaus thair is sa many Fuillis,
Rydand on hors, and sum on muillis :   25
Heir I have brocht gude chaffery,

Till ony fuill that listis to by ;
And speciallie for The Thrie Estaits,
Quhair I have mony tender maits :
Quhilk causit them, as ye may se,
Gang backwart throw the haill cuntrie,   5
Gif with my merchandise, ye list to mell,
Heir I have Folie Hattis to sell.
Quhairfoir, is this Hat wald ye ken ?
Marie, for insatiabill merchant men :
Quhen God hes send thame abundance,   10
Ar nocht content with sufficiance ;
Bot, saillis into the stormy blastis,
In winter, to get greater castis :
In mony terribill great torment,
Against the Actis of Parliament.   15
Sum tynis thair geir, and sum ar drounde,
With this, sic merchants sould be crounde.

DILIGENCE.

Quhom to, schaips thou to sell that Hude ?
I trow, to sum great man of gude.

FOLIE.

This Hude to sell richt faine I wald,   20
To him that is baith auld, and cald :
Reddie till pas to hell, or heavin,
And hes fair bairnis sax, or seavin ;
And is of age fourscoir of yeir,
And taks ane lasse to be his peir :   25
Quhilk is nocht fourteine yeir of age,
And joynis with hir in mariage :

Geifand hir traist, that scho nocht wald
Rycht haistelie mak him cuckald.
Quha maryes, beand sa neir thair dead,
Set on this Hat upon his head.

DILIGENCE.

Quhat Hude is that, tell me I pray thee ?   5

FOLIE.

This is ane halie Hude, I say thee ;
This hude is ordanit, I thee assure,
For Spirituall Fuillis, that taks in cure,
The saullis of great Diocies,
And regiment of great Abesies,   10
For gredines of warldlie pelfe,
Than can nocht, justlie, gyde them selfe.
Uthers saullis to saife, it settis them weill,
Syne sell thair awin saullis to the Deuill.
Quha ever dois sa, this I conclude,   15
Upon his heid set on this Hude.

DILIGENCE.

Folie, is thair ony sic men,
Now, in the Kirk, that thou can ken ?
How sall I ken them ?

FOLIE.

Na, keip that clois.   20

Ex OPERIBUS EORUM COGNOSCETIS EOS :

And Fuillis speik of the Prelacie,
It will be hauldin for heresie.

REX HUMANITAS.

Speik on hardlie, I gif thé leife. 10

FOLIE.

Than, my remissioun is in my sleife.
Will ye leife me to speik of Kings?

REX HUMANITAS.

Yea, hardlie speik of all kin things.

FOLIE.

Conforming to my first narratioun,
Ye ar all Fuillis, be cok's passioun! 15

DILIGENCE.

Thou leis, I trow, this Fuill be mangit.

FOLIE.

Gif I lie, God, nor thou be hangit:
For, I have heir, I to thé tell,
Ane nobill cap imperiell,
Quhilk is nocht ordanit, bot for doings
Of Empreours, of Duiks, and Kings, 5
For princelie, and imperiall Fuillis,
Thay sould have luggis, als lang as muillis.
The pryde of princes, withoutin faill,
Gars all the warld rin top ouir taill,
To win thame warldlie gloir and gude, 10
Thay cure nocht schedding of saikles blude.
Quhat cummer have ye had in Scotland,
Be our auld enemies of Ingland?

Had nocht bene the support of France,
We had bene brocht to great mischance.
Now, I heir tell the Empreour
Schaippis for till be ane conquerour,
And is muifing his ordinance,   5
Against the nobill King of France,
Bot, I knaw nocht his just querrell,
That he hes for till mak battell.
All the Princes of Almanie
Spainze, Flanders, and Italie,   10
This present yeir, ar in ane flocht:
Sum sall thair wages find deir bocht.
The Paip, with bombard, speir, and scheild,
Hes send his armie to the feild.
Sanct Peter, Sanct Paull, nor Sanct Androw,   15
Raisit never sic an oist, I trow.
Is this fraternall charitie,
Or furious folie, quhat say ye?
Thay leirit nocht this at Christis scuillis:
Thairfoir, I think them verie fuillis.   20
I think it folie, be God's mother,
Ilk Christian prince to ding doun uther:
Becaus, that this Hat sould belang them,
Gang thou and part it, evin amang them.

 The Prophesie, withouttin weir,   25
Of Merling beis compleit this yeir:
For my gudame, the Gyre Carling,
Leirnde me the Prophesie of Marling,
Quhairof I sall schaw the sentence,
Gif ye will gif me audience: 30

Flan, fran, resurgent,
Simul Hispan viribus urgent:
Dani vastabunt,
Vallones valla parabunt:
Sic tibi nomen in a,
Mulier cacavit in olla:
Hoc epulum comedes.

DILIGENCE.
Marie! that is ane ill savorit dische.

FOLIE.
Sa, be this Prophesie plainlie appeirs,
That mortall weirs sall be amang Freirs:
Thay sall nocht knaw weill, in thair closters,
To quhom thay sall say thair Pater Nosters. 5
Wald thay fall to, and fecht with speir, and sheild,
The feind mak cuir, quhilk of them win the feild.

Now, of my Sermon have I maid ane end,
To Gilly-Mowband I yow all commend:
And I yow als beseik, richt hartfullie, 10
Pray for the saull of gude Cacaphatie,
Quhilk laitlie drownit himself into Lochleavin,
That his sweit saull may be above the Heavin.

DILIGENCE.

Famous Pepill, hartlie, I yow requyre,
    This lytill sport to tak in patience;
We traist to God, and we leif ane uther yeir,
    Quhair we have failit, we sall do diligence,
    With mair plesure, to mak yow recompence;   5
Becaus we have bene sum part tedious,
    With mater rude, denude of eloquence,
Likewyse, perchance, to sum men odious.

[Adew, we will mak no langar tary,
    Prayand to Jesu Chryst, our Salviour,   10
That be the requeist of his moder Mary,
    He do preserve this famous Auditour,
    Withowt that grittar materis do ineure,
For your plesour we sall devyse ane sport,
    Plesand tyll every gentill creatour,   15
To raiss your spreitis to plesour and confort.]
      Now, let ilk man his way avance,
      Let sum ga drink, and sum ga dance:
    Menstrell, blaw up ane brawll of France.
      Let sé quha hobbils best: 20
    For I will rin incontinent.
To the tavern, or ever I stent:
And pray to God Omnipotent,
    To send yow all gude rest.

Rex sapiens, æterne Deus, genitorque benigne,
  Sit Tibi perpetuo gloria, laus, et honor.

APPENDIX.

THE AULD MAN AND HIS WIFE.

A Preliminary Interlude.

NAMES OF PERSONS IN THIS INTERLUDE.

Nuntius, *the Messenger*.
The Cotter.
The Cotter's Wyfe.
Fyndlaw of the Fute-band.
The Fuill.
The Auld Man.
Bessy his Wyfe.
The Courteour.
The Marchand.
The Clerk.

Heir begynnis the Proclamation of the Play maid by David Lynsayis of the Month Knicht, in the Playfeild, in the moneth of [blank] the zeir of God 155[blank] zeiris.

THE PROCLAMATION MAID AT COWPAR OF FYFFE.

NUNTIUS.

RICHT famous Pepill, ye sall undirstand
   How that ane Prince, richt wyiss and vigilent,
Is schortly for to cum in to this Land;
   And purpossis to hald ane Parliament,
   His Thre Estaitis thairto hes done consent   5
In Cowpar Toun, in to thair best array
   With support of the Lord Omnipotent;
And thairto hes affixt ane certane day.

With help of Him, that rewlis all abone,
   That day sall be within ane litill space: 10
Our purpose is on the Sevint day of June,
   Gif weddir serve, and we haif rest and pece,
   We sall be sene in till our Playing place,
In gude array, abowt the hour of sevin.
   Off thristiness that day I pray yow ceiss,   15
Bot ordane us gude drink aganis ellevin.

Faill nocht to be upone the Castell-hill.
   Besyd the place quhair we purpoiss to play;

With gude stark wyne your flacconis see ye fill,
   And hald yourself the myreast that ye may.
   Be not displeisit, quhat evir we sing or say;
Amang sad mater howbeid we sumtyme relyie.
   We sall begin at sevin houris of the day: 5
So ye keip tryist, forsuth we sall nocht felyie.

COTTER.

I sall be thair, with Goddis grace,
Thocht thair war nevir so grit ane prese,
   And formest in the fair;
And drink ane quart in Cowpar toun,   10
With my gossep Johne Williamsoun,
   Thocht all the nolt sowld rair.

I haif ane quick divill to my Wyfe,
That haldis me evir in sturt and stryfe:
   That warlo, and scho wist   15
That I wald cum to this gud Toun,
Scho wald call me fals ladrone loun,
   And ding me in the dust.

We men that hes sic wickit wyvis,
In grit langour we leid our lyvis,   20
   Ay dreitland in diseiss.
Ye Preistis hes gret prerogatyvis,
That may depairt ay fra your wyvis,
   And cheiss thame that ye pleiss!

Wald God I had that liberty,   25
That I might pairt, as weill as ye,
   Without the Constry Law!
Nor I be stickit with a knyfe,

> For to wad ony uder wyfe
>   That day sould nevir daw.

NUNTIUS.

War thy wyfe deid I see thow wald be fane.

COTTER.

Yea, that I wald, sweit Sir, be Sanct Fillane.

NUNTIUS.

Wald thow nocht mary fra hand ane uder wyfe ?   5

COTTER.

Na, than the dum divill stik me with ane knyfe !
Quha evir did mary agane, the Feind mot fang thame
Bot, as the Preistis dois, ay stryk in amang thame.

NUNTIUS.

Than thow mon keip thy chestety, as effeiris.

COTTER.

I sall leif chest as Abbottis, Monkis, and Freiris.   10
Maister, quhairto sowld I my self miskary,
Quhair I, as Preistis, may swyve, and nevir mary ?
        [*Heir sall entir the Cotter's wyfe.*

WYFE.

Quhair hes thow bene, fals ladrone Loun ?
Dryttand, and drinkand, in the toun ?
Quha gaif thé leif to cum fra hame ?   15

COTTER.

Ye gaif me leif, fair lucky Dame.

THE AULD MAN AND HIS WIFE.

WYFE.

Quhy hes thow taryit heir sa lang?

COTTER.

I micht not thrist owtthrow the thrang,
Till that yone man the Play proclamit.

WYFE.

Trowis thow that day, fals Cairle defamit,
To gang to Cowpar to see the Play? 5

COTTER.

Yea, that I will, Dame, gif I may.

WYFE.

Na, I sall cum thairto sickerly;
And thow salt byd at hame, and keip the ky.

COTTER.

Fair lucky Dame, that war grit schame,
Gif I that day sowld byid at hame. 10
Byid ye at hame; for cum ye heir,
Ye will mak all the Toun asteir.
Quhen ye ar fow of barmy drink,
Besyd yow nane may stand for stink;
Thairfoir byid ye at hame that day, 15
That I may cum and see the Play.

WYFE.

Fals Cairle, be God! that sall thow nocht,
And all thy crackis sall be deir coft.
Swyth Cairle, speid thee hame speidaly

Incontinent, and milk the ky,
And muk the byre, or I cum hame.

COTTER.

All sall be done, fair lucky Dame.
I am sa dry, Dame, or I gae,
I mon ga drink ane penny or twae.   5

WYFE.

The divill a drew sall cum in thy throte,
Speid hame, or I sall paik thy cote
And to begin, fals Cairle, tak thair ane plate.

COTTER.

The Feind ressaif the handis that gaif me that!
I besoik yow, for Goddis saik, lucky Dame,   10
Ding me na mair this day, till I cum hame;
Than sall I put me evin in to your will.

WYFE.

Or evir I stynt, thow sall haif straikis thy fill.
    [*Heir sall the Wyfe ding the Carle, and he sall
      cry, Goddis mercy!*

COTTER.

Now wander and wa be to thame all thair lyvis,
The quhilk ar maryit with sic unhappy wyvis!   15

WYFE.

I ken foure wyvis, fals ladrone loun,

Baldar nor I, dwelland in Cowpar toun.

COTTER.

Gif thay be war, ga thow and thay togidder,
I pray God nor the Feind ressaif the fidder.

FYNDLAW of the Fute-Band.

Now mary! heir is ane fellone rowt!
Speik, Sirris, quhat gait may I get owt? 5
   I rew that I come heir.
My name, Sirris, wald ye undirstand,
Thay call me FINDLAW of the Fute-Band:
   A nobill man of weir.
Thair is na fyifty in this land 10
Bot I dar ding thame hand for hand;
   Se sic ane brand I beir.
Nocht lang sensyne, besyd ane syik,
Upoun the sunny syd of ane dyk,
   I slew with my richt hand 15
Ane thowsand, ye and ane thowsand to,
My fingaris yit are bludy, lo!
   And nane durst me ganestand.
Wit ye it dois me mekill ill,
That can nocht get fechting my fill, 20
   Noudir in peax, nor weir.
Will na man, for their ladyis saikis,
With me stryk twenty markit straikis,
   With halbert, swerd, or speir?
Quhen Inglismen come in to this Land, 25
Had I bene thair with my bricht brand,
   Withowttyn ony help,

Bot myne allane, on Pynky Craiggis,
I sowld haif revin thame all in raggis,
  And laid on skelp for skelp.
Sen nane will fecht, I think it best,
To ly doun heir and tak me rest: 5
  Than will I think nane ill.
I pray the grit God of his grace
To send us weir, and nevir peace,
  That I may fecht my fill.
                [*Heir sall he ly doun.*

THE FULE.

My Lord, be him that ware the croun of thone, 10
A mair cowart was nevir sen God was borne.
He lovis him self, and othir men he lakkis,
I ken him weill for all his boistis and crakkis.
Howbeid he now be lyk ane Captane cled,
At Pyncky Clewch he was the first that fled.   15
I tak on hand, or I steir of this steid,
This crakkand Cairle to flé with ane scheip-heid.
    [*Heir sall the Auld Man cum in leidand his
      wife in ane dance.*

AULD MAN.

Bessy, my hairt! I mon ly doun and sleip,
And in myne arme se quyetly thow creip.
 .   .   .   .

BESSY.

My gud Husband, ...   20
I pray God send yow grit honour and eiss.
    [*Heir sall he sleip, and scho sall sit besyd him.*

THE COURTEOUR.

Lusty Lady! I pray yow hairtfully,
Gif me licence to beir yow cumpany.
Ye se I am ane cumly Courteour,
Quhilk nevir yit did woman dishonour.

MERCHAND.

My fair Mistress! sweitar than the lammer,   5
Gif me licence to luge in to your chalmer,
I am the richest Merchand in this toun :
Ye sall of silk, haif kirtill, hude, and goun.

CLERK.

I yow beseik, my lustie Lady bricht,
To gif me leif to ly with yow all nicht.   10
And of your guoman lat me schut the lokkis,
And of fyne gold ye sall ressaif ane box.

FUILL.

Fair Damessell, how pleiss ye me ?
I haif na mair geir nor ye sie :
Swa lang as this may steir, or stand,   15
It sall be ay at your command :
Na, it is the best that ever ye saw.

BESSY.

Now welcome to me aboif thame aw !
. . . .
Bot se gif ye can mak remeid,
To steill the key fra undir his heid.   20

FUILL.

That sall I do, withowttin dowt,
Lat se gif I can get it owte.
Lo heir the key! do quhat ye will.

BESSY.

Na, than lat ws ga play our fill.
         [*Heir sall thay go to sum quyet place.*

FYNDLAW of the Fute-Band.

Will nane with me in France go to the weiris,   5
Quhair I am Captane of ane hundreth speiris?
I am sa hardy, sturdy, strang, and stowt,
That owt of hell the Divill I dar ding owt.

CLERK.

Gif thow be gude or evill, I can not tell,
Thay ar not sonsy that so dois ruse thame sell;   10
At Pyncky Clewch, I knew richt woundir weill,
Thow gat na creddence for to beir a creill;
Sen sic as thow began to brawll and boist,
The commoun weill of Scotland hes bene loist.
Thow cryis for weir, but I think peax war best: 15
I pray to God till send us peice and rest,
On that conditioun, that thow, and all thy fallowis,
War be the craiggis heich hangit on the gallowis.
Quha of this weir hes bene the foundament,
I pray to the grit God omnipotent,   20
That all the warld, and mae, mot on thame wounder,
Or ding thame deid with awfull fyre of thunder.

THE AULD MAN AND HIS WIFE.

FYNDLAW.

Domine Doctor, quhar will ye preiche to morne?
We will haif weir, and all the warld had sworne.
Want ye weir heir, I will ga pass in France,
Quhair I will get ane Lordly governance.

CLERK.

Sa quhat ye will, I think seuer peax is best, 5
Quha wald haif weir, God send thame littill rest!
Adew Crakkar, I will na langer tary!
I trest to see thee in ane firy-fary.
I trest to God to see thee, and thy fallowis,
Within few days hingand on Cowpar gallowis! 10

FYNDLAW.

Now art thow gane, the dum Divill be thy gyd?
Yone brybour was sa fleit, he durst not byid.
Be woundis and passionis had he spokkin mair ane word,
I sowld haif hackit his heid af with my swerd.
[*Heir sall the Gudman walkin, and cry for Bessy.*

AULD MAN.

My bony Bessy, quhair art thow now? 15
My Wyfe is fallin on sleip I trow;
Quhair art thow, Bessy, my awin sweit thing,
My hony, my hairt, my dayis darling?
Is thair na man that saw my Bess,
I trow scho be gane to the Mess. 20
Bessy, my hairt, heiris thow not me?
My joy, cry peip! quhair evir thow be.

. . . .

BESSY.

Quhat now, gudman? quhat wald ye haif?

AULD MAN.

No thing, my hairt, but yow I craif.
Ye haif bene doand sum bissy wark.

BESSY.

My hairt, evin sewand yow ane sark
Of Holland claith, baith quhyt and tewch.   5
Lat pruve gif it be wyid annewch.
    [*Heir sall scho put the sark over his heid, and
    the Fuill sall steill in the key agane.*

AULD MAN.

It is richt very weill, my hairt,
Oure Lady, lat us nevir depairt.
Ye ar the farest of all the flok,
Quhair is the key, Bess of my lok?   10

BESSY.

Ye reve, Gudman, be Goddis breid,
I saw yow lay it undir your heid.

AULD MAN.

Be my gude faith, Bess, that is trew.
That I suspectit yow, sair I rew.
I throw thair be no man in Fyffe,   15
That evir had sa gude ane wyfe.
My awin sweit hairt, I hald it best
That we sit down, and tak ws rest.

FYNDLAW.

Now is nocht this ane grit dispyte,
That nane with me will fecht nor flyte?
War Golias in to this steid,
I dowt nocht to stryk af his heid.
This is the swerd that slew Gray Steill,   5
Nocht half ane mile beyond Kynneill.
I was that nobill campioun,
That slew Schyr Bewas of Sowth-Hamtoun.
Hector of Troy, Gawyne, or Golias,
Had nevir half sa mekill hardiness.   10
    [*Heir sall the Fuill cum in with ane scheip-heid
        on ane staff, and Fyndlaw sall be fleit.*
Wow, now, braid Benedicite!
Quhat sicht is yone, Sirris, that I see.
In nomine Patris et Filii,
I trow yone be the Spreit of Gy.
Na, faith it is the Spreit of Marling,   15
Or sum Scho gaist or Gyrgarling.
Allace for evir! how sall I gyd me?
God, sen I had ane hoill till hyd me!
But dowt my deid yone man hes sworne,
I trow yone be grit Gow-mak-morne.   20
He gaippis, he glowris, howt welloway,
Tak all my geir, and lat me gay!
Quhat say ye, Sir, wald ye haif my swerd?
Ye mary sall ye, at the first word
My gluvis of plait, and knapskaw to;   25
Your pressonar I yeild me, lo.
Tak thair my purss, my belt, and knyfe,
For Goddis saike, Maister, save my lyfe.

Na, now he cumis for to sla me;
For Godis saik, Sirris, now keip him fra me;
I see nocht ellis bot tak and slae:
Now mak me rowme, and lat me gae.

NUNTIUS.

As for this day, I haif na mair to say yow: 5
On Witsone Tysday, cum see our Play I pray yow,
That samyne day is the Sevint day of June,
Thairfoir, get up right airly and disjune:
And ye Ladyis, that hes na skant of leddir,
Or ye cum thair, faill nocht to teme yowr bleddir.
I dreid, or we haif half done with our wark,
That sum of yow sall mak ane richt wait sark.

NOTES.

NOTES.

ANE DIALOG BETUIX EXPERIENCE AND ANE COURTEOUR.

BOOKS FIRST AND SECOND, Vol. 1., *page* 223.

"THIS historical work, as it is the largest, is certainly the last of the labours of Lyndsay. How long he was compiling *the Monarchie* it is impossible to tell, as he has left nothing which can enable us to judge of the quickness of his composition, or of the time that this poetical history required. He has, however, given us a chronological calculation, in his fourth book, which clearly evinces that the work was finished at the end of 1553. In his *Epistle Nuncupatorie*, the author tells his *lytil quair* to

Ga first till James, our prince and protectour,
And his brother our spiritual governour.

But James, Earl of Arran and Duke of Chatelherault, relinquished the regency of Scotland to the Queen-mother, on the 10th of April 1554, so that the work must have been finished before this great event took place by a formal act. The first edition of this elaborate work is said in the title-page to have been 'Imprintit at the command and expensis off Doctor Machabæus. In Capmanhouin. Quod Lyndsay, 1552.' This titlepage is universally acknowledged to have been feigned, for the purpose of deception. The author, we see, avowed himself, but the printer skulked behind a deceptious titlepage. Such was the shoal on which the printer was afraid to wreck his all. Yet is it apparent that this Dialogue of Lyndsay was not printed either at Copenhagen, or London, or at Rouen : but at St. Andrews, by Jhone Skott.

Mr CHALMERS, in another part of his edition, resumes the subject, and says.

"LYNDSAY, who seems to have exhausted all his merriment in the *Historie of Squyer Meldrum*, sat down to write his *Dialog of the miserabill Estait of this Warld*, in the vain hope of benefiting mankind by his labours. Musing on the misery which he saw daily increase on earth, notwithstanding his efforts of twenty years, he tried to divert himself and to instruct others by a Dialogue betweeen Experience and a Courtier, on the instability of states, and the sad changes of sublunary things. He had lived to see much of that instability within his own country, and he was in the frequent habit of giving vent to his feelings in order to make others feel.

"Warton regards *The Dreme* and *The Monarchie* as the principal of Lyndsay's preformances. In the Prologue to the *Dreme*, the critic sees in Lyndsay strong talents for high description and rich imagery. In his Prologue to the *Monarchie* our poet has, perhaps, outdone himself in a grand display of the higher qualities of his art; in elegant metaphors, artful fictions, mythological retrospections, and picturesque recitals. Nor ought we to be surprised at this exhibition of poetic talent, when we recollect that, after rejecting the *mischeant muses, beforetime used in poetrie*, he beseeched the great God himself to be his *heavenlie muse*. Yet, at this elevation, Lyndsay seems not to have delighted to remain for any length of continuance, out of his natural port of level thinking, and colloquial writing.

"After his brilliant prologue of seven-line stanzas, consisting of ten-syllable verse, he proceeds to his historical poem, which, like other *universal histories* at the revival of learning, begins with the creation of the world, and ends with the day of judgment. This poem is said by Warton to contain much learning, but when we advert to his facilities, from preceding writers in prose and rhyme, he can only be allowed to have made a great display, without much exertion of original thought, or literary retrospect. This Dialogue between Experience and a Courtier is the largest of Lyndsay's labours. This mode of conducting a narrative, by means of an imaginary mystagogue, was adopted from Boetius, says the learned historian of English Poetry. Our *Maker* now enters a park which was decorated well by dame Nature, where he saw the sun rise, and heard the birds sing, like other poets, who seem all to have taken their pleasure in such inspired inclosures, and where he was joined by Experience. They now ran over the story of the world together, making such remarks as occasion offered, or the purpose required. This history is written merely on the plan of the *old romances*, with a religious cast. At length Experience left the poet, and the dialogue ended as the evening approached.

> When Phœbus downwart dois descend
> Toward his palice in the occident.
> —CHALMERS.

THE EPISTIL TO THE REDAR.—So in the original editions by Scot, 1554, and by Jascuy, 1559. In the edition by Charteris 1568, and subsequent impressions, including that of Chalmers, the title is changed to:—THE EPISTILL NUNCUPATORIE OF SCHIR DAVID LYNDSAY OF THE MONT, KNIGHT, ON HIS DIALOG OF THE MISERABILL ESTAIT OF THE WARLD.

"The Epistill *Nuncupatorie* of Lyndsay may be considered as somewhat analogous to the *L'Envoy* of the ancient English Poetry: Yet, was this *Epistill* always printed, till the present edition, *before* the Monarchie, though certainly with no propriety, or usefulness. This *Epistill* was certainly written while the Regent Arran still governed Scotland, and during the year 1553."—CHALMERS.

The Epistill was no doubt written by Lyndsay after he had finished the Dialog, and Chalmers has so placed it, at the end, with the above note. I think it preferable, however, to allow it still to retain its original position.

Chalmers omits to notice that the Epistill is not given by Purfoote in any of his three English editions of Lyndsay, in the years 1566, 1575, and 1581.

Line 12.—*Our Quene.* Mary Stuart succeeded to the throne on the death of her father, King James the V., 14th December 1542. She was then an infant of only six days old. Unfortunately for herself and her country, she was sent for her education to France, setting out from Dunbarton in April 1548; and she remained in that country not only till her marriage with the Dauphin, 24th of April 1558, but until her return to Scotland, as a youthful widow, 20th of August 1561.

Line 26.—*James our Prince and Protectour.*

James, Earl of Arran, Lord Hamilton, was created in 1548. Duke of Chattelherault in France, and during the Queen's minority, as next heir to the crown, failing her issue, he was chosen Regent or Governor 20th of December 1542. After a period of eleven years, he was constrained to resign this high office, when the Queen Dowager, Mary of Guise, was proclaimed Regent of Scotland, on the 12th of April 1554. (*See* Knox's History, vol. i., p. 242, note.)

Line 27.—*And his Brother, our Spiritual Governour And Prince of Preistis in this Natioun.*

John Hamilton, Abbot of Paisley, was the natural brother of the Governor. He arrived from France on the 18th of April 1543. Some time after Cardinal Beaton's death in 1546, but before 1549, he was promoted to the See of St Andrews; which entitled him to be called "the Prince of Preistis."

Line 30.—*Under thare feit.* This address or profession of submission, *Be thay content, etc.*, sounds very strange coming from one like Lyndsay, who, by taking refuge in the Castle of St Andrews, when besieged by the said Governor, after the Cardinal's murder in 1547, seemed to have cast in his lot with Knox and the early Reformers.

Line 235.—*Malmontrye* for *Mammontry,* idolatry, in the earlier editions, was altered in 1582, and other copies to *Mahumetrie,* a reading adopted by Chalmers, without any reference to the older name.

In "the Gude and Godly Ballates" (p. 63, edit. 1868) is

a Carol or Song against Idolatrie, one verse of which explains this word.

> Quha dois adorne Idolatrie,
> Is contrair the Haly writ;
> For stock and staine is *Mammontrie*,
> Quhilk men may carue or quhite.

Line 538.—*Gentyll Redar.* "This apology for writing in the maternal language, was also made by Chaucer and Lydgate, by Gawyn Douglas, and Wedderburn, the author of the Complaynt of Scotland, 1549."—CHALMERS.

Lyndsay not only urges on Prelates the propriety of allowing the people to pray and read the Scriptures in a language they could understand, as necessary for salvation, but likewise, that for the benefit of the Commonwealth, the Laws of the kingdom should be made accessible in the vulgar tongue.

In the course of time, various changes in this respect took place in the proceedings of civil as well as ecclesiastical courts, registration of deeds, &c., by adopting the common vernacular language. One instance may be noticed. In the Register of Burgesses admitted in Edinburgh, commencing at the end of the fifteenth century, on the 15th of March 1560-61, it was ordered, "That all Actis, &c., in this Book be written and extracted in oure awin maternall toung."

Line 985.—*And maid thame breikis of levis grene,*
That thair secretis suld nocht be sene.

In the English reprints of Lyndsay *breikis* is changed to *breeches*; and this word occurs in all the editions of the Geneva translation of the Bible: In the first edition "Printed at Geneva by Rouland Hall, 1560," in Gen. iii. 7, we have, "And they sewed fig-tree leaves together, and made themselves *breeches*," with this marginal gloss:—"*Ebr.* Thinges girde about them to hide their privities."—We frequently hear of a copy of the *Breeches Bible*, as something of wonderful rarity and value, upon the supposition that the phrase was peculiar to one edition. The Genevan version in which it occurs was so often reprinted between the year 1560 and

1615, or even down to 1640, that it would be no easy matter to reckon them. Bassandyne's Bible at Edinburgh in 1576, and Hart's in 1610, have *breeches* as in the Genevan and English copies. In Coverdale's earlier version, 1537, &c., the word employed is *apurns*, being only a variety of spelling *aprons*, in our present authorized translation. In the earlier Wykliffe versions of the fourteenth century the words come nearer the German text, in these words :—"Thei soweden togidre leaves of a fige-tree, and maden hem breches;" or, in a similar version, "maden breches to hem self."

Line 1355.—*The Barne is till us borne.* This in the edition 1597, as Chalmers points out, *is to be borne*, referring to the words of Isaiah, ix. 4, predicting the birth of our Saviour.

Line 1628.—*Nemrod, that beildar was of Babylon* (or the Tower of Babel.) Lyndsay chiefly follows Orosius, who has confounded this Tower with the great city of Babylon erected at a later period. According to some old writers, including St Jerome, this Tower still formed the centre of the city, round which structure the temple of Belus was built. See note to line 2087.

Line 1967.— . . . . *that greit Citie*
The quhilk was callit Ninivie.
The founder of Nineveh, the capital of the Assyrian, the greatest empire in the world, is here assigned to Ninus; while Nimrod is called the founder of Babylon; Nimrod being the third, and Ninus the fifth in descent from Noah. See lines 1628, 1960, and 2087.

Line 1979.—*Ane Monarchie that men doth call*
Of quhome I find Four principal
Quhilk hes rung sen the Warld began.
Lyndsay in his account of the Four great Monarchies has not sufficiently distinguished the Babylonian or Chaldean from the Assyrian, which he reckons as the First; the Next, was the Medo-Persian; the Third, the Macedonian or

Grecian; and the Fourth, the Roman, which according to the Prophet Daniel's interpretation of Nebuchadnezzar's dream, should bruise every other kingdom to pieces; but which itself should afterwards be divided into ten lesser kingdoms.

Line 1980.—The five great ancient Monarchies were Chaldæa, Assyria, Babylonia, Media, and Persia. Of these empires, established from the remotest times in the valley of Tigris and Euphrates, a late writer says, it may be considered doubtful whether the banks of the Euphrates or the Nile was the earliest seat of civilization and royal power. (Philip Smith's Ancient History, vol. i., p. 188.) The four Monarchies, according to Lyndsay, as stated in the above note, were Assyria, Persia, Greece and Rome.

Lines 2000, 2087, &c.
The frequent references to Diodorus Siculus, afford sufficient proof that Lyndsay had studied this old historian with great care. He was, as his name indicates, a native of Sicily; and flourished during the times of Julius and Augustus Cesar. His "Historical Library," a kind of universal history, written in Greek, extended to forty books, in which he incorporated extracts from many older authors, whose works have perished. A portion of the existing fifteen books of the original Greek was first published at Basel in 1539. It is not likely that Lyndsay knew much if anything of Greek, but the work was accessible in a printed form to the Scottish poet in the Latin version by Poggio Bracciolini the Florentine.

Line 2280.—*Behald, in every kirk, and queir*
Throch Christendome, in high and low,
Imageis maid with mennis hand
To quhome bene gyffin divers names.

On these lines CHALMERS says, "Lyndsay here justifies, by his enumeration of Saints, the remark of Warton, that our old poets are never more happy than when they get into a catalogue of persons and things." In separate notes he gives explanations of the characteristic symbols attributed to the several Saints, mentioned in the lines that follow, on which it would be quite unnecessary to enlarge.

Line 2508.—*On thair Feist day* . . .
   Thay beir ane auld stock Imaye throuch the Toun.
Respecting the fate of this auld stock Image or wooden figure of St Giles, and the tumult that took place at the annual procession of priests through the Streets of Edinburgh on the saint's day, the 1st of September 1558, (of which Knox has given a very graphic and humourous description not unworthy of Sir David Lyndsay), see Knox's Works, vol. i., pp. 259, 558, and the preface to the Bannatyne Club volume, "Registrum Cartarum Ecclesiæ Sancti Ægidii de Edinburgh," &c. 1859, 4to.

Lines 2664, 2689. *Loreit, Lawreit.* The chapel of Loretto, near Musselburgh. See note, infra, p. 354.

"The chapel of *Lariet*, near Musselburgh; a great place of pilgrimage, where there lived a hermit, who pretended to work miracles, which roused the indignation of Lyndsay. To this shrine James V. made a pilgrimage, from Stirling in 1536, in order to procure a propitious passage to France in search of a wife. In 1543 the Earl of Hertford, during his destructive voyage to the Forth, destroyed with other objects of greater consequence, 'The chapel of the Lady of Lauret.'" (*Merlin's Life*, 1641, p. 313.)—CHALMERS.

Line 2937.—*The fair Maydin of France,*
   Danter of Inylis ordinance.
The fair maiden of France, the daunter of Englishmen, was the celebrated Joan of Arc, who, instigated by supposed visions, assumed, at the age of 27, the character of one inspired to deliver her country from the usurpations of the English. This was in the year 1425, and she especially distinguished herself at the siege of Orleans—hence her name. the Maid of Orleans. Her final condemnation to the stake, having been burned alive in the market-place of Rouen, reflects undying disgrace on the English monarch and his saintly advisers.

Line 3029.—*Ethesias he dois specifie*
The noumber of the great Armie,
Sayand, &c.

Such is the reading in all the editions of Lyndsay. Not finding the name of Ethesias in any work among the writers of antiquity, it occurred to me whether by mistaking the letter C for E the reference might not have been to the Greek historian Ctesias. Upon examination this conjecture proved to be well founded. Only portions of his great work have been preserved in the extracts given by Photius, Diodorus Siculus, Plutarch, and other ancient authors. Here again Lyndsay was indebted to the Latin version of Diodorus.

ANE DIALOG BETUIX EXPERIENCE AND
ANE COURTEOUR.

BOOKS THIRD AND FOURTH.

Vol. II. *pages* 1 *and* 57.

Line 3456.—*Bastailyeis.* "Strongholds. Several of the Border-strengths in Roxburgh and Berwickshire, were called *bastile*-houses."—CHALMERS.

In old English, "*Bastile*, a temporary wooden tower, used formerly in military and naval warfare. Sometimes the term is applied to any tower or fortification."—HALLIWELL.

Line 3477.—*The Dead Sea.* Lyndsay, in the lines that follow, quotes Orosius for its extent, as being 52 miles in length and 14 miles in breadth. The statements of early writers in such matters are seldom very exact. According to the latest and best authorities, the Dead Sea is about 39 or 40 geographical miles long from north to south, and 9 or 10 miles wide from east to west, surrounded with lofty ridges, varying on the different sides from 1500 to 2500 feet above the water.

Line 3613.—*Carioun at lenth.* "John Carion's Chronicle,

which, says Bayle, Carion did not write. Carion wrote a
Sketch, which was enlarged and improved by Melanchthon.
It was translated into English by Gwalter Lynne, and
printed at London 1550. Carion was born in 1499, and
died in 1538. Carion's Chronicle was the greatest of
authorities among the Reformers. It was translated into
many languages."—CHALMERS.

Line 4097.—Lyndsay has here quoted from Josephus the
number of Jews who were reckoned to have been slain or
taken prisoners at the destructive siege of Jerusalem. To
account for the vast number of persons within the walls of
the City at the time of the siege, the Jewish historian
explains that, during a cessation of hostilities, Eleazar, the
leader of one of the factions in Jerusalem, on the feast
of unleavened bread, opened the gates of the inmost
court of the Temple, and admitted into it such of the people
as were desirous to worship the Most High. (Josephus'
Wars of the Jews, v., iii. 1.) On such an announcement the
inhabitants from all parts of Judæa flocked to the city to
avail themselves of this unwonted spiritual privilege, and
were thus drawn like "sheep to the slaughter."

Line 4245.—In the earlier editions this title reads, *The
Fyft Spirituall Monarchie*, &c. In the London edit., 1566,
and subsequent copies, it is more correctly given. "The
First Spirituall and Papall Monarchie." The author himself
expressly limited his "Dialog" to the Four Great Monarchies:
The Assyrian, the Persian, the Greek, and the Roman
Empires. The Spiritual or Papal Monarchy, he here intro-
duces, as it were, incidentally.

Line 4424—*David of Scotland, Kyng*. Bellenden in his
translation of Hector Boyce's Chronicles of Scotland, B.xii.,
ca. 17, says "Kyng David biggit xv. Abbayis in Scotland,
quhais namis ar, &c. . . . Sindry prudent men nathing
apprisis the greit liberalitie of King David toward the
Kirk, for he dotat the Kirk sa richely with the landis
pertenand to the Croun that his successouris micht not

sustene thair Riall estait efter hym sa weil as thai did afore.
. . . . Thairfoir the wise prince, King James the first (quhen he cum to Davidis sepulture at Dunfermelyng) said, *He was ane soir Sanct for the Crown*, as he wald mene, that Kyng David left the Kirk ouir riche and the Crown ouir pure. For he tuke fra the Crown (as Maister Johne Mair writtis in his Cronikles) lx.M.li. [£60,000] Scottis," &c. Edinburgh c. 1540, fol. C. lxxxvi.).

In the Satyre of the Thrie Estatis, line 2976, the author also refers to the fifteen Abbacies which were founded by David the first, and says—

> King James the First, roy of this regioun,
> Said, that he was ane sair Sanct to the Croun:
> I heir men say, that he was sumthing blind
> That gaif away mair nor he left behind.

Line 4666.—*The pure Preist thynkis he get no rycht,*
Be he nocht styled like ane Knight,
And callit Schir afore his name,
As Schir Thomas and Schir Wilyame.

" Such (says Chalmers) was the practice in Chaucer's time; they were called the Pope's Knights." Dr Jamieson, in his Dictionary, has a long disquisition on this term. Knight or Cnecht was an Anglo-Saxon word for servant, but usually applied to military service, and it may have been given to Priests as the Pope's servants or soldiers, perhaps in derision. Until the Reformation *Dominus* or SIR was given to such of the inferior Clergy or Priests of the Church of Rome who had not studied, or at least obtained the degree of Master of Arts, in some University either at home or abroad. For instance, we always find ' Master (never Sir) Gawyn Douglas,' afterwards Bishop of Dunkeld; and ' Sir (never Master) John Knox,' the Reformer; owing to the fact that the one had taken his academical degree, the other not. In these cases Master invariably preceded the Christian name. Afterwards indeed ' Master Knox,' in a general sense, was occasionally used as a mark of respect, but always without the Christian name, in speaking of the Reformer.

Lines 5172.—Here and elsewhere in place of *Anti-Christ*, the editions of Jascuy and other early copies have *Ante-Christ*. The scribe or printer of these copies not marking the essential difference in the prefix *Anti*, from the Greek, *Against, In opposition to;* and *Ante*, from the Latin, *Before, Previous to*.

Lines 5295 to 5298,
  Of quhilkis ar by gone, sickirlye
  Fyue thousand, fyue hundreth, thre and fyftie ;
  And so remanis to cum but weir,
  Four hundreth with sewin and fourtye yeir.
Lyndsay's words, as above, in the earlier impressions, (including that of Charteris 1592,) evidently refer his calcultions as dating from the Creation. The World, according to Carion's explanation, shall continue 6000 years, of which 2000 were from the Creation of Adam to Abraham; 2000 to Christ's Incarnation; and 2000 should therefore be to the World's end. Five thousand therefore is a correct enough reading. But CHALMERS says, "By a strange blunder, every edition before that of 1597 has put *fyve*, for *ane* : The context shows, that Lyndsay was calculating the *by-gone* years ; in order to ascertain the years to come : And it thus appear, that Lyndsay was writing this *Fourt buik* in 1553, though the Printer has put 1552, in the Colophon."

Whether we read *ane* or *five*, this cannot be said to change the matter, except as regards the point from which the calculation of "the by-gone years" was made. Lyndsay's calculation was evidently from the date of the Creation, not from the Birth of Christ, or after the lapse of the first four thousand years.

This, however, is a passage with which subsequent printers thought they might use their own discretion in altering. In Purfoote's editions 1566, 1575, and 1581, these lines read,—
  Of which are passed, so may I thriue,
  A thousande fyue hundred sixty fyue :
  And so remaines, as doth appear
  Foure hundred fyue and thirty yeare.

In the editions 1614, &c., we have :
>Of which are bygone sickerlie,
>A thousand five hundreth three and fiftie ;
>And so remaines to come but weere,
>Foure hundreth seven and fourty yeir.

In still later editions, 1634, &c., we have this variation:
>Of which are by-gone, as I weene
>A thousand, sixe hundreth ten and thirteene ;
>And so remaines to come, but were,
>Three hundreth, threescore and eighteene yere.

Line 5417.—*I saw Pape Julius manfully*
>*Pass to the feild triumphantly*
>*With ane richt awful ordinance,*
>*Contrair Louis the King of France.*

"Julius II., who took the field in person, in 1510, against Louis XII., died 21st February 1513-14 : Louis died in 1515."—CHALMERS.

From these lines some writers have inferred that Lyndsay had served a campaign in Italy in 1510, but this seems to be not in the least probable. See Memoir.

Pope Julius II. was elected on the 1st November 1503, and crowned the 19th of that month. He died in February 1513.

Line 5703—*Be gret gyrsome, and dowbyll maill.* In edit. 1582 so *gersome,* the same as Grassum, or the sum paid to a landlord by a tenant on entering upon the lease of a farm, with double maill or rent.

Line 5840.—*Of rank wytcheis.* I don't know where Lyndsay may have found the name of the Witch of Endor ; or why he should have fixed upon Atholl, Argyle, and part of Galloway, along with Savoy, as peculiarly the abodes of witches.

Line 6325—*And sped me home, &c.* In the next line the later editions have Oritoir, Oritore. As the English editions vary in several words; the concluding stanza, as a specimen of the liberty used in altering the text, may be quoted literally from that of 1566—

And hyed me home with hart right sorye :
And entred my quiet Oratorye :
I toke paper and their began to write
This misery, that ye haue hearde before.
All gentell Readers hartely I implore,
For to excuse this that I did indite ;
Though Ipocrites will haue at me dispite
Which would not their craftines were scande
Let God be Judge, and so I make an ende.

ANE SATYRE OF THE THRIE ESTAITIS.

Vol. II. *page* 107.

So far as can be discovered, Lyndsay's Satyre, or Play, exists only in two forms : the one, in the Manuscript collections of George Bannatyne, written in the year 1568 ; the other, in the old printed edition, at Edinburgh, by Robert Charteris, 1602. In the former, the Play is subdivided into a series of eight Interludes, by omitting large portions, or, to use the transcriber's own words, "levand the grave matter thareof, becaus the samyne abuse is weill reformit in Scotland, praysit be God." The text of the printed edition was adopted by Chalmers ; and, indeed, there could be no alternative, in order to exhibit the progress of the Play in its regular course. Pinkerton, in his " Scotish Poems, reprinted from Scarce Editions," had previously given these Interludes from an inaccurate transcript of Bannatyne's MS.; but before his collection was published in 1792, he obtained the use of a printed copy and subjoined a large number of additional passages, rendering the whole a strange piece of patchwork. Sibbald, in his " Chronicle of Scottish Poetry,

1802," also included most of these Interludes, and at the same time printed a limited impression of the Satyre in a separate form, ostensibly from Bannatyne's MS., but interpolating large portions from the old printed text, and altering or attempting to disguise the coarse, objectionable words and phrases which unfortunately disfigure this most remarkable production.

Chalmers is very severe on these editions by Pinkerton and Sibbald. He himself adhered slavishly to the old printed copy, and makes no use of the earlier text of Bannatyne's MS., which commences with the preliminary Interlude of "THE AULD MAN AND HIS WYF." This is not contained in the edition of 1602, and it was rejected by Chalmers as spurious, not on account of its indelicacy, but upon very inconclusive reasoning, "that the play had been acted many years before this Interlude was written, by whatever hand." (Works, vol. i., p. 65.) This Interlude no doubt contains allusions to events in the year 1547; but Mr. Chalmers might have remembered that as the Play was represented on different occasions, the Interludes were varied, and other changes made, which now we have no means of ascertaining; while the coarse broad humour which this Interlude exhibits, affords but too unequivocal marks of Lyndsay's hand, to leave any doubt in regards to its authorship.

I thought it preferable, however, with some omissions in the present edition, to subjoin this Interlude as an Appendix to this volume, distinct by itself, rather than attempt to connect it with the Play.

Chalmers asserts in the most positive terms the existence of two editions of the Play printed by R. Charteris, in 1602 and 1604. The original title is as follows: "ANE SATYRE of the Thrie Estaits, in commendation of vertew and vituperation of vyce; Maid be Sir Dauid Lindesay of the Mont, alias, Lyon King of Armes. At Edinburgh Printed be Robert Charteris, 1602. Cvm privilegio regis." After a careful examination and comparison of all the accessible copies I have come to a different conclusion. In particular, I

have compared the identical copies which he mentions, that of 1602, which was in his own collection, and the other called 1604, which belonged to Mr. Caley. Both these are now in the Library at Britwell House. The second copy wants the title, in place of which it has a detached title-page, intended for a re-issue of Lyndsay's Works in 1604. But both copies of the Play have the same colophon, dated 1602, as follows:—
"Printed at Edinburgh be Robert Charteris. An. Do. MDCII. And are to be sauld in his Buith on the North-side of the Gait, at the Westside of the auld Prouosts Closhead."

It is indeed not a matter of any great importance to settle this point; but as Chalmers is so dogmatic, I endeavoured, by careful examination, to ascertain the fact that only one edition actually exists.

In all the copies I have examined, the last leaf has the same colophon dated 1602. Why should this date have been retained, if reprinted in 1604?

Mr CHALMERS, in his remarks, "On the Chronology of Lyndsay's Poems," says, in regard to "The Play, or SATYRE ON THE THREE ESTATES:"

"This remarkable Drama of a rude age was undoubtedly presented at Epiphany 1539-40, before the King and Queen, the court, and country, on the Playfield, near Linlithgow. It must necessarily have been written some years before. The King is everywhere spoken of as still unmarried; but he changed his unmarried state in 1537, so that this Play must have been written before that year both of joy and of sorrow. Among the many fools whom Lyndsay satirizes, he ranks the insatiable merchantmen:

> Quhen God has sent them abundance
> Ar nocht content with sufficiance;
> Bot, sailis into the stormy blastis
> In *Winter*, to get greater castis
> In mony terribill great torment
> *Against the Acts of Parliament.*

"The Satirist alludes both generally and specially to the

noble acts of Parliament; to the acts honorabill made by
our Prince in *the last* parliament because they are baith
gude and profitabill. The whole context of this singular
Drama evinces, then, that it was originally written, or at
least finished, in 1535. It was first acted on the Playfield
at Coupar in Fife during the year 1535; and indeed much
of the scene is laid in Fife, where several men and things
are mentioned which must have been very familiar to the
people of that shire. It was acted at Linlithgow by the
express command of the King, on the day of Epiphany
1539-40. And it was a third time presented *beside* Edinburgh in presence of the Queen regent, a great part of the
nobility, and an exceeding great number of people, 'fra ix
hours afore none till vi hours at even;' as we learn from
Henry Charteris, the bookseller, who was present, no doubt.
It is to be remarked, however, that the *Satyre on the three
Estatis*, like *the Rehearsal*, when acted by Garrick and Cibber,
admitted of recent retrospection and temporary allusions.
An accurate eye, adverting to the dates, may trace Lyndsay's
interpolations for the purpose of alluding to late events, in
order to *elevate and surprise* the unpractised auditors."

 In reference to this statement I would simply remark, that
no evidence can be produced to show that the Play, as
Chalmers asserts, was first represented at Cupar in Fife in
1535; and that any supposed allusions to the personal character of James the Fifth in the play, are equally unwarranted
or inconclusive. Besides this, on the allusions which Chalmers
says "must have been very familiar to the people of that
shire," surely it might have occurred to him that such allusions would not be so familiar when the play was represented
either at Linlithgow or Edinburgh.

 The Interludes in Bannatyne's MS. begin on folio 164,
and end on folio 210. In printing these from the MS.,
Pinkerton says, "The preceding pages were printed before
any copy of David Lyndsay's Satyre, or Play, came to the
hands of the Editor, that piece being extremely scarce.
Having at length been so fortunate as to procure the loan

of the edition printed at Edinburgh in 1602, 4to, the following variations have appeared between the Play and the Interludes here published:

"The Play presents one continued succession of action, undivided into Interludes. The order is also different, as will appear by the following statement, comparing these Interludes with the printed text of the Play."

In copying portions of Pinkerton's statement, special references to the pages of the MS. are made, as well as to the lines in the present edition.

Interlude I. THE AULD MAN AND HIS WIFE is wanting in the printed copy of 1602; but from the Prologue it palpably formed part of the Play on the occasion of its representation at Cupar in Fife.—See pp. 315-328 in this volume.

After the Proclamation and this first Interlude (fol. 168) is written, "Heir begynnis Schir Dauid Lyndsay [is] Play maid in the Grenesyd besyd Edinburgh, quhilk I [haif] writtin bot schortly be Interludis, levand the grave mater 'thereof becaws the samyne abuse is weill reformit in Scotland, praysit be God; quhairthrow I omittit that principal mater, and writtin only sertane mirry Interludis thairof, verry plesand, begynning at the first part of the Play."

In another part (fol. 177) he writes, "Here followis certane mirry and sportsum Interludis, contenit in the Play maid be Schir Dauid Lyndsay of the Month, knycht, in the Playfeild of Edinbur^t, to the mocking of abusionis usit in the cuntré be deverse sortis of Estait." And, at the beginning of another Interlude (fol. 196^b.), "I tak heir bot certane schort pairtis out of the speichis, becauss of lang proces of the Play."

Interlude II. HUMANITIE AND SENSUALITIE begins the Play (Edit. 1602, pp. 1-20), vol. ii., Pages 113-136, and concluding with the SOUTAR AND HIS WIFE, Pages 168-174.

MS. fol. 168.

NOTES. 349

Interlude III. THE PUIR MAN AND THE PARDONER. This begins the second part of the Play (Edit. 1602, pp. 64-80). Pages 197-214.
MS. fol. 177.

Interlude IV. THE SERMON OF FOLLY. This concludes the Play (Edit. 1602, pp. 144-155). Pages 299-312.
MS. fol. 182.

Interlude V. FLATTERY, DECEIT, AND FALSEHOOD MISLEAD KING HUMANITY (Edit. 1602, pp. 20-38). Pages 136-152.
MS. fol. 187.

Interlude VI. THE THREE VICES OVERCOME TRUTH AND CHASTITY (Edit. 1602, pp. 39-63), Pages 152, &c.
MS. fol. 192.

Interlude VII. THE PARLIAMENT OF CORRECTION (Edit. 1602, pp. 80-109), (but numerous passages omitted). Pages 215-254.
MS. fol. 195.

Interlude VIII. THE PUNISHMENT OF THE VICES (Edit. 1602, pp. 109-145), (with still larger omissions). Pages 255, &c.
MS. fol. 203.

"Heir endis the schort Interludis of Sr Dauid Lyndsayis Play, maid in the Grenesyd besyd Edinbur^t, in anno 155[4] zeiris." MS. fol. 210.

Page 119, line 5.—*The Bowis.* This may have been a local allusion to the Nether-bow, and to the Upper or West-bow of Edinburgh.

Page 122, line 18.—*The Monks of Bamirrinoch.* "Balmirinoch, a well-known monastery in Fife, whence the Elphinstons in 1604 derived an unfortunate title. The satire is sly and severe."—CHALMERS.

Page 122, line 26.—*The buik sayis, Ommia probate.* This i

rather a perversion of the Scripture injunction, "Prove all things: hold fast that which is good." (Omnia autem probate: quod bonum est tenete.) 1 Thessal. v. 21.

Page 133, lines 21 and 22, are evidently the words of Hameliness, although not so marked either in the old printed copy or in Chalmers.

Page 135, line 17.—*That garris, &c.* "That makes our guiders, or rulers, all want *grace*, the effect of God's influence." *Die befoir thair day:* "The allusion to the Scotish kings, who mostly all died prematurely."—CHALMERS.

Page 143, line 4, and p. 304, line 1.—*Tullilum.* The third order of the Carmelites or Begging Friars of the order of the Blessed Mary of Mount Carmel. They obtained the name of White Friars from the colour of their outward garment. Their convent of Tullilum, situated a little to the west of the city of Perth, was founded in the reign of Alexander III. in the year 1262. Upon the dissolution of Religious houses, at the period of the Reformation, the lands and rents of this convent, instead of being granted to some courtier or neighbouring proprietor, were fortunately annexed to the Hospital of king James VI. at Perth. Some of the Charters of Tullilum are printed in a volume called "The Book of Perth, by John Parker Lawson," Edinb. 1847, 8vo.

Page 147, line 10.—"*Now the Vycis cumis:* These are the *old vice,*" mentioned in the *What you Will* of Shakespeare. The vice was *the fool* of the old *Moralities*, saith Johnson, who holds that *Punch* is the legitimate successor of *the old vice,* But the *vycis* of Lyndsay's *Satyre* were more *knaves* than *fools.* This character was always acted in a *mask,* and probably had its name, saith Steevens, from the old French word *vis,* for which they now use *visage.*"—CHALMERS.

Page 148, line 6.—This line, omitted in the old printed text, is supplied from Bannatyne's MS. It is not noticed by Chalmers.

Page 151, line 4.—*And all Christendome.* "We have here a sequence of witticisms, consisting of alliterations and comparisons of small things with great: Danskin with Denmark: Spittefeild with Spaine; Renfrew, a small shire, with the realm of France; Ruglan, a little town in Lanarkshire, with Rome; Corstorphine, a small parish with Christendome."— CHALMERS.

Page 155, line 5, to p. 156, line 5.—*And mak betwix us sikker bands.* "It is curious to remark that almost the whole of this *counsel* of the *Vyces*, with a slight variation or two, is copied from Lyndsay's *Complaynt.*"—CHALMERS. See vol. i. lines 187-214.

Page 162, line 2.—*This is the New Testament, in English toung, and printit in England.* This of course refers to Tyndale's translation. It was first printed abroad in 1525, but all the attempts to suppress it only encouraged the appearance of numerous impressions, which found their way into this country, and were extensively circulated before Henry the Eighth granted premission to have copies printed in England in the year 1537.

Page 168, line 1, &c.—The old printed text affords no authority for giving what follows, on the line 1411, as a separate INTERLUDE. But the emendation was required, as this interlude interrupts the progress of the Play—and it was evidently intended to amuse the lower classes of the auditors.

Page 200, line 3.—*At Session, na Senzie.* "The present Court of Session, was established, in May 1532. The word *senzie* is supposed to mean the *assizes*, MS. Glos. It is, however, certain, that it meant the *consistory;* the purpose of the poet being to satirize both the civil and the ecclesiastical courts.—CHALMERS.

Page 200, line 16.—*The town of Air.* "The town of Air, is here brought in merely for the rhyme. The poor man lived at Tranent, a place of ancient colliery; and to carry coals to Edinburgh, on his mare, was a natural circumstance; but the town of Air had no connection with the man and his mare. What a *quibble* was to Shakespeare, according to Johnson, a *rhyme* was to Lyndsay, the fatal Cleopatra, for whom he lost the world, and was content to lose it. Yet is the story well, and ably, and artfully told."—CHALMERS.

Page 215, line 1.—This title is not found in the old printed copies, and has been supplied.

Page 257, line 7.—*Micht I him get to Ewis-durris.* "Ewis-doors is the name of a narrow pass between Teviotdale and Ewesdale. The river Ewes, a small and very clear stream, runs a short course between two ranges of green hills, and falls into the Esk at Langholm. An alarming account of this defile may be found in Thoresby's diary, vol. i., p. 105, Lond. 1830, 2 vols, 8vo."—IRVING's Hist. of Scotish Poetry p. 379, note.

Page 257, line 12.—*Throuch Dysert Mure.* "The Moor of Dysert, a town in Fyfe, between the Earl of Rothes' house and the ferry at Kinghorn."—CHALMERS.

Page 257, line 19.—*The Water of Annet.* "Annet (says Chalmers) for the rhyme: the Water of Annan, Dumfriesshire." This is not a satisfactory explanation, if we think how far Common Thift after crossing the Forth would have to ride had he stolen Lord Lyndsay's horse. The river of Annan falls into the Solway Firth seventy-mine miles from Edinburgh. It is much more likely that Lyndsay referred to the stream or rivulet named Annat, or Cambus, which flows into the Forth nearly a mile above the town of Doune, and which takes its rise in the mountianous district of Perthshire. This, at least, was not half the distance of the other, and the horse-stealer might reckon himself as safe from pursuit in that quarter as in the borders of England.

Page 271, lines 10-12, and 16, 17.—These lines are repeated by Lyndsay in his "Dialog on the Monarchie."—See vol. ii., p. 41, lines 4527-4529, and 4548, 4549.

Page 281, line 14.—*It is devysit*, &c. "In those times, and long before, there was a practise of passing an act of Parliament during every session, at least, at the commencement of every reign, providing that 'The freedome of Halie Kirk suld be keeped.'—Skene."—CHALMERS.

Page 283, line 12.—*Of the maist cunning Clarks of this regioun.* "In May 1532 there was erected by Parliament 'a College of cunning and wyse men, baith of Spiritual and Temporal Estate, for doing of justice in all civile actionis,' and this was followed by a whole code, for the better regulations of this College of Justice.—See the Black Acts."—CHALMERS.

This collection of Acts of Parliament, printed *in black letter* at Edinburgh, 1566, has long been known technically as "*The Black Acts,*" to distinguish it, perhaps, from Skene's volume, printed in a different type, in 1597.

Page 289, line 22.—*To tell your namis.* "Those are the names of most of the west Border families of that age. In the Paper Office, there is a letter from Thomas Musgrave to Lord Burleigh, in 1583; giving that intelligent statesman a very minute account of the several rivers and dales on that Border, with the several families living on them, together with their marriages and alliances. The Nixons, the Rutledges, the Taylors, the Graymes, the Battesons, the Elliotts, the Armstrongs, the Irwyns, the Forsters, the Nobles, the Pandours, the Bells, are very numerous. Some of those who are mentioned by Lindsay, though not in Lord Burleigh's letter, may have been persons that were more noted for their robberies than known for their connections."— CHALMERS.

Page 299, line 7.—*Gang serve the Hermeit of Laureit.* "The hermit at the chapel of Loretto, at the east end of the town of Musselburgh, which was a famous place of pilgrimage in the time of Lyndsay, who cries out against it in his Exclamation against Idolatry, in the *Monarchie:*—

   And specially, that hermeit of Laureit,
   He pat the commoun pepel in beleif,
That blynd gat sicht, and crukit gat their feit,
   The quhilk the palzeard na way can appreif." – CHALMERS.

In "The late Expedicioun in Scotlande," under the Earl of Hertford, in May 1544, among the places "brunte and desolated by the Kinges army," we find "parte of Muskelborowe towne, with *the chapel of our Ladye of Lauret.*"

Page 308, line 16.—*Bot sailis . . . in Winter.* "In 1535, passed an act 'that na man sail into Flanders, bot twise in the yeir,' 4 Ja. V., c. 31. In the same session it was also enacted 'that na schip saill with staple gudes, fra Simon's day and Jude's, quhill Candlemes.' 4 Ja. V., c. 25. Such were the *actis* to which Lyndsay alluded."—CHALMERS

Page 313, line 1.—*Famous Pepill, &c.* "The conclusion of *Candlemas-day.* Similar conclusions, however, are not uncommon. The old mystery which is distinctly known in the drama of England, is so like that of the 'Satyre of the Three Estates,' that we might suppose that Lyndsay had seen it, though it is not easy to tell where."—CHALMERS.

The old Mystery alluded to, entitled "Candlemas Day, or the Killing of the Children of Israel," was written A.D. 1512, and is preserved in a MS. vol. in the Bodleian Library (Ken. Digby's MSS. No. 133.) with thys note, "Ihan Parfre did write thys booke." It seems to have been first printed by Hawkins, in his Origin of the English Drama, vol. 1. 1773.

GLOSSARY.

A, *a frequent prefix to many words, which are common to the Scottish and the Old English.*
Abak, *back, backward, behind.*
Abais, *to abash, to confound.*
Abayis, *abbeys.*
Abandoun, *at random, at liberty.*
Abesses, *abbacies.*
Abill, abyll, *proficient, fit.*
Abone, *above.*
Abouten, *about.*
Abrade, brade, *to issue, to spread abroad: also to press, drive, or force.*
Abufe, *above.*
Abuilze, *to dress, equip.*
Abuilzement, *dress, clothing, harness.*
Abusioun, *abuse.*
Address, *to prepare, to array, to set about.*
Adjutory, *helper.*
Adoun, *down, downward.*
Adrad, adred, *in dread, afraid.*
Afeir, *fear.*
Aff, *off, out of, from.*
Affamysit, *famished.*
Afferis, *affairs.*
Afferis, *belongs.*
Affeiritlye, *affrightedly.*
Afferand, *proportioned.*
Affye, *to confide, to rely, to trust: also, to promise, to engage.*
Afore, *formerly.*
Affore, *before.*
Aforenens, *opposite to.*
Afforrow, *before.*
Affraye, *fear.*
Affraytlye, *affrightedly.*
Agane, *against.*
Agit, *aged.*
Agone, *ago, gone.*
Aggrege, *to aggravate.*
Aggrise, *to affright; also to attack.*
Ah, *but; and so.*
Ahint, *behind.*
Aige, *age.*
Aik, ake, *oak.*
Aill, *ale.*
Ain, awin, *own.*
Air, *oar.*
Air, *heir.*
Air, *assize.*

Air, *early*,
Airtis, *direction, points of the compass.*
Aisay, *easy.*
Aisement, *accommodation, convenience.*
Ait, *oat, oaten.*
Aith, *oath.*
Alb, *a long white vestment or surplice worn by the priest at mass.*
Ald, auld, *old.*
Alege, *to relieve, to absolve from allegiance,*
Algate, *always.*
Alite, alyte, *a little.*
Alkin, *all kind of.*
All-Hallows, *All-Saints day.*
All-Hallow-mass, *the feast of All-Saints, first of November.*
Allace, *alas.*
Allanerlie, *only, solely.*
Allowe, *to applaud, to approve.*
Alluterlie, *entirely, wholly.*
Almaist, *almost.*
Almarie, aumrie, ambry, *cupboard.*
Almes, *charity, alms.*
Als, *as.*
Als, *also.*
Alswyth, *instantly.*
Alycht, *enlighten.*
Alykewyis, *likewise.*
Alyte, *a little.*
Amangis, *amongst.*
Amesit, *satisfied.*
Amiabyll, *lovely.*

Amid, amyd, *amidst.*
Amland, *ambling.*
Amangis, *among.*
Amorettis, *love-knots, favours.*
Amove, *to move.*
Amyral, *admiral.*
An, *one.*
And, *if.*
Ane, *a, an.*
Ane, *one.*
Anent, *opposite.*
Aneuch, *enough.*
Anew, *enough.*
Anis, *once.*
Anker, *a hermit, an anchorite.*
Anone, anon, *presently.*
Anoye, *annoyance.*
Ansenze, *sign.*
A per se, *an incomparable person, a nonsuch.*
Apert, *brisk, free, open.*
Appardoun, *pardon.*
Appeisit, *appeased.*
Appleisit, *satisfied.*
Applyable, *docile,*
Appoventybll, *terrible.*
Aragne, *a spider.*
Arblaster, *a crossbow.*
Arc, ark, *a chest.*
Areik, *to reach, to reach to.*
Argh, airgh, *tardy, slow, indolent.*
Arkis, *arches.*
Arles, arles-penny, *earned, earnest-money given on making a bargain.*
Armeit, *hermit.*
Armonye, *harmony.*

GLOSSARY.

Armyne, *the fur of the ermine.*
Arreir, areir, *backward.*
Artailye, *weapons of war.*
Artalyeit, *armed.*
Arthetica, *gout.*
As, *if, than.*
As, ase, *ashes.*
Ascens, *ascent.*
Aschamit, *ashamed.*
Ask, *a water-newt, a small animal of the lizard kind.*
Askar, *at a distance.*
Aspye, *to lie in wait for, to watch in ambush.*
Ass, *ashes.*
Assaill, *attest.*
Assailze, *an assault.*
Assaut, *an assault.*
Assay, *to essay, to try.*
Assaye, *attack, onset.*
Assege, *besiege.*
Asseisit, *fixed.*
Assoilze, assoilye, *to absolve, to acquit.*
Assoinze, *an excuse, an exemption: also, to excuse.*
Assyth, *satisfaction.*
Astound, *astonished, confounded.*
Astrologis, *astrologers.*
At, *that.*
At anis, *at once.*
Ather, *each.*
Atonis, *at once.*
Attentike, *authentic.*
Attir, *purulent matter.*
Attircop, *a spider, a poisonous insect.*

Atwene, atween, *between.*
Atwix, *betwixt.*
Aucht, *property, possession.*
Aucht, auchtin, *eight, eighth.*
Auchtsum, *eightsome, consisting of eight.*
Auctorite, awtoritie, *authority.*
Auctour, *author.*
Aughtest, *shouldst.*
Auld, *old, ancient.*
Aulter, *altar.*
Auncetours, *ancestors.*
Aunter, *adventure.*
Aureate, *golden, polished.*
Avenand, *affable, comely, elegant.*
Aventure, *adventure, accident, chance.*
Aver, *a sorry horse, a workhorse.*
Avise, avyse, *advice.*
Avouterie, *adultery.*
Awalk, *to awake.*
Awe, *to owe.*
Awin, *own.*
Awsterne, *austere.*
Ay, *even.*
Aye, *at the time.*
Aye, *yes.*
Ayenst, *against.*

B

Babee, bawbee, *a halfpenny.*
Babil-bearers, *tale-bearers.*
Babbis, babis, *babes, young children.*
Bachileris, *bachelors.*

GLOSSARY.

Bad, bade, *desired, offered.*
Bad-ling, *of a bad nature, a bad person.*
Bade, *stayed, did abide.*
Bailfull, *miserable, woful, sorrowful.*
Baill, *sorrow.*
Baillis, *flames.*
Bailzies, *magistrates of burghs next in rank to the provost.*
Bair, *naked.*
Bair, *pierced.*
Bair, *to bear, to bring forth.*
Baird, *to adorn with trappings.*
Bairn-teame, *progeny, offspring.*
Bairnis, barnis, *children.*
Bais, *bass.*
Bait, *beat.*
Bait, bate, *boat.*
Baith, *both.*
Baittand, *feeding.*
Bak, *bat.*
Bald, bauld, *bold.*
Baldar, *more furious.*
Balengar, *a kind of small sloop or barge.*
Balme, *oil of consecration.*
Ban, *to curse.*
Band, *a bond, engagement.*
Band, *did bind.*
Bandis, *bonds, engagements.*
Banesis, *banishes.*
Baneist, baneiss, *banished.*
Banis, *bones.*
Banrent, baneret, *a knight made in the field.*

Bar, *shut, faster.*
Barbour, *barbarous.*
Bardyng, *trapping.*
Bare, *a boar.*
Barfit, *barefooted.*
Bargane, *wrangling, contention, skirmishing.*
Barganer, *wrangler, quarreller.*
Barm, *yeast.*
Barn, *child.*
Barnis, *children.*
Barratt, *trouble, distress.*
Barres, *fences.*
Barrow-trammis, *the poles, or shafts of a barrow.*
Bassenet, *helmet, head-piece.*
Bastailyeis, *fortresses.*
Baston, *a staff, a cudgel, a baton.*
Bate, bait, *did bite.*
Batye, *invigorating, generous.*
Bawburd, *whore.*
Bawburdie, *whoredom.*
Bawtie, *a familiar appellation for a dog.*
Baxter, *a baker.*
Be, *by.*
Be, *before.*
Be I, *if I be.*
Becht, *tied, bound.*
Beckis, *bows.*
Become, *happened.*
Bedelve, *to delve, to dig, to bury.*
Bedene, bedeen, *immediately, directly, forthwith, outright.*
Beft, *beat, beaten.*
Begaird, *variegated.*

GLOSSARY.

Begairit, *besmeared.*
Begane, begone, *overgone, overwhelmed.*
Begarie, *besmear.*
Beggartie, *state of beggary.*
Beggis, *bugs.*
Begouth, *began.*
Behald, *behold.*
Behecht, *promised.*
Behest, behete, *a promise, a vow.*
Behuffit, *behoved.*
Beid, *a prayer.*
Beild, *resource.*
Beild, *built.*
Beir, *vaunt.*
Beir, *indure.*
Beir, beiris, *bear, bears.*
Beiris, *a rattling noise, commotion.*
Beir, *barley.*
Beis, *bees.*
Beis, *is, is to be.*
Beisy, *busy.*
Bek, *nod.*
Beke, beik, *to bask, to warm.*
Bell, *to fight, to contend.*
Bell, book, and candle (to curse by) *was the old form of excommunication.*
Bellical, *warlike.*
Bellie-blind, *a person blindfolded, for the purpose of playing at a sport called* bellie-blind.
Beltit, *belted, beaten.*
Belyve, belive, *quickly, instantly.*

Ben, *along.*
Bend, *bow.*
Bend, *a bound, spring, leap.*
Bene, (auxil. v.) *am, is, are, be.*
Bene, *happy.*
Benefites, *benefices.*
Bening, *benign, gracious, favourable.*
Benk, *a bench, a seat.*
Bennison, benesoun, *a blessing, benediction.*
Bent, *fields.*
Beriall, *gem, sparkling.*
Berne, *fellow.*
Beseik, *beseech.*
Besene, *appearance.*
Besprenge, *to sprinkle.*
Bested, bestade, *circumstanced.*
Bestial, *beasts, cattle.*
Besy, besyn, *busy, employed; also, to busy.*
Besynes *business.*
Bet, bett, *better.*
Betaucht, *recommended, committed.*
Betrais, *betray.*
Betwix, *betwixt, between.*
Bewis, *boughs.*
Bid, *to ask, to request, to invite: also, to order, to command, to offer.*
Biddin, *remained.*
Big, bigg, *to build.*
Biggyngis, *buildings.*
Bikker, *a fight, a skirmish.*
Bin, *am, is, are.*
Bir, *a whizzing, or rattling noise.*

Bird, *a young girl, a wench.*
Birnyng, *burning.*
Birneist, *polished.*
Birst, *burst.*
Bismair, *a term of reproach to any worthless woman.*
Black-bybill, *a funeral prayer for the remission of the sins of the dead.*
Blair (for bleir), *to cry, to weep.*
Blaitie-bum, *blockhead.*
Blan, *ceased.*
Blasphemationis, *blasphemies.*
Blawin, *blown.*
Ble, blee, *colour, complexion, hue*
Bledrand, *drivelling, babbling.*
Bleir, *to blur, obscure the sight.*
Bleirit, *dimmed.*
Blenkis, *glances.*
Blin, blinn, *to cease.*
Blithe, blyth, *glad, cheerful, happy.*
Blude, *blood.*
Blunt, *stupid.*
Blys, *bliss.*
Bocht, *bought.*
Bocking, *retching, vomiting.*
Bode, *an offer, a bid, or bidding.*
Bode, *an order, command.*
Bode-worde, *a message, an ominous message, tidings.*
Bodum, *bottom.*
Bogill, *spectre.*
Boird, *bored, cut.*
Boisis, *casks;* auld boises, *a contemptuous term applied to drunkards.*

Bo-keik, *bo-peep.*
Boldin, *swelled, overcharged.*
Boll, *a dry measure which contains 4 firlots, or 16 pecks.*
Bolt, *arrow.*
Bonair, *courteous.*
Bonjour, *good day.*
Bonnokkis, *cakes.*
Bony, *beautiful.*
Bordall, *brothel.*
Bordourit, *encircled.*
Borgh, *borrow.*
Borne, *carried.*
Borrel, borel, *rude, coarse, belonging to the common people.*
Borrow, *surety.*
Borrow, *a burgh, borough.*
Bost, *menace.*
Bostous, *rough.*
Bot, *only, but, unless, without.*
Bote, bute, *compensation, satisfaction, amends, remedy, help.*
Boteles, buteles, *irremediable, irreparable, helpless.*
Botis, *boats.*
Boucheour, *butcher.*
Bouk, *a body, the body.*
Boumbard, *cannon.*
Boun, *to go, to bend one's course.*
Boun, *ready.*
Boun, *to make ready, to equip, to dress.*
Boundin, *bound.*
Boundis, *reach.*
Bourd, *jest.*

GLOSSARY. 361

Bousteous, *boisterous*,
Bow, the vulgar pronunciation of boll, *a dry measure*.
Bow, *a fold of cattle*.
Bowis, *bulls of the Pope*.
Bowtit, *darted*.
Bowtit, *measured*.
Brae, bra, bray, *an acclivity, the face of a hill, a height*.
Braggar, *braggart*.
Bragget, bragwort, *a kind of mead, a fermented liquor*.
Braid, *broad*.
Braik, *to break*.
Braikand, brekand, *breaking*.
Brais, *embrace clasp*.
Bran, *brawn*.
Brand, *sword*.
Brank, *prance*.
Brankand, *swaggering*.
Brat, *a rag, a clout, a coarse or torn mantle or apron*.
Braull, *bluster*.
Braunis, *the calfs of the legs*.
Brawl, *quick dance or tune*.
Braye, *an acclivity*.
Brayis, *banks*.
Break, *rob*.
Breid, *altar*.
Breik, *breech, backside*.
Breikkis, *breeches*.
Brekand, *breaking*.
Bren, *to burn*.
Brether, *brother*.
Breve, *compose, dictate*.
Brevis, *composes*.
Brid, *a bird*
Bridel, *a wedding, a nuptial festival*.

Brig, brigg, *a bridge*.
Brim, *fierce*.
Broch, brogh, (for borch), *a surety*.
Broder, *brother*.
Broche, *a small piece of wood or metal worn on a woman's breast to support her stomacher, brooch*.
Brok, *badger*.
Brotekins, *buskins*.
Brouster, *brewer*.
Browderit, *embroidered*.
Bruch, *burgh*.
Bruke, bruik, *to possess*.
Brume, *broom*.
Brybour, *devourer, thief, greedy thief*.
Brycht, *bright*.
Bryggis, *bridges*.
Brym, *eager*.
Brynt, *burned*.
Bryste, *burst, break up, sever*.
Bud, *bribe*.
Bug-abo, *a hobgoblin, a bugbear*.
Bugil, *a bugle-horn*.
Buird, *board, stall*.
Buith, *booth, shop*.
Buit, *shop*.
Bukis, *books*.
Buller, *bellow*.
Bulryng, *boiling, stormy, gurgling*.
Bummil-baty, *a simpleton, a booby, an idle fellow*.
Bun, for *bum*.
Bunden, *bound*.
Burall, *beryl*.

Burde, *board.*
Burdon, *a pilgrim's staff.*
Bure, *bore.*
Burgeon, *a bud, a shoot, the young sprig of a tree.*
Burges, *a burgess.*
Burneis, *to burnish, polish.*
Burrowstoun, *a burgh town.*
Bursin, *burst.*
Bus, *bush.*
Busk, *bush.*
Busk, *to dress, to equip.*
But, *without.*
Bute, bote, *help, remedy, compensation, satisfaction.*
Buttock-maill, *an ecclesiastical fine in lieu of public penance.*
By, *besides, without.*
By, bye, *to buy.*
Byd, *tarry.*
Byde, *endure.*
Bydand, *remaining.*
Byik, *nest.*
Byill, *ulcer.*
Byre, *cow-house.*
Byngis, *heaps.*
Byrn, byrne, *to burn.*
Bystour, *malcontent.*

C

Cace, *case.*
Cace, *chance.*
Cadger, *a person who carries petty commodities about the country in panniers.*
Cadye, *merry, playful.*

Caiche, *a game of hand-ball.*
Caill, *coleworts.*
Caipis, *caps.*
Cair, *lamentation.*
Cairfull, *full of care.*
Cairt, *chariot.*
Calde, *cold.*
Calff, *chaff.*
Calsay, *causeway.*
Campioun, *a champion.*
Can, *to know.*
Can (for gan), *began.*
Cant, canty, *cheerful, lively.*
Cantel, *a fragment, a piece, a division.*
Cap, *a wooden cup or bowl.*
Capel, *a horse, a work-horse, a sorry horse.*
Cappis, *capes, gowns.*
Cap-out, *to drink out, to leave nothing in the cup.*
Caribaldis, *censorious.*
Cariounis, *carcases.*
Cariage, *service due by tenants in men and horses to their landlords.*
Cark, *care, anxiety, penuriousness, sordidness.*
Carle, cairle, *a churl, surly fellow, an old man.*
Carlin, *an old woman.*
Carpe, *to cavil.*
Carrail, *the burgh of Crail in Fife.*
Carteleinis, *wiles.*
Cartis, *cards.*
Carvoure, *carver.*
Cas, *chance.*

GLOSSARY. 363

Cassin, *cast down.*
Cast, *trick, contrivance, chances of profit.*
Caterve, *a catarrh.*
Cat-harrow, to draw at the cat-harrow = *to thwart one another.*
Catyve, *worthless.*
Cauld, *cold.*
Cautele, cawteill, *a quirk, a caution.*
Cavell, *an ignorant fellow.*
Cawsa, *causeway.*
Cawsay-packer, *a street-walker*
Cedull, *a schedule, a writing.*
Celsitude, *highness.*
Certes, *truly, verily, surely.*
Chaifery, *merchandise, wares.*
Chaft-blade, *jaw-bone.*
Chaip, *to escape.*
Chais, *to chase.*
Chalmer, *a chamber.*
Chalmerlain, *a chamberlain.*
Chanonnis, *canons.*
Chapit, *escaped.*
Chaplarie, *a scapulary.*
Chapman, *a pedlar.*
Chartereris, *Carthusian friars.*
Chease, *choose.*
Cheip, *to chirp, or squeak.*
Cheir, *a chair, a seat.*
Cheir, *aspect.*
Chene, cheinzie, *a chain.*
Cherisit, *cherished.*
Ches, *chess.*
Chesit, *chose.*
Chest, *chaste.*

Cheve, *to achieve, to come to an agreement or conclusion.*
Chevisance, *an agreement, or composition, an achievement.*
Child, cheild, *a page, a youth of high birth.*
Chiragra, *the gout in the hand.*
Chirurgiane, *a surgeon.*
Circuite, *circuit.*
Cincq and Syce, *five and six.*
Cinque-pace, *a kind of grave dance regulated by the number five.*
Claggit, *besmeared.*
Claggokis, *draggletails.*
Clais, claithis, *clothes.*
Claith, *screen.*
Clam, *climbed.*
Clan, clann, *a tribe, a race, a family.*
Clatter, *to tattle, or talk much.*
Clatteraris, *tattlers, tell-tales.*
Clattryng, *earth covered.*
Claucht, *snatched.*
Cleik, cleikis, *to catch hold of, to snatch.*
Cleikand, *snatching.*
Cleir, *fair.*
Cleithyng, *clothing.*
Clekit, *hatched.*
Clekk, *to hatch.*
Clenelie, *fully.*
Clenge, *to cleanse.*
Clepe, cleip, *to call, to name.*
Clerk, clark, *a scholar, a person in holy orders.*
Clethit, *clothed.*

Cleuch, cleugh, clough; plur. cleuchis, *a hollow between steep banks, a ravine, a narrow glen,*
Clim, *to climb.*
Clip, clippe, *to embrace, to grasp.*
Clippis, *hooks, grappling irons.*
Clips, *eclipse.*
Clippit-heid, *a head having the hair cut off; the tonsure of the monks.*
Cloiffis, *the clefts.*
Clois, *alley, court.*
Cloke, *cloak.*
Clout, *patch-rag.*
Clout, *cuff, blow.*
Cluke, *claw.*
Clynand, *rattling.*
Cluddis, *clouds.*
Clyppit, *shorn.*
Coactit, *subjected, restricted.*
Coattis, *taxes.*
Cod, *a pillow.*
Coffe, *merchant, hawker.*
Coft, *bought.*
Cog, cogge, *a boat.*
Coiffis, *hawkers.*
Coill, *coal.*
Coill, *a cowl, a hood.*
Coilyearis, *colliers.*
Coistis, *expenses.*
Coit, *coat.*
Collatioun, *a conference.*
Colpots, *coalpits.*
Com, cum, *to come.*
Come, *became.*
Comin, *come.*

Commends, *benefices.*
Commoun, *to communicate.*
Commounyng, *conversation.*
Companarie, *good fellowship.*
Companye, *to accompany.*
Companzeoun, *companion.*
Compare, *equal.*
Compleis, *to please, to satisfy.*
Compositioun, *admission into society.*
Compositours, *arbiters.*
Compte, *reckoning.*
Comptes, *countesses.*
Compt, *count, number.*
Comptit, *regarded.*
Con, (for cony) *a rabbit.*
Condampnit, *condemned.*
Conding, *due, merit.*
Conduct, *leadership.*
Conductis, *conduits.*
Confeittis, *sweetmeats.*
Confortand, *comforting.*
Conjunit, *conjoined.*
Conqueis, *to acquire.*
Consait, *thought, idea.*
Consociabill, *agreeable.*
Consuetude, *custom.*
Constry, *consistory, or ecclesiastical court.*
Contemptioun, *contempt.*
Contenis, *contains.*
Contrackis, *contracts.*
Contrair, *against, contrary to.*
Contramand, *to countermand.*
Convenabyll, *suitable.*
Convoy, *insinuation.*
Coppare, *cup-bearer.*
Corbie, *the raven.*

GLOSSARY. 365

Corce, *a body.*
Cordynar, *a shoemaker.*
Corncraik, *the landrail.*
Cornis, *grain.*
Corrump, *to corrupt.*
Corrynoch, *the funeral cry of the Scoto-Irish women.*
Corsis, *persons.*
Cors-present, *a mortuary or funeral gift to the Church.*
Cot, *coat.*
Cottar, *a cottager,*
Coulpe, *a fault.*
Count, *an account.*
Countring, *muttering.*
Coup, *fall.*
Coup, *to overturn, to upset.*
Courlyke, *short.*
Courtesse, *civil, well-bred, courteous.*
Courticiane, *a courtier.*
Courticience, *courtiers.*
Couth, *known, familiar, common.*
Covatyce, *covetousness.*
Cove, *a cave.*
Cover, *cower, to recover.*
Covyne, *a combination, a secret agreement, an intrigue.*
Cowhubie, *a stupid fellow, a booby.*
Cowp, *to buy and sell, to traffic.*
Coy, coye, *quiet, still.*
Crabing, *displeasing.*
Crack, *story.*
Crack, crak, craik, *a loud and sudden sound, the report of a cannon.*

Crack, *break.*
Craft, *"men of craft" craftsmen, tradesmen.*
Craftie, *ornately made, ingenious.*
Craftieness, *workmanship.*
Craif, *crave, implore.*
Craig, craiggis, *the throat, the neck.*
Craig, *a rock, a rocky cliff or precipice.*
Craik, *to speak harshly or disagreeably, to importune.*
Crak, *chat.*
Crakkis, crakkand, *boastful talk.*
Cramosye, *crimson-coloured.*
Cranie, *the skull.*
Creill, *a wicker basket, a pannier.*
Creis, cresse, *to crisp, to wrinkle, to rumple.*
Creische, *grease, fat.*
Creischie, *greasy.*
Crofte, *cultivated land.*
Crok, *an old ewe.*
Crone, crune, *a deep sound, a hum, a murmur.*
Crone, crune, *to utter a hollow sound, to hum, to speak or sing plaintively.*
Cruciate, *tortured, excruciated.*
Crukit, *crooked, lame.*
Crysme, *the anointing ointment used in Sacred ceremonies.*
Cubiculare, *groom of the bedchamber.*

GLOSSARY.

Cude, *a white linen cloth in which a child was wrapped at its baptism.*
Cuisse, cusse, cusche, *armour for the thighs.*
Cuist, *cast.*
Cuittis, *ancles.*
Cuitchours, *gamblers.*
Cuke, *a cook.*
Culum, *the tail, the fundament.*
Cumit, *come.*
Cumde, *come.*
Cummer, *a female gossip.*
Cummer, *bother.*
Cummerles, *cumberless.*
Cumpanarie, *companionship.*
Cun, con, *to know; also, to learn, to study.*
Cun, *to try, to prove, to taste.*
Cun, *to acknowledge, or give.*
Cunning, *agreement.*
Cunzie, *money, coin.*
Cuppill, *a couple, a brace; also, to couple, to join.*
Cure, *care.*
Cures, *charges, employment.*
Curis, *offices.*
Curcorlaous, *miserly.*
Curlyke, *churlish.*
Curnis, *small quantities.*
Cursour, *charger.*
Curtill, *sluttish.*
Custroun, *a pitiful fellow, a shallow pretender.*
Cut, cute, *trifle.*
Cyper, *cypress.*

D.

Da, *doe.*
Dade, dadie, *father.*
Daffing, *fooling.*
Daft, *foolish, mad.*
Daine, *gentle, modest, lowly.*
Dait, *destiny.*
Damais, *damask.*
Dame, *mother.*
Dampne, *to condemn, to damn.*
Dang, *beat.*
Danskin, *Dantzic.*
Dant, *chastise.*
Dantit, *trained.*
Danting, *subduing.*
Dase, *to stupify, to dull or blunt the faculties.*
Daw, *to dawn.*
Dayis-derlyng, *a term of endearment.*
Dc, *die.*
Debait, *complaint.*
Debaitit, *contested.*
Debt, *duty.*
Decerne, *decree.*
Deck't, *decked.*
Decorit, *decorated.*
Decore, *display.*
Decrcitis, *decrees.*
Dede, *dead.*
Dedeinze, *to disdain.*
Dec, *die.*
Defaid, *faded, decayed, wasted.*
Defame, *infamy, disgrace.*
Defendit, *forbidden.*
Deficill, *difficult.*

GLOSSARY.

Deft, *ready, apt;* also *neat, spruce.*
Degeist, *composed.*
Deid, *death, dead.*
Deid, *action, procedure.*
Dejectit, *ejected.*
Deil, dele, *a part, a portion, a quantity, much.*
Deil, *to act, or interfere with a person.*
Deill, *the Devil.*
Deill, *portion.*
Deir, *hurt, injury.*
Deir, *injurious.*
Deit, *died.*
Delatioun, *delay.*
Delatouris, *accusers.*
Delyverlie, *nimbly, freely.*
Deme, *to censure, to judge, to condemn.*
Dempster, *the officer who pronounced the judgments of a court.*
Deneir, *a piece of money.*
Deneiris, *money, pence.*
Depart, *divide, separate.*
Depaynt, *painted.*
Deploratioun, *lament.*
Deprysit, *disgraced.*
Derflie, darflye, *vigorously, actively.*
Dern, *to hide, to conceal, to seclude.*
Dernlie, *secretely, hiddenly.*
Derth, *dearth, famine.*
Descryve, *describing.*
Despitous, *despiteful, malicious, merciless.*

Destreyne, *to vex, to distract, to constrain.*
Detfull, *due.*
Deve, *to deafen, to stun with noise.*
Devyce, *pleasure.*
Devyse, *bequest.*
Devyse, *relate.*
Devorit, *destroyed.*
Devoyd, *to go out of.*
Deyand, *dying.*
Diffamit, *disgraced.*
Dicht, dight, *to dress, to equip, to prepare.*
Difficil, *difficult.*
Digne, *worthy.*
Dillation, *delay, remand.*
Dillatoris, *delays.*
Din, *dun, tawny.*
Dinnis, *sounds.*
Ding, *worthy.*
Ding, *strike, beat, knock.*
Dirk, *dull, obscure, dark.*
Discryve, *to describe, narrate.*
Diseiss, *strife, contention.*
Disesperance, *despondency.*
Disherisit, *stript.*
Disherisoun, *disinheriting.*
Disjune, *breakfast.*
Dispaird, *hopeless.*
Disparit, *hopeless.*
Dispend, *to expend.*
Dispense, *expense.*
Displeasouris, *grief.*
Dispone, *convey, dispose of.*
Dispyte, *indignity, contempt.*
Dispyte, *defiance, in dispyte, without mercy.*

367

Dispyit, *anger.*
Dissagysit, *disguised, arrayed.*
Dissaver, *a deceiver.*
Dissimul, *to dissemble.*
Distenyng, *staining, scorching.*
Distrubill, *to trouble, to vex, to disturb.*
Dite, diting, *to compose, indyte, dictate.*
Do, *make.*
Doand, *doing.*
Dochter, *daughter.*
Doitit, *did dote.*
Doitit, doited, *silly, foolish, stupid.*
Dok, *backside.*
Dole, dule, *grief, sorrow.*
Dolent, *sorrowful.*
Dome, *sentence, judgment.*
Donke, *dank, moist.*
Donkis, *moistens.*
Dornik, *damask stuff used for hangings.*
Dortour, *dormitory.*
Dotit, *endowed.*
Doublett, *a doublet.*
Douchtie, *valiant, strong.*
Doun-dang, *overthrew.*
Doungin, *cast or struck down.*
Dounthring, *overthrow.*
Doung (for dung), dungin, *cast down, struck.*
Doure, *severe.*
Dout, *fear.*
Dow, *dove, pigeon.*
Dow, *deserves.*
Dowe, *avail, deserves.*
Dowbill, *double.*

Dowtance, *doubt.*
Doytit, *stupid, drivelling.*
Draiff, *grains, refuse.*
Draik, *a drake.*
Dré, *to do, suffer.*
Dreid, drede, *dread, fear, doubt;* also *to dread, to fear, to doubt.*
Dreifland, *soaking.*
Dres, *redress.*
Drest, *punished.*
Dreveland, *speaking incoherently.*
Drew, *drop.*
Droggis, *fæces.*
Drouth, *drought, thirst.*
Drowkit, *drenched.*
Drowrie, *a love token, a present, a gift, a jewel.*
Drugg, *to drag.*
Dryte, *exonerare ventrem.*
Dubbis, *puddles.*
Ducheries, *duchies.*
Duches, *duchesses.*
Duddroun, *slut.*
Duke, *a duck.*
Dulce, *sweet.*
Dulcore, *sweetness.*
Dule, duill, *grief, mourning.*
Dullit, *saddened.*
Dully, *doleful.*
Dume, day of, *the day of Judgment.*
Dung, *beat, struck.*
Dungeoun, *a tower, a castle, a fortified castle;* also, *a keep, a prison.*
Dunt, *a blow, a stroke.*

GLOSSARY.

Duntibouris, *harlots, courtezans.*
Duplicandum, *a duply, (a law term.)*
Dure, *hard, severe, inflexible.*
Durlie, *rudely, harshly.*
Duschit, duscheit, *dashed down.*
Dwine, *to pine, to waste, to decay.*
Dycht, *dressed, equipped.*
Dyk, *a wall.*
Dyke-lowparis, *wall leapers, thieves.*
Dyng, *worthy.*
Dynt, *experience.*
Dynt, *blow.*
Dyte, *compose, indite.*
Dyting, *writing.*
Dyvour, *bankrupt.*

E

E, *eye.*
Ebure, *ivory.*
Ee, *eye.*
Edder, *the adder; a species of serpent, a viper.*
Edificate, *ameliorated.*
Effamisch, *to famish.*
Effectuouslie, *ardently.*
Effeiris, *becomes.*
Effeiris, *affrights.*
Effrays, *terrors.*
Eft, *again, often.*
Efter, *after.*
Efterwart, *afterwards.*
Eftsone, *soon after, in a short time.*

Egg, *to incite.*
Eggis, *eggs.*
Eik, *increase, add to.*
Eild, *age, manhood.*
Eine, *eyes.*
Eirar, *rather.*
Eird, *earth.*
Eiris, *ears.*
Eis, *ease.*
Eis, *eyes.*
Eisit, *eased.*
Eitand, *eating.*
Eith, *easy.*
Eitis, *eats.*
Eke, *also, likewise.*
Eldaris, *ancestors.*
Eliphand, *the Elephant.*
Ellis, *else, otherwise, already.*
Elriche, *hideous, ugly, terrible, applied to a person; wild, gloomy, dreary, applied to a place.*
Elwand, *yard measure.*
Eme, *uncle.*
Emottis, *ants.*
Empriouris, *emperours.*
Empryis, *emprise, an enterprise, an undertaking.*
Enarm, *to arm.*
Endlang, *along.*
Ene, *eyes.*
Eneuch, *enough.*
Ensew, *follow.*
Enterit, *entered.*
Entres, *entrance.*
Eoll, (for Æolus,) *the god of the Winds.*
Eris, *ears.*

VOL. II. 2 A

Errand, *wandering.*
Erst, *first, before, heretofore.*
Eschaip, *escape.*
Eschamit, *ashamed.*
Eschew, *to avoid, to shun.*
Esperance, *hope.*
Espoventable, *terrible.*
Essoinze, *an excuse.*
Etand, *eating.*
Etarne, *eternal.*
Etin, *giant.*
Eth, eith, *easy.*
Eusdaill, *a dale on the river Ewis, in Dumfriesshire.*
Everilk, *every.*
Evin, *straight, exact, equal, on guard.*
Evyr, *ivory.*
Exame, *examine.*
Exempne, *question.*
Exercitioun, *employment, executive, practice.*
Exerst, *exercised, employed.*
Expreme, *express, show.*
Extinct, *to extinguish.*

F.

Fa, fae, fay, *a foe.*
Facund, *pleasing, graceful.*
Fader, *father.*
Faik, *portion.*
Faill, *fault.*
Failyies, *faults, misdoings.*
Failyeit, *failed.*
Faim, *foam,* also *to foam.*
Faine, *glad, gladly.*
Fair, *betide.*

Fair, *to pass, go, proceed.*
Fair, *affair.*
Fais, *foes.*
Fald, *to fold, to put in a fold;* also *to double.*
Faldome, *fathom.*
Faldingis, *folds.*
Fall, *fail.*
Fall, *befall.*
Fallow, *fellow.*
Falset, *falshood.*
Fals, *false.*
Falt, *faulty, criminal.*
Falt, *want.*
Faltit, *sinned.*
Faltour, *sinner.*
Fameill, *family.*
Fameill, *female.*
Fa-men, *foemen, foes, enemies.*
Fand, *found, tried.*
Fane, *willing.*
Fang, *seize, molest.*
Far, *fear.*
Fare, *journey.*
Farsis, *antics.*
Faucht, *fought.*
Fauldit, *folded.*
Fay, *foe.*
Fé, fee, fey, *cattle, sheep, property, money, the wages of a servant.*
Fead, *enmity.*
Fecht, *fight.*
Fechtyng, *fighting.*
Fedderis, *feathers.*
Feddrem, *feathers, plumage.*
Fede, *enmity.*
Feid, *enmity, feud.*

GLOSSARY. 371

Feigh, *an interjection expressive of abhorrence or disgust.*
Feild, feld, *a field.*
Feildit, *fought.*
Feill, *know.*
Feill, *knowledge, sense, perception.*
Feil, fele, *many, several, much.*
Feind, *an enemy, the devil.*
Feinyeit, *invented, feigned, insincere.*
Feinze, *deceave.*
Feir, *aspect, appearance.*
Feir, *apprehension.*
Feird, ferd, *fourth.*
Feirie, *fiery, impetuous.*
Feirs, fearse, *fierce.*
Feis, *wages.*
Feit, *hired.*
Feit, *feet.*
Feiralie, *actively.*
Fell, *to befall.*
Fell, *woful, awful, fiery.*
Fell, *unenclosed land.*
Fell, *destroy.*
Fellown, felloun, *terrible.*
Feminine, *womankind.*
Fence, *to fence the Court, a forensic term, to proclaim the sitting of the Court.*
Feud, *to provide for, also to defend.*
Ferd, *the fourth.*
Feris, feiris, *companions.*
Ferleis, *wonders.*
Fery-fary, fierie-farie, *great ado, smart bustle.*
Ferme, *rent, farm.*

Ferme, *firmly.*
Festnit, *fixed.*
Fet, fett, *to fetch, to gather, to purchase.*
Few, *a lease.*
Fey, *unfortunate.*
Fidder, fither, futher, fouther, *cart load, an indefinite quantity considered as a whole.*
Figour, *effigy.*
Fillokis, *young women.*
Fine, *end.*
Fireflaucht, *lightning; a flash of fire.*
Firth, *forest.*
Fistand, *cuffing.*
Fit, fitt, *a song, a short poem, a division or part of a poem.*
Flag, *an opprobrious term applied to a woman.*
Flagartie, *flouncing.*
Flam, *custard.*
Flamand, *flaming.*
Flammis, *flames.*
Flane, flain, *an arrow.*
Flap, *stroke.*
Flatlyngis, *flatly.*
Flaw, *flew.*
Fle, *frighten.*
Fleich, *wheedle.*
Fleicheing, *flattering.*
Fleid, *cowardly.*
Fleimit, *driven away.*
Fleit, *abound.*
Fleitand, *floating.*
Fleme, *drive away.*
Flend, *run away.*
Fleschers, *butchers.*

Fleyd, fleyit, *frightened.*
Fleure, flewre, *smell, flavour.*
Flichterand, *fluttering.*
Flicht, *flight.*
Flings, *upbraids.*
Flit, *to remove, to change the place of abode, to migrate.*
Flobbage, *phlegm.*
Flocht, *fright, panic.*
Flokkis, *flocks.*
Flouris, *flowers.*
Flouris, *youth.*
Flude, *river.*
Flure, *floor.*
Fluriste, *flourishing.*
Flycht, *flight.*
Flyngand, *dancing.*
Flypit, *turned inside out.*
Flyts, *scolds.*
Flyte, *rage.*
Fold, *earth, the earth.*
Folkis, *folk, people.*
Foly-hat, *a fool's cap.*
Follysche, *foolish, weak.*
Fonde, *founded.*
Fon, *fondle, play.*
Fond, *foolish.*
Fone, *foes.*
For, *because, because that.*
Force, *care, matter.*
Forcie, *powerful.*
Forde, *for it.*
Fordwart, *a precaution, a paction, an agreement.*
Fordwarte, *forward.*
Foreland, *sea-shore.*
Fore-grandschir, *forefather.*
Forfair, *perish, wear.*

Forfaltit, *forfeited.*
Forfalt, *forfeited.*
Forgane, *over against.*
Forleit, *to forsake, to quit, to give up, or over.*
Forlorne, *undone.*
Formose, *beautiful, fair.*
Fornent, fornenst, *over against, opposite.*
Forquhy, forthy, *because, therefore, for this reason.*
Forsuith, *indeed, forsooth.*
Fortherit, *induced.*
Forthink, *regret, grieve.*
Foryeild, forzeild, *to repay, to reward; also to punish.*
Foryet, forzet, *forgot.*
Founderit, *fell.*
Fow, *drunk.*
Fow, *fill.*
Fra hand, *off hand.*
Fra, *from.*
Fraid, *freed.*
Fray, *fright, fear.*
Freik, *forward fellow.*
Frelie, *worthy.*
Fremit, *foreign.*
Frenyeis, *fringes.*
Fresche, *fresh.*
Frist, *credit.*
Fruct, fructis, *fruit, fruits.*
Fructuall, *fruitful.*
Frugge, *a rug, coarse woollen bed cover.*
Fruschit, *crushed.*
Frutage, *fruit.*
Frynasie, *frenzy.*
Fude, *fellow.*

GLOSSARY. 373

Fuffe, *whiff, puff.*
Fuffling, *shaking, wincing, flapping.*
Fuilyeit, *trampled.*
Fuilis, *fools.*
Fulfillit, *well stored.*
Fule, *fool.*
Full, *completely, perfectly.*
Fundin, *found.*
Fure, *went.*
Furris, *fields.*
Furth, *forth, out.*
Fut, fute, *foot.*
Futtit, *footed.*
Fyill, *to pollute, defile.*
Fyles, *defiles.*
Fyne, *end, purpose.*
Fyreflaucht, *lightning.*
Fyve syis, *five times.*

G

Ga, *go.*
Gab, *the mouth;* also, *talk, prating.*
Gaddis, *rods.*
Gaif, *gave.*
Gaill, *chant.*
Gailyeonis, *galleys.*
Gaird, *guard.*
Gaining, *requirement.*
Gairth, *garden.*
Gais, *goest.*
Gaist, *ghost.*
Gait, *goat.*
Gait, gaittis, *the way, ways.*
Galay, *a kind of great gun.*
Galbarte, *mantle.*
Galmoundis, *gambols, capers.*
Galyeardlie, galzeartlie, *gallantly.*
Gambis, gammis, *gums.*
Game, *sport.*
Gamond, *caper.*
Gan, gane, *began.*
Gane, *gone.*
Ganer, *gander.*
Ganestand, *withstand.*
Gaude, *a trick, a prank.*
Gang, *go.*
Gant, *yawn.*
Gar, *cause.*
Garmoundis, *garments, liveries.*
Garnisoun, *company.*
Garris, *makes, compels, causes.*
Garth, *field, garden.*
Gart, *caused, made.*
Gearking, *foppish.*
Geaslyngis, *goslings.*
Geid, *went, walked.*
Geill, *jelly.*
Geir, *property, accoutrements.*
Geis, *geese.*
Genners, *engenders.*
Gent, *pretty.*
Geve, *if.*
Ges, *guess.*
Get, gettis, *to obtain, obtainis.*
Ghaist, *ghost.*
Gif, *give.*
Giglottis, *wantons, fools.*
Gird, *a stroke, a blow;* also, *to strike, to hit.*
Girning, *distorting the countenance with anger.*
Glader, *gladdener.*

Glaid, *gladden.*
Glaikit, *thoughtless, stupid.*
Glaiks, *tricks, a game of deception.*
Gled, *the kite, a kind of hawk.*
Glennis, *valleys.*
Glore, *glory.*
Glorifeit, *glorified.*
Glowris, *stares.*
Gluifis, *gloves.*
Gnarr, *to snarl, to growl.*
Gnarre, *a hard knot, or bump, a knot in wood; metaphorically, a churl.*
Gob, gab, *the mouth.*
God-bairn-gift, *the present of a godfather at the baptism of a child.*
Goik, *cuckoo.*
Goldspink, *goldfinch.*
Gome, gume, *a man.*
Gonet, *horse.*
Gor, (glengore) *the venereal disease.*
Gorman, gormand, *glutton.*
Gossop, *a neighbour.*
Governance, *command.*
Gowland, *howling.*
Gowles, *red.*
Gragit, *excommunicated.*
Graip, *feel.*
Graith, *harness, goods, articles.*
Gram, *wrath, mischief, grief.*
Gram, *ireful, furious, mischeivous.*
Grandgore, *venereal disease.*
Grandschyre, *forefather.*
Grange, *a farm, a farm-house.*

Grane, granis, *groan, groans.*
Graniter, *keeper of a granary.*
Grave, (for grove), *a bush of wood.*
Greabyll, *agreeable.*
Gre, *degree.*
Grene, *green.*
Greislie, *grissly, frightful.*
Greit, greityng, *weep, weeping.*
Gret, *great.*
Grew, *Greek.*
Grice, *grey fur.*
Grief, *to grieve.*
Grim, *grimace.*
Grippit, *griped, compressed.*
Grote, *small coin value* 4d.
Ground, *foundation.*
Grounder, *founder.*
Grume, *fellow.*
Grund, *ground.*
Grundin, *sharpened.*
Grunschyng, *complaining, grumbling.*
Gruntill, *snout.*
Grunzie, *snout.*
Gryce, *pig.*
Gryntaris, *bailiffs.*
Grym, *cruel.*
Gubernation, *government.*
Guckit, *foolish.*
Gudame, *grandmother.*
Gude, *worth.*
Gude-man, *husband.*
Guddis (for guidis), *possessions.*
Gudlie, *goodly.*
Gudlingis, *alloys, or base metal.*
Guerdonyng, *rewarding.*
Guse, *a goose.*

GLOSSARY. 375

Gustyng, *tasting.*
Gut, *gout.*
Guyder, *leader.*
Gyder, *pilot.*
Gyle-fat, *cooling-vat.*
Gyn, *art.*
Gyse, *deception.*
Gyse, *fashion.*
Gyir Carlyng, Gyre Carling, *a witch of gigantic size and appearance.*
Gyrsome, *a premium given for the lease of a farm.*

H

Habbie gown (for haberzeon), *a breast-plate, coat of mail.*
Habitakle, *habitation.*
Haboundance, *abundance.*
Habyll, *able, qualified, amenable.*
Hackit, *choped.*
Hag, *notch.*
Hagbutteris, *musketeers.*
Haifing, haiffand, *having.*
Haikney, *horse.*
Hail, *to heal, to cure.*
Haill, *wholly, whole, entire.*
Haillilie, *wholly.*
Hailsum, *wholesome.*
Hais, *hoarse.*
Haistit, *hastened.*
Hait, *hot.*
Hait, *heat.*
Hakkit, *choped.*
Hald, *hold.*

Halflings, *half, partly.*
Hals, *neck.*
Haly, *holy.*
Halyeir, *whole year.*
Hame, *home.*
Hanclethis, *ancles.*
Hand, *bargain.*
Hap, *chance, opportunity.*
Hape, *chance.*
Hapnit, *happened.*
Happit, *covered.*
Harbrieles, *without shelter.*
Hard, *heard.*
Hard on, *contiguous to.*
Hardines, *defiance.*
Hardlie, *boldly.*
Harknit, *hearkened.*
Harld, harlit, *dragged, pulled.*
Harlot, *a worthless person of either sex.*
Harlotrie, *the trade of a harlot, lewdness, ribaldrie.*
Harmes, *sufferings, injuries.*
Harmisay, *have mercy.*
Harne pan, *skull.*
Harnis, *brains.*
Harow, harrow, *an exclamation for help.*
Hart, *heart.*
Hartlie, *heartily, heartfully.*
Hasardie, *gaming.*
Hasarture, *gamester.*
Hat, *hit.*
Hauld, hald, *hold.*
Hauld, *hold, place, habitation.*
Hayif, *name.*
Hecht, *promised.*
Hecht, *promise.*

Hede-werk, *head-ache.*
Hege-skraper, *niggard.*
Heid, *behead.*
Heidlangs, *headlong.*
Heipit, *heaped.*
Heirbis, *herbs.*
Heirschyp, *devastation, plundering excursion.*
Heklit, *pulled, fastened.*
Helie, *haughty.*
Hent, *seized.*
Heretouris, *heirs, heritors.*
Heires, *nobles.*
Herield, *tribute.*
Heryit, *plundered.*
Herywalter, *net.*
Hete, *to promise, to vow.*
Heuch, heugh, hew, *a height, a steep bank, a cliff.*
Hewis, *hues.*
Heych, *high.*
Heynd, *gentle.*
Hiddie, *giddy.*
Hie, *high.*
Hiech, *high.*
Hichtit, *raised.*
Hiear, *higher.*
Hingand, *hanging, suspended.*
Hint, *clasped.*
Hippis, *the hips.*
Hippit, *applied to the hind parts.*
Historiciane, *historian.*
Ho, *hold, stop.*
Hobbeld, *mended, cobbled.*
Hobbils, *dances.*
Hobland, *hobbling.*
Hoch, *leg.*
Hoggis, *year-old sheep.*

Hoilsum, *wholesome.*
Hoir, *hoary, gray.*
Hole, *whole.*
Holkit, *excavated.*
Hollyng, *holly.*
Holm, howm, *a flat on the side of, or surrounded by, water.*
Holtis, *woods.*
Hore, *withered, bare.*
Horn, *outlaw.*
Hose, hois, *stockings.*
Host, hoist, *a cough.*
Houlet, *owl.*
Hound, *to hunt, drive away.*
Hountaris, *hunters.*
Houris, *prayers.*
Housel, *the Eucharist, the consecrated bread.*
How, *a hollow.*
How, *night-cap.*
Howis, *houghs.*
Howit, *hooted.*
Hoyis, *the forensic cry Oyez, at making a proclamation.*
Hude, *hood.*
Huirsone, *whoreson.*
Humlock, *a polled cow.*
Humyl, *humble.*
Humilie, *humbly.*
Hummil - bummill, *muttering speech.*
Hunder, hundreth, *a hundred.*
Hurdaris, *hoarders.*
Hurdies, *buttocks.*
Huris, *whores.*
Hurly-burly, *much ado.*
Hydropesie, *dropsy.*
Hy, *haste.*

GLOSSARY.

Hye, *high.*
Hycht, *hight.*
Hynd, *behind.*
Hynde, *hind.*
Hyne, *hence, hereafter.*
Hyrald, hyreild, *a fine extorted by a superior on the death of his tenant.*
Hyre, *reward.*

I.

Ignorantis, *ignorant persons.*
Ilk, *each.*
Ilke, *every.*
Illude, *delude.*
Ill-fairde, *ill-looking.*
Illuster, *illustrious.*
Imbroudit, *embroidered.*
Impit, *grafted.*
Impone, *impose.*
Importabyll, *intolerable.*
Impresonit, *imprisoned.*
Impyrand, *domineering.*
Impyre, *empyreal.*
Immundicitie, *uncleanness, corruption.*
Inclusit, *shut up.*
Incontinent, *immediately, without delay.*
Incounsolable, *not to be counselled.*
Indeficient, *abundant.*
Induryng, *during.*
Ineure, *happen.*
Infetching, *inbringing.*
Infortune, *misfortune.*
Ingent, *huge.*

Inglis, *English.*
Ingyne, *ability, intellect.*
Innarrabyll, *inexpressible.*
Innis, *lodgings.*
Inopportune, *inconvenient.*
Insolence, *folly.*
Instrument, *a written document given in proof of any deed of a court.*
Intellibill, *not to be told.*
Intendit, *proceeded.*
Intendiment, *intention, purpose.*
Intill, *into.*
Ipocras (for Hippocrass), *an aromatic wine.*
Ipocrasie, *hypocrisy.*
Ire, *anger, rage.*
Irk, *annoyed.*
Irne, *iron.*
Ise, *I shall.*

J.

Ja, *the jay.*
Jaip, *a jest, a trick.*
Jaip, *to debauch.*
Jangle, *to wrangle, to create dissension.*
Jangler, *a wrangler, a mischief-maker.*
Jo, *joy, my dear, a sweetheart.*
Jois, *joys.*
Jonet, *a jennet, a small handsome horse.*
Jowrye, *the land of Judæa.*
Juge, *a judge.*

GLOSSARY.

Juggis, *dregs.*
Junit, *joined.*
Junne, *join.*
Jurden, *a chamber-pot.*
Jure, *law.*
Justice Airis, *the periodical circuits of the King's Justiciaries.*
Justing, *tilting.*

K.

Ka, *a Jackdaw.*
Kaill, *broth made of cabbage.*
Keiste, *dug.*
Ke, *jackdaw.*
Keik, *to peep, to look.*
Keipit, kepit, *kept.*
Keitching, *kitchin.*
Kekell, *cackle.*
Ken, *direct.*
Ken, *know.*
Kend, kende, *known.*
Kendyll, *kindle.*
Kene, *daring.*
Kepith, *tend.*
Keppit, *caught.*
Kest, *opened.*
Keste, *cast.*
Kewis, *instructions, line of conduct.*
Kilt, *tuck up.*
Kin, kyn, *kindred, relations, family.*
Kirk, *church.*
Kirtil, *tunic, short petticoat.*
Kist, *a chest, or box, used as a coffin.*

Kittil, kittle, *to tickle.*
Knaif, knave, *a boy, a serving boy, a servant.*
Knaifatica, *a mean, low pedlar.*
Knarry, *knotty.*
Knapskaw, *head piece.*
Knaw, *know.*
Knawin, *known.*
Knawleging, *acknowledgement.*
Knellis (saul), *bells tolling.*
Kow, *custom, tax.*
Kow, *a cow.*
Kow, *branch, twig.*
Kow-clink, *harlot.*
Krake, *break.*
Kuik, *cook.*
Ky, kye, *cattle, cows.*
Kyith, keith, *make manifest.*
Kynrent, *kindred.*
Kynrik, *kingdom.*
Kyte, *belly.*

L

Lack, *fault, blame, disgrace.*
Lackit, *reproved.*
Ladder, *backward.*
Laddis, *servants.*
Ladronis, *low women.*
Laid, *servant.*
Laidlie, *filthy.*
Laif, *remainder, rest.*
Laif, lave, *a loaf.*
Laik, *want, require.*
Lair, *school.*
Laird, *lord, proprietor.*
Laiser, *leasure.*
Laithlie, *loathsome.*

GLOSSARY.

Lak, *reproach.*
Lake, *disgrace.*
Lakkis, *depreciates.*
Lamber, lammer, *amber.*
Lame, *lamb.*
Land, *country.*
Land folk, *country-people.*
Land wart, *the Country, in opposition to Town.*
Lang, *long.*
Langis, langith, *belongs.*
Langsum, *tedious.*
Lansing, *bounding.*
Lap, lape, *leaped.*
Lappit, *enveloped, surrounded.*
Lardis, *lords.*
Lassis, *girls.*
Lat, *cease.*
Lat, *let, permit.*
Lat be, *let alone.*
Lauborit, *laboured.*
Lauch, *laugh.*
Laute, *loyalty.*
Lave, *remainder.*
Laverock, *the lark.*
Law, *low, make humble.*
Law, *a hill.*
Lawlye, *lowly.*
Lawit, *ignorant, humble.*
Lawrer, *laurel.*
Lawtie, *fidelity.*
Lay, *let go to waste.*
Layid, *humble.*
Layik, *laymen.*
Layser, *leasure.*
Lear, *a liar.*
Leche, leiche, *a physician or surgeon.*

Lede, *lead.*
Ledder, *a ladder.*
Ledder, *leather, the skin.*
Lee, *a lie.*
Leich, leche, *to cure, to heal.*
Leid, *lied.*
Leid, *language.*
Leid, *lead.*
Leif, *believe.*
Leif, *live.*
Leif, *leave, relinquish.*
Leifful, leifsum, *lawful.*
Leill, *faithful, true, honest.*
Leir, *learn.*
Leirand, *learning.*
Leis, *order, ceremony.*
Leise, *to lose.*
Leit, *let, allowed.*
Leit, *language.*
Lemant, lemand, *shining.*
Lemis, *beams, rays.*
Lemman, *illicit lover.*
Len, *lend.*
Lende, *a loin.*
Lendis, *the loins, the back.*
Lenth, *length, lengthen.*
Lesing, leising, *lying.*
Lestand, *lasting.*
Lesit, *lost.*
Let, lett, *to forbear, to hinder, to stop.*
Leven, *lightning.*
Lever, *rather.*
Levit, *lived.*
Leuch, *laughed.*
Levis, *leaves.*
Leysour, *leasure.*

GLOSSARY.

Libellis, *writings.*
Licence, *leave.*
Licents, *licentiates.*
Lichtit, lychtit, *alighted.*
Liddir, *loathsome fellow.*
Liddir, *awkward, backward.*
Lift, *firmament.*
Lig, ligge, *to lye.*
Liggis, *leagues.*
Like, lyke, *to like, to please, to be pleased.*
Limmer, *jade, scoundrel.*
Ling, *a line.*
Lith, *a joint, a limb.*
Loch, *lake.*
Lod sterre, lod sterne, *the Pole star.*
Loft, *storey.*
Loge, *to lodge.*
Lok, *restraint.*
Lorimer, *saddler.*
Lore, *instruction.*
Louch, *a lake.*
Loun, *worthless fellow, rogue.*
Loup, loupe, *leap.*
Lout, *to stoop, to bow, or bend the body.*
Lovyng, *praise.*
Low, *to bellow.*
Low, *a flame.*
Lownis, *idle fellows, rascals.*
Lowng, *the lungs.*
Lowrance, *the fox.*
Lows, *open.*
Lowsit, *loosed, released.*
Lox, *locks.*
Lucken, *shut, closed.*

Lucky, *a familiar term used in addressing a woman.*
Ludges, *lodgings.*
Lufe, *love.*
Lufe, *palm of the hand.*
Luffis, *love's.*
Luferay, *livery.*
Lufe-takin, *a love token.*
Luffaris, *lovers.*
Luffer, *the liver.*
Lugs, luggis, *the ears.*
Luiffillis, *handfuls.*
Luke, *see, look.*
Lukis, *reads, peruses.*
Lumis, *limbs.*
Lunzie, *loin, back,*
Lupis, *wolf.*
Lurden, *rogue.*
Lurdoun, *unmannerly.*
Luris, *tempters.*
Lurke, *hide.*
Lusty, *lovely, fruitful.*
Lustye, *pleasant.*
Lustie, *beautiful.*
Lustelie, lustellie, *pleasantly.*
Lustiheid, *pleasantness, pleasure.*
Lyart, *hoary.*
Lycam, lykam, *a body.*
Lycht, *light.*
Lychtit, *alighted.*
Lychtleit, *slighted.*
Lychtleyand, *slighting.*
Lyffis, *lives.*
Lyk, lykand, *like.*
Lymbe, *limbo, place of durance.*
Lymmis, *limbs.*

Lyne, *lain.*
Lyng, *charge, rush.*
Lyte, *little.*
Lythe, *sheltered.*
Lythquo, *the town of, or palace of Linlithgow.*
Lyre, *skin.*
Lyste, *will, please.*
Lyttill, *little.*

M

Ma, *more.*
Mahown, *Mohammed, the Devil.*
Maid, made, *committed.*
Maid, *procured.*
Maiglit, *mangled.*
Maik, make, *a mate, a consort, an equal, a match.*
Maill, *meal.*
Maill, *taxation.*
Mairattour, *moreover.*
Maist, *utmost.*
Maister, *a master.*
Maisterie, maistrie, *superior power, the mastery.*
Mak, *make.*
Mak yow forde, *take advantage of.*
Makand, makkand, *making.*
Makkar, *author.*
Maleson, *malediction, curse.*
Malmontrya (for Mamontrie), *idolatry.*
Malysoun, *curse.*
Man, *must.*
Manassyng, manesyng, *menacing, threatening.*
Mandement, *a command, an order.*
Mane, *complaint.*
Mangit, *confounded, deranged.*
Maugre, *in spite of.*
Mansweir, *perjure.*
Mansweit, *meek.*
Mapamound, *map of the world.*
Marchand, *merchandise, freight.*
Mareguildis, *marigolds.*
Mark, merk, *a Scottish silver coin value thirteen pence and one-third of a penny sterling.*
Marinall, *mariner.*
Marrow, *companion, equal.*
Martrik, *a fur.*
Marvill, *marble.*
Maseris, *macers, ushers.*
Masking-fat, *brewer's vat.*
Matier, *body.*
Matutyne, *in the morning.*
Maves, maveis, *the thrush.*
May, *a virgin, a young woman.*
May, *can.*
Mayn, *strength, power, might.*
Medcinair, *physician.*
Meg, for *Margaret.*
Mekle, meikle, *much.*
Menze, meinze, *company, family, crew.*
Meir, *mare.*
Meisit, *appeased.*
Mekill, *much.*
Mell, *meddle.*

Mence, *grace.*
Mendis, *amendment, satisfaction.*
Mendit, *remembered.*
Mene, *explain.*
Menever, *a white fur.*
Menge, *to mix, to confound.*
Menis, *esteems.*
Merciall, *martial.*
Merle, merll, *the blackbird.*
Merchetis, *the money paid to a lord for his right to the virginity of a tenant's daughter at her marriage.*
Mes, *the Mass.*
Mesel, *a leper.*
Mesken, (for misken) *misknow.*
Mesoure, *measure.*
Messane, *a small dog.*
Midding, *dunghill.*
Mid-eard, *the earth.*
Mightful, *mighty.*
Mint, *attempt.*
Mirk, *dark.*
Mischevit, *hurt.*
Miscuikit, *mismanaged, spoilt,*
Misericorde, *mercy.*
Miseritie, *misery.*
Misgydit, *led astray.*
Misken, *mistake.*
Misknawis, *mistakes.*
Misordour, *confusion.*
Misouris, *measures.*
Misse, *fault.*
Mister, *need.*
Mistoinit, *mistuned, discordant, out of tune.*

Mo, *more.*
Mocks, *mockers.*
Moit, *mote,*
Mollet, moylie, *amble, gently.*
Mon, *must.*
Mone, *moon.*
Monethis, *months.*
Monunday, *Monday.*
Mony, *many.*
Monyeoun, *minion.*
Monyfauld, *intestines.*
Monyste, *admonished.*
Morne, *to-morrow.*
Mort, *die.*
Mostouris, *musters, parades.*
Mot, *may.*
Mow, *a jest.*
Mow, mowe, *the mouth.*
Mowe, *beak.*
Mowis, *jest.*
Muck, *dung.*
Muck, *to clear of dung.*
Mufe, *cause.*
Mummill, *mumble.*
Munzeoun, *minion.*
Murmell, *complaint.*
Murnit, *tossed restlessly.*
Mute, *speak, articulate.*
Mycht, *might, strong.*
Mychtis, *powers.*
Myddis, *midst.*
Mylyeoun, *million.*
Myn, *less.*
Myne allone, *myself.*
Myne, *my.*
Mynnie, *mother.*
Myreast, *merriest.*
Myrk, myrke, *dark, gloomy.*

Myrknes, *darkness.*
Mys, *fault, error.*
Myscheant, mischeand, *evil, wicked.*
Myskend, *disowned.*
Myttanis, *gloves.*
Mytour, *mitre.*

N

Na, *no.*
Na, *now.*
Namelye, *principally.*
Nane, *none.*
Nar, *to snarl.*
N'as, *was not.*
Natheles, *nevertheless.*
Ne, *not.*
Ne, *nor neither.*
Nedis, *requires.*
Neif, *fist.*
Neir, *near, almost.*
Neirs, *kidneys.*
Neis, *nose.*
Nether, *lower.*
Nichtbour, *neighbour.*
Nippit, *curtailed, pinched.*
Nocht, *nothing.*
Nocht, *not.*
Noder, *neither.*
Noe, Noy, Noye, *Noah.*
Nois, *dirt.*
Nold, *would not.*
Nolt, *cattle.*
None, *noon.*
Nonis, *nonce, occasion.*
Nor, *than, may.*
Noryce, *nurse.*

Not, *know, not.*
Noter, *a Notary.*
Nother, *neither.*
Novellis, *news.*
Nowmer, *number.*
Nowreis, *nurse.*
Noy, noye, *vex, vexation, destruction.*
Nuikit, *cornered.*
Nuke, *corner.*
Nummer, *number.*
Nycht, *night.*
Nyll, *will not.*
Nynt, *ninth.*

O

Oblyssit, *obliged, bound.*
Observance, *respect, duty.*
Occararis, *usurers.*
Occident, *the west.*
Och, *oh, alas, woe.*
Ocht, *aught.*
Ociositie, *ennui.*
Of, *by, from.*
Off, *out of.*
Offertour, *an anthem chanted during the offering.*
Oist, *host, army.*
Oliphantis, *elephants.*
On, *during.*
On lyve, *alive.*
Ony, *any.*
Or, *ere.*
Oratour, *oratory.*
Ordinance, *order of place, array, settlement, place, appointment.*

GLOSSARY.

Ordinance, *cannon.*
Orient, *the east.*
Orisioun, *prayer.*
Oritore (see oratour), *a study, a place for saying prayers.*
Orphelenis, *orphans.*
Ouer, (pron. ou'r), *over.*
Ouerdrive, *pass away.*
Ouirman, *oversman, arbitrator.*
Ouersene, *overlooked, excused.*
Ouersene, *overseen, examined, viewed.*
Ouersylit, *obscured.*
Ouirset, *overcome.*
Ouirthorte, *athwart.*
Oule, *owl.*
Oulkis, *weeks.*
Outher, *either.*
Outterit, *ran out of the course.*
Overscyll, *deceive.*
Ower (for ou'r), *over.*
Oyste, *host, army.*
Oyl dolic, *olive oil.*

P.

Paise, *to raise, or bear up, to poise.*
Pak, pack, *a load, package, burden.*
Padoks, *frogs.*
Paikaris, *beater, stamper.*
Paiks, *strokes, chastisement.*
Pailyeoun, *pavilion.*
Pairt, *depart.*
Pais, *paces.*
Paist, *repast.*

Pak, *decamp.*
Pallet, *crown of the head.*
Palyard, *a born beggar, an imposter.*
Palzeoun, *pavilion.*
Panis, *pains.*
Pans, *to think.*
Pantonis, *slippers.*
Pape, *the Pope.*
Papyngo, *the Parrot.*
Pardoner, *a trafficker or seller of the Popes Indulgences.*
Paregall, *parallel.*
Parischoun, *parish.*
Pas, *pass, go.*
Pasche, *Easter.*
Pasis, *paces.*
Passis, *surpasses, excels.*
Passionis, *agonies.*
Passioun, *suffering.*
Pastance, *pastime.*
Pat, *put.*
Patrone, *example, pattern.*
Paupis, *breasts.*
Pavin, *a grave and stately dance.*
Payntouris, *painters.*
Peax, *peace.*
Pedder, *a hawker, pedlar.*
Peggrell, *beggarly.*
Peice, *peace.*
Peild, *peeled, bald.*
Peipand, *peiping, whineing.*
Peiris, *equals.*
Peirte, *pert, impudent.*
Pek, *peck, the fourth part of a firlot.*
Pellour, *robber.*

GLOSSARY.

Penetratyve, *penetrating.*
Penny-braid, *penny breadth.*
Penseil, *banner.*
Perdie, *truly, by God.*
Peregal, *equal.*
Peremtouris, *peremptorily.*
Perfay, *truly, by my faith.*
Perfurneis, *accomplish.*
Perfyte, *perfect.*
Perqueir, *off hand.*
Perrell, but perrel (for peregal), *without equal.*
Perse, *Persia.*
Person, *a parson.*
Pertendand, *succeeding.*
Pertinat, *pertinacious.*
Pew, *a cry.*
Pharisience, *Pharisees.*
Phlegeton, *a river of Hell.*
Physnomie, *physiognomy.*
Piete, *pity, condescension, good nature.*
Pieteous, *piteous.*
Pik, *pitch.*
Pille, peille, *to rob, to plunder*
Pirmityvis, *rules, laws.*
Pistil, *an epistle.*
Pith, *strength, marrow.*
Placebo, *a courteour, a sycophant.*
Placebo, *to sing the Placebo in the Roman Catholic service.*
Plaige, *region.*
Plaint, *complain.*
Plait, *mail.*
Plak, *a Scots coin equal to the third of an English penny.*
Plasmatour, *the Creator.*

Plat, *flattened.*
Plate, *a stroke with the open hand.*
Platfute, *a term of reproach, splay-footed.*
Platt, *closed, placed.*
Playand, *playing.*
Playfeir, *playmate.*
Pleid, *dispute.*
Pleinzie, *complain.*
Plene, *complain.*
Pleneis, *to fill.*
Plenischit, *furnished.*
Plesance, *pleasure.*
Plesoure, *pleasure.*
Plet, *plaited.*
Pleuch, *plough.*
Pley, *to plea, to contend.*
Pley, *plea.*
Polesye, *benefit.*
Poleysie, *policy, estate.*
Poplesye, *apoplexy.*
Populaire, *people.*
Porte, *gate.*
Portouns, *a Mass book.*
Portratour, *figure.*
Poulder, *dust.*
Poulderit, *powdered.*
Pown, *peacock.*
Practiciane, *practitioner.*
Practick, *practise.*
Practyke, *policy.*
Prais, preis, *tumult.*
Precell, *excel.*
Precellent, *excelling, super-excellent.*
Preclare, *supereminent, illustrious.*

VOL. II.   2 B

Precordiall, *most cordial.*
Preif, *prove, taste, try.*
Preinis, *pins.*
Preis, *endeavour, attempt.*
Preisit, *presumed.*
Prencis, *princes.*
Prent, *stamp, impress.*
Preplesand, *most pleasing.*
Prepotent, *most powerful.*
Presoun, *prison.*
Preterit, *past.*
Prettike, *practice.*
Preve, *try.*
Prevene, *prevent.*
Prick, *to ride hard, to gallop.*
Prime, *the first Canonical hour.*
Principate, *principal, chief.*
Prochane, *near, next.*
Proffect, *profit.*
Promovit, *promoted.*
Propone, *propose, announce.*
Propynis, *gifts.*
Prosternit, *prostrated.*
Proudely, *lavishly.*
Proviance, *management, conduct.*
Proviance, *providence.*
Provost, *the chief magistrate of a Scottish borough.*
Prunyeand, *trimming.*
Pryis, *valued.*
Pryse, *prize.*
Pryse, *praised,* also *price,* also *prize.*
Pudlit, *puddled.*
Puddingis, *the intestines.*
Puissance, *power.*
Pulchritude, *beauty.*

Pungityve, *pungent, sharp.*
Punis, puneis, *to punish.*
Punyst, *punished.*
Punytioun, punisioun, *punishment.*
Purchais, *emolument.*
Purcheist, *acquired.*
Pure, *poor, unfortunate.*
Purellis, *poor people.*
Purfeillit, *wrought, or ornamented about the edge.*
Puris, *poor.*
Put, *to jog or push gently.*
Putane, pewtane, *a whore.*
Putour, pewtour, *a whoremonger.*
Pye, pyot, *the Magpie.*
Pyke, *pick, snatch.*
Pykthankis, *parisites.*
Pyne, *pain, torment.*
Pynit, *tormented.*

Q

Quaif, *band.*
Quair, *a quire of paper, a stitched book.*
Quart, *measure.*
Queint, *neat, artful, subtil, strange.*
Queir, *choir.*
Quell, *to kill.*
Quene, *wench.*
Querrell, *quarry.*
Querrell-hollis, *quarry holes.*
Quha, *who.*
Quhair, quhare, *where.*
Quhais, *whose.*
Quhalis, *whales.*

Quham, *whom.*
Quharethrow, *whereby, whereof.*
Quhat, *what.*
Quheill, *wheel.*
Quhen, *when.*
Quhether, *whether.*
Quhile, *sometimes.*
Quhilk, quhilks, quhilkis, *who, which, what.*
Quhill, *until, whilst.*
Quhilum, *of late, some time ago.*
Quhimperand, *whimpering.*
Quhin, *a whin.*
Quhissill, *whistle.*
Quhite, *white.*
Quhittle, *a knife.*
Quho, *who,*
Quhose, *whose.*
Quhow, *how.*
Quhowbeit, *howbeit.*
Quhryne, *whine.*
Quhyle, *while.*
Quhylumis, *at times.*
Quick, *live, living.*
Quintacensoris, *backbiters.*
Quod, *said.*
Quyke, *live.*
Quyte, *free.*
Quyetlie, *quietly.*

R.

Ra, *roe.*
Race, *course of events.*
Rache, *a dog.*
Ractis, *racks.*
Ra-fell, *roe-skin.*
Ragment, *rhapsody, discourse. accusation.*
Raid, *afraid.*
Raid, *anchorage.*
Raid, *rode.*
Raif, *rave.*
Raif, *tore asunder.*
Raife, *declare.*
Raiffell at the rakkett, *play at tennis.*
Raik on raw, *walk in file.*
Raipe, *rope.*
Rair, *roar, cry.*
Rais, *rose.*
Rak, *matter.*
Rak, *wrack, wreck, ruin, destruction.*
Rakkett, *noise and confusion.*
Rakles, *careless, graceless.*
Ramp, *to stamp, to prance, to caper.*
Rander, *order, make.*
Randoun, *a hurry, a random motion.*
Rang, *reigned.*
Ranson, *a ransom.*
Raploch, *coarse woollen cloth.*
Rath, raith, *soon, quick, early.*
Ratton, rattounis, *a rat, rats.*
Raucht, *reached.*
Raveand, *vague.*
Ravis, *raves.*
Raw, *row, rank.*
Rax, *stretch.*
Raye, *array.*
Rebaldrie, *ribaldry, wicked conduct.*

GLOSSARY.

Rebauldis, *ruffians.*
Recantit, *discharged.*
Record, *celebration, relation.*
Recure, *to recover.*
Red, *parted, separated.*
Reddyng, *putting in order.*
Redolent, *sweet smelling.*
Reft, *taken by violence.*
Reft, *tossed.*
Refute, *refuge.*
Regiment, *management, government.*
Regiment, *rule, law.*
Regnand, *reigning.*
Regne, *a kingdom, a reign.*
Regratour, *wrong.*
Rehabilit, *reinstated.*
Reid, *red.*
Reid, red, *advise.*
Reidwod, *furious.*
Reif, *pillage, robbery.*
Reiffaris, *robbers.*
Reiffis, *takes away, robs.*
Reik, *tumult.*
Reik, *reach.*
Reik, *smoke.*
Reill, *roam.*
Rejosit, *rejoiced.*
Relent, *assuage.*
Relyie, *rally, banter.*
Remede, *remedy.*
Remord, *remember.*
Rent, *revenue.*
Renze, *a rein.*
Repair, *resort.*
Repleadgeand, *redeeming.*
Repreve, *to reprove.*
Requiem, *the Service for the dead.*

Rerd, reird, *sound, noise.*
Reset, *abet.*
Resort, *come.*
Resoun, *reason.*
Restringityve, *astringent.*
Rethor, *an orator, a rhetorician.*
Retraitit, *reversed.*
Retrevit, *rejected, avoided.*
Reuin, *ruin.*
Reuth, *pity.*
Reve, refe, *a stewart, bailiff, overseer.*
Reve, *dream.*
Rever, *robber.*
Revaris, *plunderers.*
Revin, *torn.*
Revyst, *wrapt.*
Rew, *repentance, mourn, pity.*
Rew, *a row.*
Rewarris, *robbers.*
Rewland, *governing.*
Rewle, *law, rule.*
Rewlit, *revealed.*
Rewme, *humour.*
Rewme, *a realm, a kingdom.*
Rewyne, *ruin.*
Richt, rycht, *right.*
Richtwis, *righteous, just.*
Rickill, *confused heap.*
Riftit, *belched, broke wind.*
Rig, rigg, *the back, also a ridge.*
Rin, rinn, *to run.*
Ring, *reign.*
Ringis, *realms, kingdoms.*
Rink, *race, course.*
Rink roume, *course room.*
Rippit, *scrape, dilemma.*
Rivis, *split.*

GLOSSARY.

Riven, *torn*.
Roche, rochis, *a rock, rocks*.
Rock, *distaff*.
Rocket, *surplice*.
Roiploch, *home-spun cloth*.
Rokkis, *distaffs, spindles*.
Rokkit, *restrained*.
Rolpand, *crying, croaking*.
Rome-raker, *a trafficker in relics, indulgences, pardons, or benefices*.
Rondel, *a short poem, or song which ends as it begins*.
Rone, *crustation*.
Rong, *reigned*.
Roste, *tumult*.
Round, roune, *whisper*.
Roundand, *whispering*.
Roukis, *rooks*.
Roung, *reigned*.
Roupit, *croaked*.
Route, *to bellow*.
Roustit, *rusted*.
Roustye, *unpolished*.
Rout, *stroke*.
Rout, *company*.
Rout, *fill*.
Rowbourris, *a wine measure, large vessels for holding wine*.
Rowkand, *huddling*.
Rowme, *room*.
Rowst, *rust*.
Rowpand, *croaking*.
Rowte, route, *noisy crowd*.
Royatouslie, *riotously*.
Roye, *a king*.
Royne, *a quean*.

Rubeator, *a robber, libertine*.
Rude, *cross*.
Rude, *the complexion*.
Ruffeis, *ruffians*.
Rug, *pull*.
Rummeis, *rumble*.
Ruther, *rudder*.
Ruscheit, *threw down, tumbled down*.
Ruse, ruisse, *praise*.
Rusticall, *provincial*.
Rute, *root*.
Rutit, *rooted*.
Rutlande, *croaking*.
Ryall, *royal*.
Rybalds, *profligates*.
Rycht, *right*.
Ryfe, *rife, frequent, common, plentiful*.
Ryn, *point*.
Ryn, *to run*.
Ryn, Rinnis, *a point, promontories*.
Ryng, ryngis, *reign, reigns*.
Ryngis, *kingdoms*.
Rype, *search*.
Rysche-bus, *rush bush*.
Ryve, *tear, rend*.

S

Sa, *so*.
Sad, *steady, solid, grave*.
Saiffer, *the Saviour*.
Saikles, *innocent, guiltless*.
Saile, *to assail*.
Saine, *to hallow by making the sign of the cross, to bless*.
Saip, *soap*.

Sair, *sore.*
Sair, *to serve.*
Sait, *seat.*
Sald, *sold.*
Sall, *shall.*
Salus, *salute.*
Samyn, *the same.*
Sandie, *a proper name, Alexander.*
Sane, *say.*
Sang, *song.*
Sanis, *sanctifies.*
Sapour, *drowsiness.*
Sapouris, *flavours.*
Sard, *stitch, mend.*
Sare, *sore.*
Sarye, *sorry.*
Sauld, *sold.*
Sark, sarkis, *a shirt, shirts.*
Sattell, *settle.*
Saulis, *souls.*
Saw, sawis, *proverb, sayings.*
Sawrles, *savourless.*
Sax, *six.*
Saylit, *sailed.*
Scaip, scape, *to escape.*
Schaik, *shake.*
Schaip, *purpose, intend.*
Schalme, *a pipe, hautboy.*
Schankis, *legs.*
Schavelings, *shaved persons, monks, or friars.*
Schaw, schew, *show, showed.*
Schaw, shaw, *a small wood, a cluster of trees.*
Scheif, sheif, *sheaf.*
Scheir, *reap.*
Schellis, *enclosures for sheep.*

Schend, shend, *to reject, to confound, to disgrace.*
Schene, *brightness.*
Schene, *shining, lovely, beautiful.*
Schent, shent, *lost.*
Schew, *showed.*
Schift, *resource, expedient, endeavour.*
Schip, *a ship.*
Schinnis, *shins.*
Schiphirds, *shepherds.*
Schir, *a name given to Priests, hence called Pope's Knights.*
Scho, *she.*
Schog, *to shake, to vibrate.*
Schonder, *asunder, sunder.*
Schone, *shoes.*
Schone, *page, servant.*
Schort, *amuse.*
Schort, *short.*
Schot, *shot.*
Schote, *shot range.*
Schouris, *showers.*
Schrevin, *confessed.*
Schrew, *curse.*
Schrift, *confession.*
Schryne, *coffin.*
Schure, *cut.*
Schutand, *shooting.*
Schrewis, *worthless person.*
Schryve, *confess.*
Schyathica-passio, *the sciatick pain, the hip rheumatism.*
Schyning, *shining.*
Schyre, *district.*
Scrip, *wallet.*
Scroppit, *contemptible.*

GLOSSARY. 391

Scroug, *brushwood.*
Scuilis, *schools.*
Scule, *school.*
Se, *see.*
See, *sea.*
See, *abode.*
Sege, *throne.*
Seigit, *besieged.*
Seil, sele, *good, happiness, prosperity.*
Seillit, *sealed.*
Seilye, *foolish.*
Seindell, *seldom.*
Seinzie, *consistory.*
Seir, *several.*
Seis, *seats, thrones.*
Seisit, *seated.*
Seisit, *settled.*
Selcouth, *strange, uncommon.*
Sely, *harmless.*
Sempyll, *simple, humble.*
Sen, *send.*
Sen, *since.*
Sener, *sir.*
Senownis, *sinews.*
Sensyne, *since then.*
Senye, senzie, *consistory.*
Senyeorie, *highness, lordship.*
Sere, *many.*
Sers, *search.*
Serve, *deserve.*
Set, *dispose.*
Set, *regard.*
Settis, *sits by, frequents.*
Seware, *Stewart.*
Sewch, *ditch.*
Sey, *sea.*
Seych, *sigh.*

Seyne, *consistory.*
Shed, *separated.*
Sib, sibb, *related, near a-kin.*
Sichand, *sighing.*
Sicker, *sure.*
Sic, sick, *such.*
Sickernes, *security.*
Side, *large.*
Sie, *see.*
Sikkerlie, *certainly.*
Sillabis, *syllables.*
Sillie, *trifling.*
Sindry, *sundry.*
Sing, *sign.*
Sittill, *subtle.*
Skair, *share.*
Skaith, *hurt, injury.*
Skant, *scarce, scarcity.*
Skap, *scalp,*
Skaplarie, *vestment worn by the Friars.*
Skar, *fright.*
Skard, *frightened.*
Skeich, *skittish, shy.*
Skelp, *stroke.*
Sker, *frighten.*
Sker, *submerged rock.*
Skowland, *overhanging.*
Skyre skaid, *scabbed.*
Sla, *to slay.*
Slaik, *abate, quench.*
Slake, *lower.*
Slakyng, *quenching.*
Sleutchers, *hangers on.*
Sleuthful, *indolent.*
Slidder, *slippery.*
Slop, *gap.*
Sloppit, *pierced.*

Sloug, *idle, lounge.*
Slycht, *ingenuity, invention, skill.*
Slyding, *uncertain.*
Smaik, *mean fellow.*
Smedie, *smithy.*
Smorde, *smothered.*
Smorit, *suffocated.*
Smuke, *smoke.*
Smurit, *smothered.*
Snaw, *snow.*
Snawdoun, *a name for Stirling Castle.*
Snell, *quick, keen, sharp.*
Snyp, *snap.*
Sobbit, *sobbed.*
Sobir, *feeble.*
Soddin, *steeped.*
Soillis, *soles.*
Solace, *entertainment.*
Solempne, *solemn.*
Solist, *to solicit.*
Solystatioun, *solicitation.*
Somer, *summer.*
Sone, sonne, *the sun.*
Sone, sonne, *a son.*
Sonsy, *well conditioned.*
Sopit, *steeped.*
Sornand, *sojourning.*
Sort, *crew, squad.*
Sortis, *ways, manners.*
Soumand, *swimming.*
Souer, *firm.*
Souertie, *security.*
Soup, *sup, fare.*
Soup, *to sob, to weep.*
Soup, *to sweep.*
Southeroun, *a name given to Englishmen.*

Sowldiouris, *soldiers.*
Sowne, *swoon.*
Sowtar, *a shoemaker.*
Spair, *to despair.*
Spair, *to grudge.*
Spaiks, *spokes.*
Sped, *conferred.*
Speid hand, *make haste.*
Speik, *bespeak.*
Speill, *climb.*
Speir, speris, *sphere, spheres.*
Speir, *enquire.*
Spence, *a place where provisions are kept, a pantry.*
Spense, *expense.*
Spill, *spoil.*
Splene, *the spleen.*
Spoilyeis (for spuilyie), *robs.*
Spoilze, *strip.*
Spousit, *wedded.*
Spreitis, spretis, *spirits.*
Sprent, *sprinkled.*
Spryngis, *dancing tunes.*
Spuilyeit, *plundered, stripped.*
Spuilyie, *plunder.*
Spur-gaid (for spur-galled), *exhausted.*
Spyit, *spied, observed.*
Squeilit, *screamed.*
Stage, stagis, *furlong.*
Staid, *situated.*
Stait, *obeisance, honour.*
Stait, *condition.*
Stak, *stuck.*
Stanche, *quench, abate.*
Stan, stane, *a stone.*
Stang, *sharp pain.*
Stank, *a ditch.*
Stankis, *ponds.*

GLOSSARY.

Stark, *potent.*
Stark, *brace, strengthen.*
Statute, *ordained.*
Staw, *stole.*
Steer, *a young bullock.*
Steid, *station, place, farm.*
Steil, *a handle, a stalk.*
Steir, *stir, move.*
Stends, *strides.*
Stent, *stop.*
Stepbarne, *stepchild.*
Sterne, *a star.*
Stervit, *killed.*
Sterris, *stars.*
Steven, *a voice, a sound, a cry, a tune.*
Stewat, *loathsome fellow.*
Stik, *stab, pierce.*
Sting, *spear.*
Stirk, *a young heifer, or bullock.*
Stirlyng, *starling.*
Stith, *stiff, strong.*
Stob, *stump of wood.*
Stockis, *trunks of trees.*
Stokkis, *blocks of wood.*
Stope, *jug, stoup.*
Stot, *a young bullock.*
Stound, *instant, shooting pain, shock.*
Stouith, *theft.*
Stoup, *pitcher.*
Stour, *battle.*
Stoure, *fight, tumult.*
Straik, *fought, struck.*
Straikis, *blows.*
Strais, *straws.*
Strampit, *trampled.*

Strang, *strong.*
Strang-wesche, *urine.*
Strands, *streams.*
Strandis, *streams, seas.*
Straucht, *direct, stretched, straight.*
Strenth, *strengthen.*
Strenthis, *fortresses, strongholds.*
Stridlingis, *astride.*
Strykken, *fought.*
Stuffat, *lacquey, hostler.*
Stump, *remnant.*
Sturt, *disturbance, annoyance.*
Styll, *title, designation.*
Styllit, *honoured.*
Sua, *so.*
Subditis, *subjects.*
Subscryve, *to subscribe.*
Sudgeorne, *delay, linger.*
Sudgeornyng, *lingering.*
Suggurit, *sweet.*
Suith, suth, *truth.*
Suld, sulde, *should.*
Sumtyme, *sometimes.*
Sunzie, *excuse.*
Suppertatioun, *support.*
Suppone, *suppose.*
Supprest, supprysit, *oppressed*
Supprisit, *surprised.*
Sute, *staff, company.*
Suth, *truth.*
Suyth, swyth, *be gone, instantly, quickly.*
Swa, *so.*
Swagis, *assuages.*
Swappit, *swung.*
Swappit, *fell down.*

GLOSSARY.

Swart, *black, swarthy, gloomy.*
Swatterit, *weltered.*
Sweitie, *perspiring.*
Sweitlie, *sweetly.*
Sweir, *lazy, unwilling.*
Sweird, *sword.*
Swelterand, *weltering.*
Swevin, *a sleep, a dream.*
Swilk, *such.*
Swyngeour, *rascal.*
Swink, *labour.*
Swomand, *swimming.*
Swoulis, *swivels.*
Swoun, *swoon, faint.*
Swyfe, swyvis, *to commit whoredom.*
Swyre, swire, sware, *the neck.*
Sychand, *sighing.*
Sycht, *sight.*
Syde, *long, large.*
Syder, *longer.*
Sydlingis, *sidewise.*
Syik, *brook.*
Syis, *times.*
Syle, *deceive.*
Syllie, *harmless.*
Syment, *cement.*
Syne, *thereafter, then, since.*
Synopier, *green.*
Syper, *cypress.*
Syre, *person of honour.*
Systerne, *reservoir, cistern.*
Syte, *mourning.*

T.

Ta, *one.*
Tabill, *backgammon, or any game played with the table and dice.*
Tabrone, taburne, *a small drum.*
Tache, *a blemish, a spot.*
Tadis, *toads.*
Tailis, *trains.*
Tailyeour, *tailor.*
Tain, taine, *taken.*
Tais, *toes.*
Tak, *a lease.*
Tak, *take.*
Takill, *an arrow.*
Takinnis, *tokens.*
Takkand, *taking.*
Talkin, *to talk.*
Tane, *taken.*
Tane, *the one of two.*
Tapessit, *tapestried.*
Targe, *a shield.*
Tarye, *tedious, wearisome.*
Tauld, tald, *told,* also *counted.*
Taverner, *sot.*
Tedder, *a halter.*
Teicheing, *teaching.*
Teichit, *taught.*
Teind, *tithe.*
Teme (for tume), *empty.*
Tene, *vexation, grief, sorrow, trouble.*
Tent, *notice, watch, heed.*
Teuch, *tough, difficult.*
Tewch, *tough, strong.*
Thack, *thatch.*
Thai, *these.*
Thair, *their.*
Thame, *them.*
Than, *then.*
Thare, *there.*
Tharetill, *thereto.*
Thay, *these.*

GLOSSARY.

Thays, thayis, *they shall.*
The, *thee.*
The, *to thrive.*
The, *the thigh.*
Thegyder, *together.*
Thesaurer, *treasurer.*
Thewis, *manners, customs, dispositions, qualities.*
Thift, *theft.*
Thiftwis, *thievish.*
Thir, *these.*
Thirl, *a perforation, a hole.*
Thirl, *to perforate.*
Thirlage, *thraldom, restriction.*
Tho, *those.*
Tho, *then.*
Thocht, *though.*
Thocht, *thought,*
Thoill, *permit.*
Thole, *endure.*
Tholis, *allows.*
Tholand, *tolerating.*
Thrang, *throng.*
Thrang, *grasped.*
Thraw, *struggle.*
Thraw, *a time, an instant.*
Thrawis, *throws.*
Threip, threpe, threap, *to allege, to aver, to argue, to reprove.*
Thresoure, *treasure.*
Threswald, *a threshold.*
Thretty, *thirty.*
Thrid, *third.*
Thriftie, *successful.*
Thrissil, *the thistle.*
Thrist, *to press.*

Thronit, *enthroned.*
Throuch, *through.*
Thryngis, *throws.*
Thye, *thigh.*
Thyne, *thence.*
Tibbe, *a proper name,* Isabel.
Tide, *happen, befal.*
Til, *till, to, unto.*
Tinsale, *loss.*
Tit, *to pull suddenly, to snatch.*
Tocher, tocher-gude, *dowry, a marriage portion.*
To, *too.*
Tods, *foxes.*
Tofore, *before.*
Togidder, *together.*
Tornayis, *tournaments.*
Tounder, *tinder.*
Toure, *tower.*
Tout, *drink.*
Towart, *docile.*
Tragedy, *a tragic narrative, or tale,* (not restricted to the Drama.)
Trail, *to drag,*
Train, *scheme, quibbles, excuse.*
Traist, *trust, reckon.*
Tramalt, *ravelled.*
Tramplit, *trampled.*
Transcurris, *runs through, traverses.*
Transfigurate, *disguised.*
Trappouris, *trappings.*
Trattyll, *mumble, prattle.*
Travell, *labour.*
Travers, *crosses.*
Tre, *a tree.*

Treddingis, *tracks*.
Treid, *trod*.
Treit, *retain, employ*.
Trenchour, *spear head*.
Trentalls, *Masses for the dead*.
Treukour, trewker, *a cheat, a sharper*.
Trew, *true*.
Trimmyll, *to tremble*
Triplicandum, *a triply,* (*a law term*.)
Trittyll, *pshaw*.
Troch, *trough*.
Trompouris, *deceivers*.
Trow, *believe, trust*.
Trucour, *rogue*.
Trump, trompe, *a trumpet*.
Trypis, *the intestines*.
Tryist, *appointment*.
Tryne, *train, retinue*.
Trypartit, *divided into three parts*.
Tulzeour, *fighter*.
Tuke, *took*.
Tumbe, *tub*.
Tumde, *emptied*.
Turcumis, *accumulation of dirt*.
Turn, *allotted work*.
Turne, *an act, a service, a duty*.
Turs, *truss, gather together*.
Turss, *pack up, hoard*.
Turtur, *turtle dove*.
Tutorye, *tutorage*.
Twa, twae, tway, *two*.
Twane, *two*.
Twistis, *twigs, branches*.
Twinne, *to part, to separate*.

Twycheing, *to touch, embrace*.
Twycheit, *touched*.
Tydie, *seasonable, neat, in good condition*.
Tyisting, *enticing, alluring*.
Tyke, *a dog, a cur*.
Tylde, *tile, bricks*.
Tyll, *to, till, so*.
Tyne, *weaken*.
Tyne, *to lose*.
Tynis, *neglects*.
Tynt, *lost*.
Tyrit, *tired*.
Tyte, *straight, directly, quickly*.
Tythands, *tidings*.
Tysday, *Tuesday*.

U.

Uder, *other*.
Umest, *uppermost*.
Umquhile, *the late, deceased*.
Unblomit, *without bloom*.
Uncouth, *strange*.
Undantit, *savage*.
Underly, *to be subject to, to undergo the consequence or punishment of*.
Undocht, *dunce*.
Undrest, *undressed*.
Uneffrayit, *undaunted*.
Uneth, uneith, unethes, *not easily, scarcely*.
Unfenyeitlie, *unfeignedly*.
Unfriends, *enemies*.
Unhable, *incompetent*.
Unleifsum, *unlawful*.
Unleill, *unfaithful, dishonest*.

GLOSSARY.

Unprovisit, *unprovided.*
Unpysalt, *unrestrained.*
Unricht, *wrong.*
Unrokit, *unprovoked.*
Unrychtis, *unrighteous.*
Unsawin, *unsown.*
Unsell, *a wretch, worthless.*
Unsely, *unhappy, unfortunate.*
Unthrall, *unsubjected.*
Untraist, *unstable.*
Untrowabyll, *incredible.*
Unwemmit, *unspotted.*
Unwerly, *unawares.*
Upaland, *the country, distinguished from town, or borough.*
Uphauld, *uphold.*
Uprevin, *torn up.*
Ure, *hap, fortune.*
Uther, *other.*
Utter, *outer.*
Utterit, *swerved, run out of the course.*
Utterance, *extremity.*

V.

Vacands, *vacancies.*
Vagers, *vagrants.*
Vaik, *vacate.*
Vaill, *valley.*
Vailith, *avails.*
Vailye quod vailye, *happen what may.*
Vailzeand, *valiant.*
Variand, *varying.*
Varlet, *a footboy, a servant.*
Vassalage, *valour, prowess, glory.*
Veirs, *verse.*

Verrayment, *verity.*
Verraye, *true.*
Veschell, *slave.*
Vesiand, *visiting.*
Vespertyne, *pertaining to the evening.*
Vesyit, *viewed.*
Vilde, *vile.*
Vilipendit, *vilified.*
Vilitie, *vileness.*
Vincuste, *vanquished.*
Visie, vesie, *view.*
Vocis, *voices.*
Volt, *vault.*
Vyld, *vile.*

W.

Wa, *sorrowful.*
Wacheman, *spy.*
Wad, *a pledge.*
Wage, *wages.*
Waif, *to swing.*
Waik, *weak, soft, moist, cloudy.*
Waill, *choose.*
Waillis, *bulwarks.*
Waillit, *selected.*
Waine, *to wish, to desire.*
Wair, *wrack, refuse.*
Waird, *to put in ward, custody.*
Wairde (for ware it), *to spend.*
Wairdit, *imprisoned.*
Wais me, *woe is me! alas!*
Wait, *knows, to be aware of.*
Wait, *wet.*
Wak, *moist.*
Wakness, *moisture.*
Wald, *would.*
Walker, *fuller.*

GLOSSARY.

Walking, *waking.*
Walkryfe, *wakefull.*
Wallie, *well.*
Wallie-fall, *good befal.*
Wallis, *waves.*
Wallope, *gallop.*
Walloway, *well away.*
Walter, *water.*
Walx, *wax,*
Wambe, *belly.*
Wamenting, *lamentation.*
Wan fortune, *misfortune.*
Wan, *gained.*
Wan, *got.*
Wand, *rod.*
Wander, *weariness.*
Wandis, *whips.*
Wands, *authorities.*
Wane, *a house, a dwelling.*
Wantonlie, *gallantly.*
War, *were.*
War, *worse.*
War, *cautious.*
Ware, *to expend, to lay out.*
Warie, warye, *to curse, to cry out against.*
Warison, *a remedy, a recompense, a reward.*
Warlo, *a wicked person, warlock.*
Wark, *work, book.*
Warldie, *worldly.*
Warst, *worst.*
Waryand, *cursing.*
Waryit, *reviled.*
Wassall, *a vassal.*
Wast, *waste.*
Wat, *know.*

Watt, *know.*
Wate, *know.*
Wattand, *waiting.*
Wawis, *waves.*
Waxin, *to wax.*
Wed, *a pledge,* also *to pledge.*
Wedder, weddir, *weather.*
Weid, *apparel.*
Weidis, *rage.*
Weill, *well, benefit.*
Weill-fairde, *good looking, handsome.*
Wein, *expect.*
Wein'd, *understood.*
Weine, *know.*
Weir, *wear.*
Weir, *delay.*
Weir, *doubtfully.*
Weir, *war, combats, quarrel.*
Weird, *fate.*
Weirlie, *warlike.*
Weische, *wash.*
Weit, *wet.*
Weld, weild, *to govern, to rule, to manage.*
Wend, *thought.*
Wend, *intended.*
Wend, *go.*
Wene, *thought, opinion, expectation.*
Wene, *to think, to imagine, expect with confidence.*
Wene (but), *doubtless.*
Weriouris, *warriors.*
Werkis, *works.*
Werp and woft, *warp and weft.*
We's, *we shall.*

GLOSSARY.

Wesche, *wash, urine.*
Weyis, *weighs.*
Weyis, *weights, scales.*
Wecht, *strong, active.*
Wha, *who.*
Whan, *when.*
While, *time, a space of time.*
Whiles, *at times.*
Whilk, *which.*
Wicht, *creature, person.*
Widcock, *woodcock.*
Widder, *to wither.*
Widdie, *a halter, the gallows.*
Widdiefow, *a knave, one who deserves a haltar.*
Will of wane, *uncertain of a house.*
Wilsum, *wilful.*
Win, *profit.*
Windyng-scheit, *a shroud.*
Winning, *earning.*
Winsum, *pleasant, merry, agreeable.*
Wirrear, *worrier.*
Wirry hen, *greedy gobbler.*
Wische, *direct.*
Wiss, *know.*
Wissen, *to grow dry, to wither.*
Withouten, *without.*
Withsay, *to gainsay, to contradict, to deny.*
Wittin, *known.*
Witsone, *Whitsuntide.*
Wobster, *weaver.*
Wo-begone, *overwhelmed with woe.*
Wod, *furious, mad.*
Wode, *wild, enraged.*

Wodder, *weather.*
Wodis, *woods.*
Woid, *wager.*
Woll, *wool.*
Woltering, *rolling.*
Womanheid, *womanhood.*
Womentyng, *lamentation.*
Won, *to dwell, to reside.*
Wone, wonne, *a dwelling-place, a house.*
Wonning, *dwelling.*
Woo, *sorry.*
Word, *worth, to be, to become.*
Wordis, *words.*
Woun, *wont, used to.*
Wounder, *wonderfully, wonderous.*
Wow, *an exclamation of surprise.*
Wower, *wooer.*
Wox, *waxed, grew, became.*
Wrache, *a wretch, niggard, miser.*
Wracheit, *wretched, miserable.*
Wrack, wrak, *a wreck.*
Wraik, *revenge.*
Wrait, *wrote.*
Wraith, *wroth, wrath.*
Wrangous, *unjust, wrongful, unlawful.*
Wreik, *retaliate.*
Wrestit, *sprained.*
Wrinks, *deceits.*
Wrocht, *wrought.*
Wrokin, *wreaked.*
Wuische, *washed.*
Wycht, *immense.*
Wycht, *strong.*

GLOSSARY.

Wychtlie, *swiftly, vigorously.*
Wydder, *wither.*
Wyf, wyfe, *a woman advanced in years, a married woman.*
Wyit, *blame.*
Wyll, *bewildered.*
Wyle, *trick, beguile.*
Wyn, *reach.*
Wyne-yaird, *a vineyard.*
Wynnis, *dwells.*
Wynnis (gains), *wins.*
Wypit, *wiped.*
Wysche, *washed.*
Wyt, *with.*
Wyt, *know.*
Wyrk, *work.*
Wyrkand, *working.*
Wys, *wish.*
Wys, *long.*
Wyste, wist, *knew.*
Wyt, *know.*
Wyt ye weill, *believe me.*
Wyte, *blame.*
Wyttin, *known.*
Wyvis, *housewives.*

Y.

Yare, *ready.*
Yairnis, *yearns for, longs, desires.*
Yamer, *to shriek.*
Yarnis, *earns for, desires.*
Yarnit, *longed.*
Yate, yet, *a gate.*
Ye, *yea.*
Yearnis, *desires.*
Yeid, *went, walked.*
Ye'ile, *you will.*
Yeir, *year.*
Yeis, *you will.*
Yet, yett, *gate, door.*
Yewt, *a roar, to cry out.*
Yistrene, *the night before, yesternight.*
Yit, *yet.*
Yneuch, *enough.*
Yon, yond, *yonder, those yonder.*
Youthage, *youth.*
Youtheid, *youth.*
Yowis, *ewes.*
Yowling, *howling.*
Yowting, *crying in pain, moaning.*
Yre, *ire, anger, wrath.*
Yschare, *usher.*
Yuill, Yule, *Christmas.*

Z.

Zald, *yeilded.*

www.ingramcontent.com/pod-product-compliance
Lightning Source LLC
Chambersburg PA
CBHW051242300426
44114CB00011B/861